The Holmes
Partnership
Trilogy

PETER LANG
New York • Washington, D.C./Baltimore • Bern
Frankfurt am Main • Berlin • Brussels • Vienna • Oxford

The Holmes Partnership **Trilogy**

Tomorrow's Teachers, Tomorrow's Schools, Tomorrow's Schools of Education

WITH A NEW FOREWORD BY Judith Lanier

PETER LANG
New York • Washington, D.C./Baltimore • Bern
Frankfurt am Main • Berlin • Brussels • Vienna • Oxford

Library of Congress Cataloging-in-Publication Data

The Holmes partnership trilogy: tomorrow's teachers, tomorrow's schools,
tomorrow's schools of education
p. cm.
Includes bibliographical references.
1. Teachers—Training of—United States.
2. Universities and colleges—Curricula—United States.
3. Educational change—United States. I. Holmes Group (1983—   ). II. Title.
LB2165.T48   370.71'1—dc22   2006028893
ISBN-13: 978-0-8204-8833-2 (hardcover)
ISBN-13: 978-0-8204-8832-5 (paperback)
ISBN-10: 0-8204-8833-X (hardcover)
ISBN-10: 0-8204-8832-1 (paperback)

Bibliographic information published by **Die Deutsche Bibliothek**.
Die Deutsche Bibliothek lists this publication in the "Deutsche
Nationalbibliografie"; detailed bibliographic data is available
on the Internet at http://dnb.ddb.de/.

Cover design by Lisa Barfield

The paper in this book meets the guidelines for permanence and durability
of the Committee on Production Guidelines for Book Longevity
of the Council of Library Resources.

■|■|■

Table of Contents

Tomorrow's Schools

Tomorrow's Schools of Education

■|■|■

The Holmes Trilogy—Again!

JUDITH LANIER

So what are these books? Where did they come from? For whom were they written? And why should they be reprinted twenty years later? These questions are addressed here so readers might better understand the social context that gave rise to the three volumes—and why their espoused challenges remain. More retrospective than historical analysis, these introductory thoughts and reflections represent "lessons learned" from the seemingly endless observations, experiences, and decisions that shaped the treatise. Over twelve years of study, dialog, writing, consensus-building, political action, rewriting, printing, and distributing the books (individually and as a set)— while also trying to implement the goals in our own universities—comprised the work. The times were demanding, but filled with excitement and learning. In reprinting and inviting reconsideration of the trilogy, the Holmes Partnership continues the learning and growth that created the organization, and continues to sustain it.

The Trilogy: Tomorrow's Teachers, Tomorrow's Schools, Tomorrow's Schools of Education

The set of books is a manifesto—a public declaration of motives and intentions by a group regarded as having some public importance at the time. Created by a group of education deans from some of the nation's leading research universities, the first two volumes were each three years in the making. The third took considerably longer, for reasons to be noted.

The gestation period for each book included shared study, dialog, and learning-from-experience as the deans considered and began acting on the ideas under consideration. Early drafts were informed by perspectives invited from persons external to the deans, including respected leaders from various schools, businesses, think-tanks, and the collegiate and K-12 policy sectors. Later working drafts were reviewed critically and revised by the deans themselves in meeting after meeting—accompanied often by intense argument and contentious debate. Throughout the time, the deans were assisted by several major foundations, the U.S. Secretary of Education, and many thoughtful faculty from a variety of schools and colleges.

Tomorrow's Teachers
(—and who, by the way, was Henry Holmes?)

No one person sat down with the idea of writing a book on the future of U.S. teaching, and teacher education. Rather, *Tomorrow's Teachers* grew out of the questions, commitments, and frustrations of three education deans who wanted to improve teaching and teacher education on their own campuses—interacting with the intellectual and political events of the day. As members of a national task force on the accreditation of schools of education, the deans became disgruntled when their efforts to question the quality of institutional standards for teacher preparation went unheeded.

The three deans—John Palmer (from Wisconsin-Madison), Bob Koff (from SUNY-Albany) and I (from Michigan State)—shared concern about the number of admittedly weak teacher education programs across the country. Knowing that hundreds of programs were accredited while hundreds of others were not, we wondered what difference it made—and to whom? Moreover, why would an institution go through the work of seeking accreditation if it didn't matter? Further, why were some of the nation's major research universities so disdainful of teacher education—and so little concerned about program quality? Why did some eschew accreditation entirely, while others made the effort and got it—even when their teacher education programs were admittedly weak? Could accreditation in teacher education mean so little that it was given easily to universities that were known for good research and promising students? Was the accrediting body afraid of rejecting the elite?

Each of us was devoted to and proud of our own universities' strength in research and development, as well as the quality preparation programs for medical personnel, engineers, architects, and other professionals. We had seen our colleague deans from these other fields argue for and receive the resources needed to enhance program quality in light of a pending accreditation review. Only seldom in teacher education did requests for resources have the desired effect. After all the norms in teacher education reflected low expectations and programs that could typically be done on the cheap, a circumstance that caused some of our own teacher education programs to languish.

Wondering why teacher education standards were not rising in any way commensurate with the growing need for quality teaching in the United States, we launched a more serious conversation. Why did the fields of teaching and teacher education appear "stuck in the past" when the twentieth century had brought significant changes to most fields requiring a college degree? Why not teaching and teacher education? What was going on to keep them seemingly "untouched" in a rapidly changing information-age society? Sharing concern and an abiding interest in quality teaching and teacher preparation, we exchanged articles and ideas on the subject soon after the accreditation task force was disbanded.

We also shared these concerns with our own university presidents and chief academic officers, as well as with other education deans in our peer institutions. We found some shared interest, and a small study network was born. The Johnson Foundation, which hosts dialog among leaders from a number of fields at their Wingspread Conference Center, agreed to host a first session. About twenty participants attended that first meeting, and, after an informative exchange, the Johnson Foundation agreed to host another six sessions.

The discourse focused on societal change and quality teaching and teacher education, as well as standards that might appropriately steer programs toward such levels. We read papers in advance and discussed the issues. Interest grew, and other academic leaders from comparable institutions wanted to participate. As word spread that some academic leaders from respected universities were examining what was considered a rather dreary subject (quality teaching and teacher education), it suddenly became more interesting and important. However, just as interest grew, so did the criticism. Rather than "Well it's about time these folks got up to steam on the subject," we heard loud grumbling instead about the "self-generated professional development sessions"—mostly from the uninvited.

The education press wanted to know what was going on, and the speculation started in earnest. Was there a conspiracy? Why were people examining a field they had so long neglected? Weren't the "right" people to address issues related to teaching quality those in institutions with a tradition of teacher preparation and the mission to prepare teachers for a given geographic area? Weren't the "right" folks to convene sessions on the subject located in Washington, D.C., at the established associations on Dupont Circle?

Accompanying the growing interest in teaching and teacher education among the Wingspread attendees was a growing national concern with the quality of U.S. education in the K-12 sector. Terrel Bell, President Reagan's Secretary of Education, organized the development and publicity of *A Nation at Risk*—a powerful rallying call for education reform. Thinking that the established higher education groups could well be reluctant to join the effort, Bell looked for a reform-minded group that might concomitantly stir the pot in the direction of change. He personally attended and contributed significantly to our meetings and offered to support more gatherings and reform initiatives.

Meanwhile, in our quest to better understand the issues, we fell upon an article about a man named Henry W. Holmes, the dean of the Harvard Graduate School of Education in the 1920s. Back then Henry Holmes shared many of the ideas that were again on the table—stating over sixty years earlier that "the training of teachers is a highly significant part of the making of the nation." He argued that "a more serious conception of the place of the teacher in the life of the nation is both necessary and timely" and urged educational and political leaders to join him in "changing the systems that support poorly trained, paid and esteemed teachers." He believed that teachers should be prepared with "the power of critical analysis in a mind broadly and deeply informed." Though he found few supporters, he succeeded in constructing a strong six-year graduate program for teachers at Harvard. Alas, it was short-lived, and, like others before him, he failed in his efforts to make school-teaching and teacher education more professional.

Another contributor to the mix came from the Ford Foundation. Ed Meade, a program officer there with a long-standing interest in teaching and teacher education, employed the services of an Englishman by the name of Harry Judge. A former education "don" (i.e., dean) from Oxford University, Harry was invited to study the leading graduate schools of education in America. He did so, and after visiting many campuses and interviewing faculty and administrators, he wrote a little book about them. The results brought few surprises, for his findings squared with the experience and discussions of those at Wingspread. The education schools and departments in most U.S. research universities managed to keep their teacher education programs in the basement. His findings were shared widely, fueling interest in doing something about it—again motivating added interest in the talk and possible outcomes from the Wingspread meetings.

At the last of the six sessions, a set of draft standards for teacher preparation was shared in the hope of achieving some consensus around them. The Secretary of Education (Terrel Bell) was there, as were representatives of several major foundations—but the education deans began to back off. They explained why the standards wouldn't work at their institutions (not enough money, insufficient faculty interest, contradictory state policy requirements, and so on.). As they were "slip sliding away," Secretary Bell took the podium—and commenced to scold the deans for their lack of fortitude and commitment to improvement. Apparently he shamed them into submission, for shortly after he left the meeting they voted to support the effort and move ahead with the agenda.

Tomorrow's Teachers and The Holmes Group (early surprises and mistakes)

Now those who gathered at Wingspread began holding meetings across the various regions of the country, and instead of "the Wingspread Deans," began calling themselves "The Holmes Group," after Henry Holmes. Holmes shared the same commitments, acted on them, and reminded the deans that failure was a real possibility. Holmes, though, had acted alone, while we would together establish new standards for teaching and teacher education. Times had changed, and there was public support for change. The members of the group worked and reworked the public commitments they would make, and they began shaping an organization to support their own continuous learning, as well as implementation of a reform agenda.

After about forty deans approved the major premises in *Tomorrow's Teachers,* a writing team was put in place, and it soon came off the presses with an official release at the Washington Press Club. The *Chronicle of Higher Education* not only wrote about the report, but it printed its contents in full—starting with front page coverage. The reporters noted their surprise that ed school leaders could appear so bold and capable. The reviews were strong and positive as *Tomorrow's Teachers* was sent to the presidents, provosts, and deans in 123 major universities in the country, with the request that they review its contents and decide if they wanted to participate in the national reform network as described. Invitations were sent to the leading research university in each state, and then to enough other major universities that there would be at least one for every 25,000 teachers across the geographic regions of the country. The text explained:

> We write as a consortium of education deans and chief academic officers from major research universities across the United States. We came together because we knew that our own schools and universities were not doing well in teacher education, and because we hoped to improve. We have probed the problems and explored remedies. This has never been easy, and often it has been painful. Pursuing the shortcomings of one's own profession, and one's own institutions, is difficult at best.
>
> It has been fruitful, nonetheless. In our nearly two years of work together we have found much to criticize in teacher education. But we have also found ourselves

wxilling to argue for radical improvements that most of us would have dismissed as impractical just a few years ago. We have decided that we must work for the changes that we believe to be right, rather than those that we know can succeed.

The Holmes Group began formally in 1983—with more than 100 founding members convening for the first time in January of 1984. They became a nonprofit organization, with bylaws, a board of directors, and a regional-national organizational structure. The staff was voluntary, though modest support for secretarial assistance was provided for meetings and communications. Local leadership was to come from the deans and chief academic officers themselves, as the work was judged integral to their roles and responsibilities as education leaders on their own campuses and in their states and nation. The organization could grow again in three to five years, but it had to remain cohesive and manageable in the beginning—and yet large enough to have impact as a movement.

The first Holmes Board convened several months after their first national meeting, following approval of the bylaws and a process for moving from an appointed to an elected board. The main issue at the time was how to deal with the realization that The Holmes Group clearly had insufficient minority representation. The administrative and faculty leaders in the nation's research universities were predominantly white, while the nation's youth that were to benefit from their R&D and improved teacher education were racially and ethnically diverse. At the outset, the organizers of Holmes were not adequately sensitive or knowledgeable about diversity issues, but they could learn—and they did.

With regret and apologies for the oversight, a number of historically black institutions respected for their R&D productivity in various fields were invited to a special meeting on the work of Holmes and its hopes for *Tomorrow's Teachers*. Though tensions were high, the issues were put on the table—and we admitted that this would not likely be the last mistake The Holmes Group would make. However, we were committed to correcting our errors as soon as we recognized and understood them. We invited their full participation in the work of Holmes, raised the financial resources to assist with their faculty travel to Holmes meetings, and committed ourselves to working seriously on the race and class issues that were endemic to America's education system.

Tomorrow's Teachers: The Big Ideas and Challenges

The essence of *Tomorrow's Teachers* emerged from several years of learning more about teaching, teacher education, and the changing nature of society. When public schools first became broadly available in the U.S., teaching went on in many one room schools as well as in big city schools. "Instructing classes" and "showing and telling" students was often provided by those knowing only a little more than the children. Books, information, and knowledge were scarce.

However, since that time, the culture shifted from an agricultural, to an industrial, to an information society, and the transformation stood the "knowledge business" on its head. The nation went from knowledge and information shortages to knowledge and information excesses. Books got fatter and heavier, and students and teachers were expected to know more . . . and more. Television and computers arrived. Now more people were expected to learn more . . . and more. High school became a requirement for everyone, and the schools were made available to racial minorities and youngsters with various handicaps. More knowledge, more work demands, more people, but not more time. Time alone stood still.

Throughout the developed world, there was also a growing focus on learning. Countries began competing for the distinction of producing highly educated youths, and America wasn't doing as well as many thought. So the backdrop to Holmes's efforts to greatly improve teaching was America's growing awareness that our schools had to become much more successful in helping students learn. However, what besides hope would make this happen? The envisioned course corrections were significant:

1 **Learning in America needed to change.** Higher expectations and more ambitious learning goals were needed, as was increased learning in quality and quantity for all people's children. *A Nation at Risk* and mountains of similar reports were already documenting the need for greater learning on everyone's part—higher levels of learning for all—fast and slow, young and old. It would help if everyone just worked a little harder in the same old ways, but such efforts would produce meager gains at best, not the significant achievement gains that were sought. But how could this happen if teaching stayed the same?

2 **Teaching in America needed to change.** The nature and norms for teachers' work were geared to America's industrial era instead of the knowledge age. Teachers instruct groups of students who are batch-processed in classes, put on assembly line, age-graded tracks, and culled for their learning agility. Some pass, some muddle through, others fail. However, if teachers must now help all students become intellectually competent, they need new tools, technologies, support structures, adaptive work habits, and professional methods that fit our world of rapidly changing information. Primitive tools, such as teachers' grade-books, chalkboards, and erasures must be enriched with modern technology. Imagine, in the absence of a sophisticated information system, asking teachers to keep track of individual students' learning progress—according to many different learning goals and many different standards in many different subjects—over time for many diverse learners. Still asked to

do this today, they are not equipped to succeed. Innovation in teaching
is a necessity—yet how can it happen if schools remain static?

3   **Schooling must change.** Just as changes in the occupation of teaching need to be invented and discovered, so do concomitant changes in
schools. The cellular unit of the classroom needs greater flexibility.
More young people and more adults are needed to share in the work of
helping each other learn. Computer use is only beginning to be fully tapped
in K-12 schools, and teacher autonomy, teamwork, and parent advocacy
is spotty. More stimulating learning environments are needed, as are many
changes yet unknown. Concerted efforts to develop, test, and study
alternatives for their learning effectiveness are called for—and who better to begin work on the challenges than the nation's research universities, in partnership with selected innovating schools? Together, they
could create "innovation sites" for educational improvement. But how
might we make this happen?

4   **Universities must change some of their approaches to research.**
Increased emphasis on programmatic, applied research in designated settings over time is needed to develop, refine, and test the new technologies and approaches to teaching and learning. Educational research
today is mostly basic inquiry, pursued by individual faculty members as
their interests and dispositions lead them. Few focus over time on the
enduring problems of teaching and learning, and few work to cumulate
findings into growing bodies of knowledge. Still fewer test the applications of their findings broadly and systematically in practice. Most education research gets reported in journals read by other college professors,
and remains unavailable to practitioners who have neither the time nor
interest to search through it all for a potential nugget of insight. Society
must be able to look to its universities for some help in this regard, for
it will not be easy to further innovation and improvement in America's
schools without them. Can't a way be found to enlist university faculty
help in addressing the nation's need for increased learning?

5   **Teacher education needs to change.** The nation's future teachers
would need greater breadth and depth of knowledge and skill if they were
to educate more youngsters more broadly and deeply than heretofore.
In addition, if tomorrow's teachers were to learn to work differently, they
couldn't learn new approaches from those teaching in the same old
ways—whether in the university or in the schools. People develop
expertise from acquiring an understanding of the key underlying principles that guide the work, watching masters of the craft perform and

explain the work, and practicing the work themselves in light of good feedback so they can make needed course corrections. Future teachers need to learn to teach differently from those working and teaching in future-oriented, innovative schools. They can only learn new teaching practices from experienced teachers who can demonstrate the new approaches while working to improve them. However, where are these places?

6   **A new institution is needed.** Today, neither school nor university faculty have the knowledge needed to adequately address the challenging goal of higher learning for all of the nation's children and youths. Systematically, the university's research and development capacity must be brought to bear on the nation's new challenges for learning, teaching, and schooling. Furthermore, just as systematically, the nation needs a way to prepare and equip teachers for new and different work. Currently, there is no place to meet either of these needs. But a synergy can result from combining the resources for meeting both needs in a single new institution, in a place where school and university faculty are disposed and equipped to collaborate on invention and discovery. It must also be a place where the school and university faculty collaborate in preparing the nation's present and future education workforce so that time and space can be made available for their learning as well. But what would such a place look like—and where would the resources come from?

Responses to many of these questions are addressed more fully in *Tomorrow's Schools: And Tomorrow's Schools of Education,* which grew out of the Group's continued study and experience over the next several years. However, partial, general answers to the questions were embedded in the vision The Holmes Group described for educating prospective and practicing teachers in their first volume. The vision is elaborated on briefly here.

Tomorrow's Teachers: Its Core Vision and Its Controversies

The recommendation getting most attention from the higher education and K-12 sectors was the idea of extending the normal four-year entry route into teaching. Then, as now, most future teachers complete their teacher preparation in four years, and then start work that has the same full professional responsibilities as the five-, ten- and twenty-year veteran teacher. Beginning teachers begin their work in classrooms where they are isolated from other adults and free to learn much of their practice the hard way—with their students.

Part of the reasoning behind the extended program recommendation was the awareness that a good liberal arts education takes four years. Thus, students who go to college to major in the liberal arts, or in a discipline such as physics or math, it takes four years. Similarly, students who major in an applied field, such as business, communications, or engineering, will also need four years, but the students don't graduate, find work, and begin assuming responsibilities identical to those of the most experienced members of the firm. Advancement typically requires further study and learning from experience.

No one could imagine how a would-be teacher could squeeze all of this learning into the same four years—a quality liberal education, a deep understanding and agility with one or more disciplinary subjects, and the training and practice needed to teach a range of diverse learners autonomously and as effectively as an experienced colleague. It just didn't seem possible, for while a number of prospective teachers are gifted individuals, many are also just ordinary college students. So The Holmes Group held to the high standard for a broadly and deeply educated teacher, and they proposed several alternative possibilities for dealing with the extended learning requirements. The new expectations were:

- *Tomorrow's Teachers* will be prepared as knowledge workers. With growth in information and knowledge occurring at an ever faster pace, future teachers need to be equipped with a broad, first-rate liberal education, as well as deep knowledge and understanding of at least one or more subjects. The old practice of having teachers simply "know a little bit about a lot of things" is no longer adequate, even for those working with young children.

- "Tomorrow's Teachers" also need to learn their teaching methods and practices from those who are themselves identified as competent teachers—both at the university and in schools. The practice of putting would-be teachers in sites where there is little if any quality control over what they are learning must end.

- "Tomorrow's Teachers" must have the opportunity to learn and demonstrate their competence through a substantial internship in real schools. An internship of some duration is needed to replace the "student teaching" of old where a neophyte could come in, meet the students, observe briefly, help out for a time, and then solo in all subjects for several weeks. Learning occurs over time, and effective teaching requires getting to know each student—understanding how they learn, how they think about various learning tasks, and what helps them progress. The challenge of complex teaching, where the teacher knows all of the students, how each one is learning, what works best for them, how to judge their work, and give them helpful guidance in many subjects is only learned over months of work—not weeks.

Because all of this learning couldn't be squeezed into four years—a five-year baccalaureate became a possibility, or a four-year baccalaureate if a student studied all year and didn't take the summers off. Another alternative was a four-year baccalaureate with one or more years of master's study. In still another scenario, a student could earn a four-year baccalaureate and enter teaching as an "instructor," pursuing added study in the evenings, weekends, or summers. However, an "instructor" would work under the guidance and tutelage of a professional teacher—not on his or her own. Whichever route was taken, teachers would only be recommended as "career professional teachers" once they passed their internship demonstration requirements and the required knowledge exams.

Tomorrow's Teachers: Reality Clashes with Hope and Vision

Once *Tomorrow's Teachers* went public, the alarms went off. Instead of being applauded for working to improve a field they had long neglected, Holmes's members were castigated for "trying to take over a field not rightfully theirs." Recognizing the leadership potential of the Holmes members, some read the report as dictating to others, provoking a "What right do *they* have to tell *us* what to do" response. As an ad hoc group, Holmes had neglected the Washington-based policy establishment—to our peril. Even in its infancy, The Holmes Group had more enemies than friends in higher education and in the organizations that represented its members.

Part of the tension arose from the extraordinary attention Holmes received, and part of it was worry that we might draw off resources currently flowing to our newfound competitors for the reform agenda. There was also disagreement, if not anger, over some of the proposed reform ideas themselves, for in one way or another change always threatens somebody's status quo.

One university administrator sent a note in with his fee payment for founding membership in Holmes, adding that he would not support additional undergraduate study or graduate work for teachers. The Holmes Board of Directors returned his check and urged him to pursue his agenda with others who shared his position. The Group didn't need those who would join them for appearances only, and they certainly didn't need members who would undercut their reform agenda and commitment. However, the returned check only led the sender to create a dissident group that would compete with and distract from the work of Holmes.

Much of the negative hoopla centered on the requirement for closer working relationships between universities and schools, as well as on added learning requirements for teaching. Nonetheless, *Tomorrow's Teachers* laid out the big ideas and organizing framework for The Holmes Group. Their mission to "improve education through research and development and the preparation of career professional teachers" was hard to argue with. Embedded in this mission were ambitious hopes and understandings for both research and teacher education, but the proposed changes in research received scant attention—lost in the swirling controversies that surrounded changes in teacher education.

Few faculty members were eager to work more closely with the schools, and the students weren't eager to exchange an earning year for another year of study and tuition. However, some of the graduate research universities were under way with teacher education offered at the graduate level, after the candidate had successfully earned a baccalaureate degree in a discipline or the liberal arts. An added year of study and internship achieved or brought them close to a master's degree where graduates could enter teaching at a higher pay level, thus compensating them for the added year over time. For most universities the idea of taking five years to prepare their teacher candidates was a scary one, for they feared that prospective teachers would go to other institutions for the faster four-year track.

Tomorrow's Schools: Principles for the Design of Professional Development Schools

Tomorrow's Schools provoked less intrigue and worry than *Tomorrows Teachers.* It was a creative, problem-solving task to think about America's schools-of-the-future, and how they could further innovation and better teacher education. With participants drawn from the elementary, secondary, college, and education policy arenas, the meetings brought distinguished practitioners and scholars together to think through the issues and challenges for these new institutions, which came to be called "professional development schools."

These were the innovation sites—real schools working in partnership with the universities for purposes of learning new ways to increase learning for everybody in them—young students, prospective teachers, and practicing faculty from the schools and the university. The PDSs, as they came to be called, would have large numbers of interns practicing in them, thereby giving some of the school faculty time to learn, study, and engage in R&D activities and helping to find new ways of bringing about better learning.

The intent was to figure out how to do this in the unique environment in which the schools and universities live—with formal, long-term relationships being developed over time—as with teaching hospitals that also have interns, residents, and collaborative research agendas. The report was subtitled "Principles for the Design of Professional Development Schools." They were to guide the collaborative study and dialog that would have to take place before actual *design principles* could be mutually drafted. Subsequently, actual experience would inform decisions about appropriate standards—and any additional funding that might be needed to carry out these new responsibilities.

Tomorrow's Schools of Education:
What Do We Want to Be Anyway?

The first two volumes—*Tomorrow's Teachers* and *Tomorrow's Schools*—took much less time to prepare than the third. In part, this was because many of the faculty and deans had already struggled with the agenda for five or six years. They knew the challenges, and how much easier it was to talk and write about them than overcome them. It was also easier to think about changing others—such as teachers and schools—than changing one's own faculty in *Tomorrow's Schools of Education.*

More likely, though, the fundamental culprit was the information-knowledge age that had placed growing demands for specialization and expansion on schools of education. Once brought to campus to develop educational knowledge and to prepare administrators and teachers for the public schools, they had long strayed from this core mission. Over the last half century, as knowledge expanded and society became more specialized, they seized many opportunities that took them further and further away from schoolteaching and student learning—and even into fields quite removed from K-12 schools.

However, the press from *Tomorrow's Teachers* and *Tomorrow's Schools* called for the education schools to struggle with their identity as a knowledge producing, knowledge extending agent of society. Whom should they serve now that everybody needed to learn for a lifetime? Just schoolteachers and counselors and administrators? Weren't the other programs that focused on education throughout society just as important? Weren't their ultimate clients now everyone—instead of just the young students in America's schools?

If schools of education went back to their original focus on research and personnel preparation for the nation's public schools, what would happen to the many programs that focus on education throughout society, be it business and industry, higher education, health and athletics, museum education, adult guidance, or rehabilitation counseling to name a few? Holmes pushed for priority setting because trying to do too much with too little inhibits impact. If education schools can do many things well, that's good. However, if doing a great many things comes at the expense of good research and personnel preparation for the nation's schools, then they should not be so accredited.

The Holmes focus on *teacher education* and R&D in schools thus threatened ed school faculty and administrators who feared a redistribution of resources to correct the straitened circumstances of teacher education. Added tension came from the fact that teacher education in most places was not an area of graduate study, and this was a problem. Advanced degrees were needed only for education specialties—e.g., administration, counseling, testing, special education, curriculum, and so on—but not for improved classroom teaching. Advanced learning was equated with leaving the classroom.

So the reach for consensus on *Tomorrow's Schools of Education* was long and tiring. It never really came, as more and more faculty and administrators sought a return to the status quo. Efforts were made to purposefully bring much of the education specialists' training and research into Professional Development Schools, but the interest was not there. Efforts were made to involve other external support groups, but the energy and will was diminishing. The deans signed off on the final report, but they did so reluctantly, for many of them remembered and feared the fate of Henry Holmes.

What Is Next for Holmes? Then and Now

Having completed the trilogy of reports, The Holmes Group chose to reconsider its own future. Now that its agenda was clear, what could they do to strengthen their institutions' resolve and their capacity to better support the proposed reforms?

The Holmes Board entered into a major strategic planning effort twelve years after their work began. In doing so, they acted on a recommendation from *Tomorrow's Schools of Education*—to bring their colleagues and allies from the schools and other professional groups into the organization as full partners. They changed their name from *The Holmes Group* to *The Holmes Partnership,* emphasizing their collaborative arrangements between universities and schools, and their emphasis on authentic partnership. They decided to keep the Holmes main office at a volunteer university with a primarily volunteer staff and to broaden their improvement mission.

So Why Revisit the Trilogy?

Because a generation of students has come through America's schools since the work began with a learning record hardly distinguished from that of the 1980s. From *A Nation at Risk* we have come to *No Child Left Behind.* The rhetoric is easy to say, easily understood, and sets a wonderful goal. Measuring student progress is an important step, but we know that weighing people doesn't make them heavier and testing students doesn't make them smarter. Only more effective approaches to the work of teaching and learning will make truly significant differences with educators equipped with the knowledge, tools, and learning environments to make their efforts increasingly productive.

So let us revisit the Trilogy because the agenda is important and remains unfinished. Let us examine it again with the universities and schools that have persevered and continued to further the work. Their faculty and graduate students can review the ideas in the Trilogy and draw on their experience to examine their relevance today—for . . . if we don't learn from history, we are bound to repeat it. Which of the ideas from back then are worth keeping? Which need to be updated, strengthened, and corrected? What should be discarded as naïve or poorly conceived at the outset—and what ideas should take their place?

Let us also return to some of the universities that abandoned the efforts. Their services are still needed, and we should urge their participation as we reconsider the early ideas. We must also note and preserve the strong parts of the work we did achieve, such as the Holmes Scholars Program that was launched to help create "the new faculty" called for in *Tomorrow's Schools of Education.* The program has added strength and diversity to our university faculty and school leadership—and must be continued.

The Holmes Partnership may wish to develop a stronger political-economic plan for establishing PDSs or Partnership Schools. Had we done this early on, the innovation and reform agenda might have taken better hold. Moreover, as part of that plan, local, state, and national linkages between and among the government agencies supporting the reform should be put in place if Partnership Schools are to be nurtured and sustained. So reconsider the ideas with policymakers in the schools and universities, and at various levels of government.

Then there are more recent initiatives that should be capitalized on as the nation continues its search for innovation and school improvement. Microsoft and the Philadelphia school district just opened a "School of the Future"—"anticipated to be the most progressive and ingenious place of public learning ever built." Let us hope that the "School of the Future" becomes a PDS or Holmes Partnership School, and let us explore many more such "partnerships" with businesses across the country.

Visiting the Trilogy a generation after the work began also begs the question about what can be done in the next generation, for the original *tomorrows* are now yesterdays, and the future for many students is not promising. What forces can be mobilized and harnessed to encourage universities and schools, in Partnership, to develop the innovative philosophies and practices needed to achieve great student learning and great teacher education? What are the new possibilities if we don't follow the guidelines proposed here? Holmes must continue to foster that learning.

■|■|■

The Holmes Group's Executive Board

DONALD P. ANDERSON
Dean, College of Education
Ohio State University

CHARLES W. CASE
Dean, College of Education
University of Iowa

NANCY S. COLE
Dean, College of Education
University of Illinois-
Champaign/Urbana

JAMES COOPER
Dean, School of Education
University of Virginia

DEAN C. CORRIGAN
Dean, College of Education
Texas A & M University

BERNARD R. GIFFORD
Dean, School of Education
University of California, Berkeley

GARY A. GRIFFIN
Dean, College of Education
University of Illinois, Chicago

ROBERT H. KOFF
Dean, School of Education
State University of New York, Albany

JUDITH E. LANIER, *Chair*
Dean, College of Education
Michigan State University

CECIL G. MISKEL
Dean, School of Education
University of Utah

FRANK B. MURRAY
Dean, College of Education
University of Delaware

JOHN R. PALMER, *Vice-Chair*
Dean, School of Education
University of Wisconsin-Madison

HUGH G. PETRIE
Dean, Faculty of Educational Studies
State University of New York, Buffalo

P. MICHAEL TIMPANE
President, Teachers College
Columbia University

■|■|■

PART ONE

A Report of The Holmes Group

Tomorrow's Teachers

■|■|■

Preface

The concern with the quality of education in the United States has extended to the nation's colleges and universities. A growing number of analysts are now urging higher education leaders to get into the thick of reform activities, and many of them are doing so. The Holmes Group began its critical analysis of teacher education in 1983. Assisted by former U.S. Secretary of Education Terrel Bell, several skeptical foundations, and a number of hopeful academic vice-presidents, the education deans forming The Holmes Group began with the modest goal of finding ways they could improve teacher education programs in universities such as their own—that is, those with research productivity as a central responsibility of the institution.

The response to their early meetings was unanticipated. A flurry of concern swirled about their discussions, as if the assembled leaders were plotting revolution. Serious thinking about the problems of teacher education and teaching in their own institutions, quite apart from the structures and strictures of established education groups, was not well received. Apparently, the business of teacher education in America has been a thriving one for higher education, and to even talk about initiatives that might disrupt its continuance, or increase its costs, threatened those profiting from the status quo.

In spite of the controversy, the deans forged ahead. They needed to provide direction in their own institutions and states, for teaching and teacher education remain troubled fields. And the deans needed to clarify their own thinking on such matters, so they could exercise responsible leadership in this period of crisis in American public education. Most of them sensed a genuine obligation to participate in the re-creation of America's schools—so they again become places of pride and a major resource for the development of a literate, productive, and cohesive citizenry.

Originally the deans hoped they would be able to develop new, higher standards for teacher education at their institutions across a fifteen-month period. But as their study and deliberation progressed, the unrealistic nature of their original time frame became apparent. In retrospect, it is not surprising that they found the problems associated with improving teacher education more complex than expected. But as the complicating issues were revealed, the deans modified their time frame, rather than their resolve. The development of sound examinations to better screen individuals entering teaching would take three to five years; apparently, the development of strong standards to better screen the institutions that prepare teachers would take a comparable amount of time.

While the fifteen-month period of study and deliberation did not produce a set of refined standards, it was productive for the emerging consortium. Necessary guidelines for the future work of the reform-minded group emerged during their time of intense discussion and consultation. A common agenda, shared understandings, and a broad outline for action commitments were identified. Described in the body of this report, the shared goals, understandings, and action commitments will guide the refinement and gradual implementation phase of the consortium, bringing greater specificity to the standards development work across the next several years. Members of the consortium will also participate in the intellectual and political activities required to ensure that future teachers prepared according to the standards have receptive environments in which to work. In time, it is expected that the emerging standards will serve as a basis for accreditation of research universities that prepare Career Professional Teachers.

More than 100 research universities in the United States have now been invited to participate in further development and study pursuant to The Holmes Group goals and reform activities described in this report. The institutions invited to become charter members of The Holmes Group have several unique features that form the basis of their consortium. They are, while encompassing a fairly wide spectrum of quality themselves, the leading research institutions in their respective states and regions. They are, by any commonly accepted standard, the top ten percent of American institutions engaged in teacher education, even though in some cases their teacher education programs are not currently among the nation's best. All the more reason for the consortium which, at its core, is simply a means by which the members can improve and reform their programs. However, the consortium has to be more than a self-help group, because its vision of the kind of professional who should be permitted to teach school in America requires the consortium to work equally hard to change the teaching profession itself. The consortium, by aligning itself with other organizations, agencies, and institutions who support its goals and general directions, wishes to see nothing less than the transformation of teaching from an occupation into a genuine profession.

Thus the consortium is organized around the twin goals of the reform of teacher education and the reform of the teaching profession. It assumes that these reforms will prosper if the nation's best universities are committed to teacher education. It assumes also that teacher education programs will be different in these institutions for all the reasons that make these institutions so academically powerful in every other respect. They are institutions that attract more than their share of the best and the brightest students; they have the faculty who, on the whole, are the nation's best and most authoritative sources of information in their fields; they command substantial resources; and, in the case of education, they are the institutions that have educated and will continue to educate the professoriate in education. If for no other reason than the fact that the teachers of teachers should do their graduate work in institutions that have exemplary teacher education programs, a consortium of institutions that educate teacher educators as well as teachers is needed. This consortium is The Holmes Group.

Judith E. Lanier, Dean
College of Education
Michigan State University

■|■|■

Acknowledgments

The study and consensus-building deliberations of the past several years culminate in the release of this report. As with all projects of such complexity, the efforts have benefited greatly from the invaluable contributions made by others. They deserve our mention as well as our expressions of gratitude.

The Holmes Group efforts have grown from their uncertain beginnings to an organization with broad participation and well-focused goals. Much of this evolution was facilitated by the Johnson Foundation's continued support of the group's deliberations. We offer our special thanks to the foundation's president, William Boyd, and vice-president, Henry Halsted. With the kind and helpful assistance of Kay Mauer, Susan Poulsen Krogh, and other fine staff of the Wingspread Conference Center, our work on these difficult issues was able to be both productive and pleasant.

We are also appreciative of the strong encouragement of former U.S. Secretary of Education Terrel Bell. Although Dr. Bell partially funded the group through the Secretary's Discretionary Fund, his most important contribution was recognizing the importance of our work and urging our leadership in taking an introspective look at teacher education in America. His strong advice to remain steadfast and courageous during periods of doubt was particularly helpful.

We also wish to recognize the support of Edward Meade of the Ford Foundation, and Alden Dunham of the Carnegie Corporation of New York. We thank them for their financial support, genuine interest, and personal involvement in the efforts leading to the formation of The Holmes Group plans. Their commitment to the improvement of schooling in America continues to evidence their own and their foundations' interest in the public good.

We would like to extend our gratitude to Gary H. Dryer, Joanne DiFranco, and Jeanette Minkel. As competent staff at Michigan State University, they gave graciously and generously of their time and talents in the providing of accounting, secretarial, conference coordination, and manuscript preparation services for the group. MSU designer Lawrence Cole created the cover and coordinated the printing for the report, and Suzanne Ludwig provided final editing services. We thank them for their kind and helpful assistance.

Finally, we must acknowledge the tremendous contribution made by the faculty and administrators of the participating institutions of higher education. The deans, academic vice-presidents, and many others gave generously of their time and energy. Their intellectual and financial resources also contributed in a most significant way in making this effort possible.

A Shared Agenda

America's dissatisfaction with its schools has become chronic and epidemic. Teachers have long been at the center of the debates, and they still are today. Many commentators admit that no simple remedy can correct the problems of public education, yet simple remedies abound. Most are aimed at teachers: Institute merit pay; eliminate teacher education; test teachers to make sure they know eighth-grade facts. Paradoxically, teachers are the butt of most criticism, yet singled out as the one best hope for reform.

Teaching must be improved, but plans for improving teaching also must be improved. This report is a contribution to both endeavors. We write as members of The Holmes Group, a consortium of education deans and chief academic officers from the major research universities in each of the fifty states. We came together because we knew that our own schools and universities were not doing well in teacher education, and because we hoped to improve. We have probed the problems and explored remedies. This has never been easy, and often it has been painful. Pursuing the shortcomings of one's own profession, and one's own institutions, is difficult at best.

It has been fruitful, nonetheless. In our nearly two years of work together we have found much to criticize in teacher education. But we have also found ourselves willing to argue for radical improvements that most of us would have dismissed as impractical just a few years ago. We have decided that we must work for the changes that we believe to be right, rather than those that we know can succeed. Much is at stake, for American students' performance will not improve much if the quality of teaching is not much improved. And teaching will not improve much without dramatic improvements in teacher education.

This report outlines our goals for the reform of teacher education. It sketches our plans for reaching those goals. And it explains our reasoning. The report is the result of two years' work, but it is only a beginning. It is a program for action for our schools and universities, one for which we will work in the years to come.

Our Goals

1　*To make the education of teachers intellectually more solid.* Teachers must have a greater command of academic subjects and of the skills to teach them. They also need to become more thoughtful students of teaching, and its improvement.

2　*To recognize differences in teachers' knowledge, skill, and commitment, in their education, certification, and work.* If teachers are to become more effective professionals, we must distinguish between novices, competent members of the profession, and high-level professional leaders.

3　*To create standards of entry to the profession—examinations and educational requirements—that are professionally relevant and intellectually defensible.* America cannot afford any more teachers who fail a twelfth-grade competency test. Neither can we afford to let people into teaching just because they have passed such simple, and often simpleminded exams.

4　*To connect our own institutions to schools.* If university faculties are to become more expert educators of teachers, they must make better use of expert teachers in the education of other teachers, and in research on teaching. In addition, schools must become places where both teachers and university faculty can systematically inquire into practice and improve it.

5　*To make schools better places for teachers to work, and to learn.* This will require less bureaucracy, more professional autonomy, and more leadership for teachers. But schools where teachers can learn from each other, and from other professionals, will be schools where good teachers will want to work. They also will be schools in which students will learn more.

We note that these goals have large implications beyond our own schools and departments of education. They reach into other parts of our universities, where most prospective teachers get most of their higher education.

Our own professional schools are part of the problem. But what of the many badly taught and often mindlessly required courses that our students, like all undergraduates, must take in the various departments of arts, sciences, and humanities? Is the weak pedagogy, the preoccupation with "covering the material," the proliferation of multiple-choice tests, and the delegation of much teaching to graduate students—increasingly, students who cannot speak English very well—not full of messages about the nature of knowledge and standards for acceptable teaching? Can we expect many good teachers to come from universities that teach their undergraduates in these ways? These problems are as real as those in our own schools and departments, and as influential for school teaching. We are pressing ahead with our own faculties, and will continue. American colleges and universities must get to work on these larger problems of teacher education. Preliminary conversations with top officials of our universities have turned up encouraging evidence of their wish to attack these difficult problems.

Our goals also lead us out, from the universities in which intending teachers study, to the schools in which they must practice. We have become convinced that university officials and professors must join with schools, and with the teacher organizations and state and local school governments that shape the schools, to change the teaching profession. Schools no less than universities are places in which teachers learn. Unfortunately that learning typically has been lonely, and catch-as-catch-can. It has been more a matter of daily survival in a difficult job than progress toward professional improvement. America's children need schools in which teachers can learn, in which teachers can thoughtfully investigate and improve professional practice. For schools in which most teachers can barely learn enough to survive are schools in which most students will do no better. Together with other educators we have much to do, to make schools better places for teachers and students.

An Agenda for Improving a Profession

Professional education prepares people for practical assignments: to teach, to heal, to design buildings, or to manage organizations. One therefore cannot consider teacher education apart from the practical assignments that we call teaching, any more than one could consider medical education apart from the practice of medicine. Unhappily, teaching and teacher education have a long history of mutual impairment. Teacher education has long been intellectually weak; this further eroded the prestige of an already poorly esteemed profession, and it encouraged many inadequately prepared people to enter teaching. But teaching long has been an underpaid and over-worked occupation, making it difficult for universities to recruit good students to teacher education or to take it as seriously as they have taken education for more pres-tigious professions. Teaching, after all, comes with large responsibilities but modest material rewards. Good teachers must be knowledgeable, but they have few oppor-tunities to use that knowledge to improve their profession, or to help their col-leagues improve. And, despite their considerable skill and knowledge, good teachers have few opportunities to advance within their profession.

As we try to improve teaching and teacher education, then, we cannot avoid try-ing to improve the profession in which teachers will practice. Here we find a curi-ous situation. While the intellectual and social demands on teachers have escalated at an astonishing rate since this century began, the nature and organization of teach-ers' work have changed only a little since the middle of the nineteenth century. We now live in an age when many elementary school students have their own microcom-puters. These students can put some of the most amazing achievements of modern science and technology to work in support of their learning. Yet their teachers are still working with the same job descriptions that teachers had in the mid-1800s, when *McGuffey's Reader* and spelling slates were the leading educational technology.

It is a painful contrast, one that embarrasses us as educators and as Americans. Consider these points. Many teachers still instruct whole classes of students in all subjects, as there is little or no academic specialization until high school. They still teach classes all day long, with little or no time for preparation, analysis, or evalua-tion of their work. They still spend all of their professional time alone with stu-dents, leaving little or no time for work with other adult professionals to improve their knowledge and skills. Nor are they thought worthy of such endeavors or capa-ble of developing the requisite expertise. But teachers have a lengthening list of responsibilities. They must teach children with many special needs and disabilities—children who were rarely in school until recently. They must supervise extensive testing and evaluation programs for their students, and try to make sense of the results. They must cope with a variety of state and federal programs and requirements and mandates. The list goes on.

The schoolteacher's job description, then, is one that none of our universities would ever visit on a member of their faculties. For they know that teachers who work under such conditions have no time left to learn themselves, to be productive schol-ars, or even to do justice to their students' homework. Yet, nearly all schoolteachers hold such creaky old jobs—even now, in the slick, high-tech years of the late twen-tieth century. The past century has seen the most amazing explosion of knowledge in human history. Science has revolutionized our understanding of nature several times over in eight decades, and no end is in sight. The social sciences have been invented and prospered, and the humanities have been enriched, expanded, and radically revised. All of this has greatly enriched and complicated our understanding of the world and of human society. Yet the jobs we assign to teachers have remained very nearly the same as they were before these great intellectual revolutions began. What is teaching if it is not bringing students into that new world of the mind? But how can teachers do such work well, when they must do it with a job that was designed for a society in which most Americans could barely read, in which books besides the Bible were rare, and in which teachers were paid in pumpkins and firewood?

If someone argued that doctors should practice modern medicine within the terms of an 1850s job description, evangelizing patients from a horse or wagon, working for low pay, wandering the countryside in search of work, and requiring no more education than one's patients, he would be ridiculed by any audience. Yet most Americans think nothing of requiring teachers to carry out a late twentieth-century assignment while locked into a mid-nineteenth century job description. Nor does it strike them as odd to then blame teachers for a job badly done.

It seems indisputable that teachers' assignments must be changed. The best education will be no antidote to demeaning jobs that make little room for what has been learned, that offer few incentives for learning more, and that are swamped with clerical and other responsibilities. The first requirement is jobs that will challenge and reward the best minds now in teaching, and that will attract others just as good. Above all else, teaching must make room for top practitioners who can lead their field to improvement. This means jobs in which fine teachers can use their pedagogical expertise to improve other teachers' work, as well as to help children. It means jobs in which teachers can become experts in a specialized area, such as curriculum development, teacher evaluation, or school management. It means jobs in which real leaders can exercise the responsibilities and reap the rewards of serious professionalism. We call these people *Career Professionals.* They would be people at the top of their field, who have proven their excellence in teaching, in their own education, and in examinations. They would play a role in education not unlike that of clinical professors in medicine.

But such a cadre could only be small—we estimate roughly one-fifth of all teachers. A majority of the teaching force should be *Professional Teachers:* people who have proven their competence at work, in rigorous professional qualification examinations, and in their own education. Their jobs would differ from those of today's teachers in their more serious educational requirements, and in the stiff standards for entry to and continuance in teaching. These would be jobs to which only bright, highly qualified people could gain entry. They also would be jobs in which teachers could continue to learn and improve—among other ways, through their work with one another and with Career Professionals. They would be jobs that could lead to a Career Professional position, if the incumbent were sufficiently gifted and willing to invest the time in advanced study and examinations.

Finally, many teachers would be novices. We call these novices *Instructors*. They would be beginning teachers, whose job would last only a few years. The entrance requirements would be flexible. Bright college graduates with a solid academic background in one or two subjects, and who could pass an entrance exam, would be welcome. So would be adults from other professions, who wanted to try out teaching, and whose knowledge of an academic field made them a safe bet to assume limited instructional responsibility. Work as Instructors would offer many talented people an opportunity for service and for learning, and it would give them a chance to explore a job about which they were uncertain. It also would enable American schools to absorb enrollment swings without the mindless responses—first hiring thousands of unqualified warm bodies, and then riffing thousands of capable teachers—that have marked the last three decades of educational history. Instructors would be qualified to teach, but their work would be supported and supervised by Career Professionals.

This array of teaching assignments would make room only for well-educated teachers. But it would recognize differences in competence, commitment, and responsibility among these teachers. It would create room for professional improvement and advancement within teaching, but it would tie these opportunities to professional expertise and commitment. This array of jobs would therefore create incentives for a constructive professionalism: for learning, for serious inquiry, and for helping others to improve.

One way to think about these jobs, then, is as a way to improve the teaching profession. But we are educators and teacher educators. As we think about preparing people for such jobs, we see the need for basic changes in teacher education. Certainly the present arrangements for educating teachers would not produce many qualified applicants. We therefore sketch below our view of the changes we must make, if our schools and departments are to produce people worthy of such assignments as we have just described. This sketch reflects our agenda for work in the coming years.

We are also university officials who work within state requirements for teacher licensing, and whose academic curricula increasingly have been driven by those requirements. The job structure just outlined implies some major changes in the criteria for teacher certification and in the university's role in that certification. We sketch these changes first.

Changes Required in Teacher Licensing

The changes we propose would establish a three-tier system of teacher licensing. Two of these certificates—Professional Teacher and Career Professional—would be renewable and could carry tenure. The other—Instructor—would be temporary and nonrenewable. Each certificate would depend upon entrance exams and educational accomplishments. The two professional certificates also would require assessment of performance on the job.

Instructor

No professional certificate should be available to a teacher who has only an undergraduate degree. The license open to Instructors must therefore be temporary. These certificates should be non-renewable, and good for no more than five years. We call these people Instructors to emphasize our belief that they should not be confused with the nation's corps of professional teachers. Since teachers should offer instruction only in the academic subjects that they know well, Instructors should be licensed only in those subjects in which they have an undergraduate major or minor. In addition, no teacher should be allowed to practice as an independent professional without at least a year of carefully supervised practice, and advanced study in pedagogy and human learning. Since beginning Instructors will have met neither of these requirements, they should be licensed to practice only under the direct supervision of a fully certified professional. These temporary certificates also would require an intensive professional development course (several months of full-time study) before candidates would be admitted to practice.

Taking and even passing college and university courses are no guarantees that the material has been learned. Thus, all Instructors should also pass a written test in each subject they will teach, prior to certification. This exam should test for their understanding of the basic structure of the discipline, and tenets of a broad liberal education. They should additionally pass a general test of their reading and writing ability, and a test of the rudiments of pedagogy. These tests would assess reasoning as well as specialized knowledge, general information, and memory. They should be sufficiently difficult so that many college graduates could not pass.

Professional Teacher

This would be the first full professional certificate. It would be granted only to teachers who had completed a master's degree in teaching. This degree would include continued study in the candidate's major or minor academic field, studies of pedagogy and human learning, work in classrooms with children who were at risk, and a full year of supervised teaching.

Professional Teachers would have to pass the same examinations in the subjects they would teach as would Instructors, and they would have to pass the same general reading and writing exams as well. If they wished to add a new major or minor field since qualifying as an Instructor, exams for them also would have to be passed prior to certification. And they would have to pass examinations in pedagogy and human learning similar to those taken in their subject fields.

But one cannot learn to practice in any profession without extensive practical experience. There is ample evidence that if intending teachers do not have carefully supervised and extensive practical experience at the beginning of their careers, most will not learn to teach well. They may learn how to keep their classes quiet and their students buried in workbooks, but they will not learn how to help them to think, to press ahead on their own, and to care for learning. Thus, no professional certificate should be granted unless the candidates have met several additional requirements.

First, they should prove their competence as practitioners. Standardized tests cannot cover this entire task. They are suited to assessing how good a student of teaching one is—just as they can assess how good a student of law, history, or physics one is. But candidates' performances on such tests are very poor predictors of their capacity to teach these things well. One cannot be a good teacher of a subject unless one is a good student of that subject; teaching cannot be content-free. But to be a good teacher, it is not enough to know a subject well as a student. One must know its pedagogy. One must know it as a teacher, and not just as a student. This is analogous to the difference, in medicine, between being a good student of anatomy and physiology on the one had, and knowing how to perform surgery on the other. The analytic knowledge of the subject is a necessary element in good surgery, but it is hardly the same thing as surgical skill.

In order to qualify as a Professional Teacher, then, candidates also should be able to demonstrate competence as teachers of academic subjects. This means practical and varied demonstrations of professional skills and knowledge. They could include carefully assembled portfolios of teaching and/or studies of one's own practice, planned exhibitions of one's teaching, and unannounced observations of the candidate's classroom performance. Whatever the form of these demonstrations, they should afford a balanced, rigorous scrutiny of candidates' practice with a variety of learning groups.

Career Professional

This would be the highest license in teaching. It would be granted to Professional Teachers whose continued study and professional accomplishments revealed outstanding achievements as teachers, and promise as teacher educators and analysts of teaching.

A first requirement would, of course, be satisfactory completion of all the requirements for the Professional Teacher license. A second requirement would be extensive experience as a Professional Teacher, with outstanding performance.

The third requirement for this license would be further specialized study, ordinarily for the doctorate either in an academic subject or in some other specialty.

For instance, many Career Professionals would take a major role in the supervision and education of practicing teachers; they might, therefore, choose to concentrate their academic studies in teacher education. Others might serve as head teachers, and specialize in instructional management. Still other Career Professionals might focus their academic studies on the assessment of student learning or in advanced study of subject matter pedagogy.

The typical way to satisfy these requirements for specialization would be a combination of successful doctoral study and demonstrations of practical competence. Thus, a candidate might present a completed doctorate in teacher education, including extensive clinical research on teachers' learning, or on alternative approaches to improving pedagogy in a subject, or some related matter. The candidate also would present evidence from practice about competence in this specialty. As noted above, these practice exams would include oral exams on teacher education, unplanned observations of work as teacher educators, and a portfolio of evidence from the study of the candidate's own practice, among other things.

But candidates for the Career Professional license might well complete these requirements for advanced study and outstanding professional practice without the doctorate. In some cases an academic thesis might be an inappropriate vehicle, and in others the candidate's field might be covered as well in clinical as in university classroom study. Candidacy for this license should therefore be open to practitioners who can demonstrate high achievement in both the study of practice and practice itself, whether or not they have the doctorate.

■ ■ ■

These paragraphs only sketch our view of the teacher licensing requirements that should be adopted, and quickly summarize the arguments for these standards. Much remains to be done before such certification standards could be put into effect. New standardized examinations in reading, writing, academic subjects, pedagogy, and the foundations of education would have to be devised and field-tested. New forms of examination for professional competence also would have to be devised and tested, so that practitioners could be certified on the basis of proven professional competence rather than competence as a student of a subject. Both of these are large assignments, the second more than the first. One of our highest priorities will be working with others in education, and with specialists in tests and professional assessment, so that we can have such examinations ready to use in five years. They will not be perfect. But we are confident that a balanced portfolio of assessment approaches can be devised, one that will allow us to discriminate those who know a subject well from those who do not, and that will allow us to discriminate those who know how to teach that subject from those who merely know it as a student.

These teacher licensing standards also imply a great deal of work for our own education schools and departments, and for our universities. We turn to those matters now.

Changes Required in Universities and Schools

Here we discuss dramatic changes in education as a field of study. We outline revisions in both the undergraduate and graduate curriculum, parallel changes in the study of pedagogy and allied fields, and the new relationships between universities and schools that will be required to support these changes.

First, the undergraduate education major must be abolished in our universities. For elementary teachers, this degree has too often become a substitute for learning any academic subject deeply enough to teach it well. These teachers are certified to teach all things to all children. But few of them know much about anything, because they are required to know a little of everything.

No wonder so many pupils arrive in high school so weak in so many subjects.

We emphasize that no teachers, even the temporary Instructors, should be allowed to teach subjects they have not studied deeply. Professionally certified teachers should teach only subjects they both know well and can teach well. Eliminating the undergraduate education major is therefore only a beginning toward improving the quality of teacher education.

How can we say this, when so many reformers argue that we need only eliminate education courses to solve the problems of poor teaching?

Our answer is simple. America already has experimented with this unfortunate idea. Most of our universities have long since eliminated most education requirements for secondary school teachers, to provide more subject matter specialization. Many universities never had serious requirements. Intending high school teachers in our universities thus take only two or three education courses. This has long been the rule.

How has this approach worked?

Not well. The last five years of reports on high schools present a dismal account of high school teaching. Most of it is dreary. Teaching consists chiefly of either dull lectures or fact-oriented workbook assignments. Most teachers exhibit no deep grasp of their subjects, nor any passion for them. Their pedagogy is as sadly lacking as their grip on the material. But these problems with their performance as teachers cannot be chalked up to weak course work in education, or insufficient course work in the subjects that they teach. These teachers had the same course work in the subjects they teach as other undergraduate majors. They had the university education that many reforms hold out as the alternative to teacher education.

What explains this result?

Part of the answer probably lies in the ways these teachers were taught in school, which seems to have been similarly dreary. But another part lies in our own universities. They strive to hire highly qualified academic specialists, who know their subjects well and do distinguished research. But few of these specialists know how to teach well, and many seem not to care. The undergraduate education that intending teachers receive is full of the same bad teaching that litters American high schools.

To eliminate the undergraduate education major would remedy none of this. In fact, it would probably worsen things. For most of the education majors in our universities are in elementary teaching, and most observers argue that pedagogy in elementary schools is better—more lively, imaginative, and considerate of students—than in high schools. Cutting out the courses that help to produce such teaching would do little good, and the evidence from high schools suggests that it might well do some evil.

But we do not argue for retaining undergraduate education majors. We argue instead that eliminating those majors without dramatically improving the academic subjects that undergraduates learn would be a sad error. To cut down on courses in pedagogy for intending schoolteachers without improving pedagogy in the universities would make a horrible joke of educational reform.

Instead, we urge that our universities take three steps to strengthen education in academic subjects, as accompaniments to the elimination of undergraduate education majors. One is to sharply revise the undergraduate curriculum, so that future teachers can study the subjects they will teach with instructors who model fine teaching and who understand the pedagogy of their material. A second step is to organize academic course requirements and courses so that undergraduate students can gain a sense of the intellectual structure and boundaries of their disciplines, rather than taking a series of disjointed, prematurely specialized fragments.

Our point is simple. If teachers are to know a subject so that they can teach it well, they need to be taught it well. Few of us are Leonardo. To become good teachers, most undergraduates need both good pedagogy and courses that help them to learn the structure of the subjects they will teach. Neither is common today.

The third major change must be in schools and departments of education. Instead of our present sprawling and often scattered courses of study, we need to devise coherent programs that will support the advanced studies in pedagogy required for solid professional education. The certification requirements outlined earlier imply sharply revised programs of research and study, leading to master's and doctoral degrees in teaching and allied fields. Elements for this work exist in nearly all of our universities, but nowhere have these elements been pulled together, and given the sense of purpose and support they require.

What would these new pedagogical studies look like?

We have no blueprint. Answering this question is a large part of our work in the next five years. We have explored the feasibility of our plan, and are convinced that it can be done. No two universities will have identical programs, but we can provide some sense of their outlines.

One important and large line of work must focus on the pedagogy of specific subjects. Generic undergraduate "methods" courses must be replaced with subject matter-oriented studies of teaching and learning. This work should be based on the best understanding—from academic research and clinical studies of practice—of good teaching and learning in specific subjects. Such studies can build on recent research on human cognition, on older lines of research in subject matter-specific teaching and learning, and on recent research on teaching.

A second important line of work should focus on teachers' learning. Here we must bring to the study of teachers' acquisition of skill and knowledge the intelligence that social scientists and practitioners have applied to the study of children's learning. There is more to be done here than in the study of pedagogy, for research on teachers' learning is still weakly developed. But some solid beginnings have been made. Improved research and practice will be essential for the improvements in teacher education that we want to promote in schools and in universities.

Additional work should be focused on the specialties mentioned above: the assessment of professional performance, and the evaluation of instruction chief among them.

These changes would require that the top officials of our universities lead the efforts for change. Many faculty members and administrators would have to work hard for years to devise and implement major revisions in university curriculum and instruction. The changes also would require unprecedented cooperation across departmental and disciplinary lines within universities. For example, changing the undergraduate curriculum as outlined above would require cooperative work among faculty members from the humanities, sciences, social sciences, and education. Faculty from these diverse realms, who rarely work together now, would have to work closely to change the structure of the curriculum, and to sharply improve the quality of teaching. Such work would not be easy.

Cooperation would also be required to reorient courses in pedagogy so that they build on a sophisticated understanding of both the subject in question and of pedagogy for that subject. Some scholars in the humanities, sciences, and social sciences have investigated these matters, as have others in education schools. But their work—while absolutely central to improving teaching and learning, in schools or in higher education—is fragmented and little esteemed in universities. If substantial change in teaching and learning is to occur, whether in schools or universities, scholars of this sort should be brought together. Their efforts should be focused on the improvement of instruction in academic subjects, and they should be supported heavily enough by their universities to recruit other good minds. If successful, their work should be central to revisions in the undergraduate curriculum, and to the development of advanced studies in pedagogy.

Finally, along with all of these changes, our schools and universities must open up new connections with schools. One connection would be to bring expert teachers into universities, as more important and more responsible participants in professional education. Good teachers have long been crucial in this respect, in their work with student teachers. But university students in the new advanced programs sketched earlier will have much to learn from the top people in teaching about pedagogy and student learning. Conversely, university faculty who are competent to teach either teachers or pupils should spend more time doing these things and studying them in schools. Such work could help to improve our understanding of instruction, and to sharpen teachers' knowledge and skills. It also would help to turn schools into places in which teachers' learning, and research on teaching and learning, are more common.

Changes of this sort are easier to describe than to carry off. Bringing expert teachers into universities will require forging new arrangements with schools, to redefine those teachers' jobs. It also may require new arrangements within the universities; for example, the ordinary criteria for university appointments do not include distinction in practice. Sending more university faculty into the schools will be no less difficult. There are few rewards for such work in the incentive structure of research universities. There are no titles, job descriptions—or even places to sit in schools—for such emissaries from higher education. And there are few precedents for managing the complex jobs that swim in the limbo between agencies.

Conclusion

Our universities must respond to the crisis in public education. As the educators of most teachers and administrators in public schools, we have some responsibility for conditions in them. We have outlined a program of action aimed at dramatically improving the quality of America's teachers and at improving the teaching profession. We have committed ourselves to work for these improvements—in both undergraduate education and in graduate professional education—in our universities. Without the sorts of change outlined here, the quality of teaching and learning in the public schools cannot improve.

But we do not argue for these changes only because of past evils. The program outlined above draws on the unique strengths of the research universities. It requires extensive research and development aimed at much-improved instruction for undergraduates. It requires a program of development and field trials of new approaches to the assessment of professional competence. It requires stepped-up research on teaching and learning academic subjects. And it requires the sort of cooperation across academic boundaries that happens easily in great universities when the problems are taken seriously enough.

The work that we propose is therefore distinctively the province of the university: study, research, and teaching. What is new in our proposals is the idea that these distinctive academic resources be focused on the problems of teacher education, and that the universities make the solution of these problems a top priority.

In a sense, then, our proposal is hardly radical. For American universities know quite well how to provide outstanding professional education. The best professional education in medicine, public affairs, business, and law that can be found in the world is found here in the United States. There is no doubt that our universities can do an equally outstanding job for teachers. The only question is whether they will.

■|■|■

A Common Understanding
of the Obstacles

The breadth of The Holmes Group agenda testifies to the problems and the complexities of the undertaking. We cannot improve the quality of education in our schools without improving the quality of the teachers in them. Curriculum plans, instructional materials, elegant classrooms, and even sensitive and intelligent administrators cannot overcome the negative effects of weak teaching, or match the positive effects of competent teaching. Although leadership, resources, and working conditions in schools influence those who enter and choose to remain in the classroom, they do not affect students' learning as directly as do teachers. The entire formal and informal curriculum of the school is filtered through the minds and hearts of classroom teachers, making the quality of school learning dependent on the quality of teachers.

The quality of teachers will not be improved unless we improve the quality of their education—and we cannot accomplish this task without changing the universities, the credentialing systems, and the schools themselves. The functions of these institutions cannot be regarded as independent of one another. As difficult as it may be, any promising reform agenda must address the interdependence of institutional functions and responsibilities. The rewards and career opportunities for teachers; the standards, nature, and substance of professional education; the quality and coherence of the liberal arts and subject matter fields; and the professional certification and licensing apparatus must all be changed together, in a mutually compatible fashion.

Serious and effective reform of teacher education is not a parochial concern for one segment of the education community. It is central to the broader reform of education, and the support of the larger community is essential to its success. The support of the constituencies that represent this larger community must be based on an understanding of the underlying problems that shape the quality and composition of the teaching force. This understanding is necessary if we are to resist the temptations to adopt superficial and symbolic reforms that will not build and reward competence but actually could worsen the problems they were meant to solve.

This section of The Holmes Group report attempts to build that understanding by illuminating the fundamental problems we have wrestled with over the past several years. Its purpose is to expose the larger educational and policy communities to our distinctive view of the obstacles to reforming teaching and learning in our schools. We hope that the lessons that we have painfully learned about existing inadequate approaches to educating teachers and improving teaching will strengthen the understanding and conviction of others to assist with the reform efforts we propose.

Overly Simple Solutions

Henry W. Holmes, dean of the Harvard Graduate School of Education in the 1920s, argued persuasively that "the training of teachers is a highly significant part of the making of the nation." Claiming that "a more serious conception of the place of the teacher in the life of the nation is both necessary and timely," Holmes urged educational and political leaders to join him in changing the systems supporting poorly trained, paid, and esteemed teachers. He pleaded with his colleagues in schools of education to prepare teachers who had "the power of critical analysis in a mind broadly and deeply informed." But he found few supporters, and while he constructed a strong program at Harvard, it was short-lived. Like a number of educational leaders before and since, Henry Holmes failed in his efforts to make school teaching and teacher education more professional.

Half a century later, why should another set of deans resurrect these same arguments, call for similar reforms, and then expect a more positive outcome? The hope, we believe, lies in our better understanding of the obstacles that blocked earlier reform efforts, and in our reform plans themselves, which are grounded in principles of effective institutional change. It is buoyed by the social circumstances that now make educational change a prominent, critical issue. This optimism, however, is countered by a deep concern that the nation will again opt for the traditionally simple solutions that have consistently failed. These failures will be repeated unless we learn from past reform efforts.

The legendary problems of teacher education in America have been lamented since the turn of the century. A rediscovery of the problems and a condemnation of the factors thought to cause the problems recur each decade, accompanied by a new exhortative report. With a remarkable sameness, these reports have admonished teacher educators for not recruiting better students and imposing higher selection and screening standards. Only the best and brightest should be entitled to teach, and the brightest should be better prepared by taking more subject matter courses—so long as they are offered outside of schools of education. Except for expanded practical study in the schools, the reports call for fewer education courses. With great consistency, the problem has been conceived as the wrong persons, studying the wrong things, in the wrong places.

Traditionally such logic has led to a simple and straightforward reform platform. Prospective teachers should be brighter and more accomplished, studying subjects rather than pedagogy, spending less time in the halls of ivy and more time in the schools. College degrees and professional teaching licenses should be awarded on the basis of performance and standardized tests of teaching and subject matter competence. For a number of very good reasons, this perennial, basically simple, and appealing agenda has gone nowhere.

The Holmes Group has identified two fundamental weaknesses in these familiar recommendations. The first is a simplistic view of the nature of the problems confronting education—a failure to appreciate the extent to which teacher education has evolved as a creature of teaching. The second is a simplistic view of how one goes about solving the complex problems of education. Would-be reformers have attempted to impose solutions, assuming that their ideas could be readily accepted and implemented without the active involvement of practitioners. We can no longer perpetuate such major oversights.

Plans to improve teacher education must be inextricably tied to plans to improve the occupation of teaching. They must be devised and tested by the school and university teachers and administrators who will be expected to carry them out. The reward structure, career patterns, working conditions, and nature of professional responsibilities in teaching will continue to influence the structure, standards, and substance of teacher education. The Holmes Group, consisting of leaders from teacher education itself, is aware of the impossibility of reforming professional schools for teachers apart from changing the structure of teaching and the career opportunities and rewards available in the K-12 schools. We acknowledge that reforming professional teacher preparation requires the full participation of practicing teachers and teacher educators. Recent scholarship in implementation demonstrates the essential role that teachers themselves play in the reform process and how critical it is to avoid assuming that initiatives imposed from above will have any predictable or desirable effects on teaching and learning.

To avoid the problems and frustrations that accompanied efforts to act on the earlier critiques of teacher education, The Holmes Group leadership endorses a reform agenda consisting of several distinctive but essentially interdependent parts. Necessarily complicating the reform agenda, our plans far exceed the simple solutions proposed in the past. In order to improve teachers' professional opportunities and teacher education, the structure of the traditional careers in teaching needs to be changed. Differences in teaching responsibilities, in turn, require substantial changes in the structure, standards, and substance of teacher education. Further, new partnerships between the schools and institutions of professional education are necessary. It is also imperative that the nature of liberal arts instruction be modified to strengthen the substance and coherence of the disciplinary backgrounds of prospective teachers. If the status quo is to change, we must reckon with these complexities.

Naive Views of Teaching

If teaching is conceived as highly simple work, then any modestly educated person with average abilities can do it. But if teaching is conceived as a responsible and complex activity that is clearly related to both group learning and individual learner success—including those children for whom learning is not easy and for whom lots of help at home is unavailable—then teaching requires special selection and preparation. The case can be made, in fact, that the nation's troubles with student learning in schools are closely tied to popular and excessively simple conceptions of teaching. The three most common views that characterize the insufficient "bright person" models of teaching must be understood.

One-way teaching

One simplistic version equates teaching with "presenting" or "passing on" a substantive body of knowledge. Another includes "presenting and keeping order," and a third elaborates these views slightly to include "planning, presenting, and keeping order." Such views assume that bright, well-educated individuals can draw on their accumulated knowledge to develop coherent, logical presentations which can be delivered and hence learned by students in orderly classrooms. A critical aspect of such models is their tendency to assume that whether or not learning takes place in any particular class is primarily an outgrowth of the students who happen to be there. The teacher's responsibility is only to develop and deliver lessons in some reasonable fashion; the onus for learning rests with the students. The characteristics of the student group and the individuals in it thus influence the lesson and mode of delivery only modestly. The teachers' responsibility basically ends when they have told students what they must remember to know and do.

The simplistic nature of these views of teaching and learning becomes readily apparent when one considers that well-educated persons could *obviously* produce an adequate presentation on some aspect of their acquired knowledge. Virtually all of them should be able to prepare a lesson which would be appropriate, maybe even outstanding, for at least some classroom of students, at some level of our educational system, somewhere in the United States. This conception blithely overlooks one of the most critical aspects of quality teaching—the extent to which the lesson is appropriate for the particular students for whom the teacher is responsible and for whom the lessons should be crafted.

Unfortunately, simple models of teaching are often most attractive to bright, studious individuals who took major responsibility for their own learning as students—once they were pointed in the general direction by a "presenting" teacher. Reasoning that it worked for them and will for others, some intellectually able teachers give only passing attention to learners and learning, insisting that to do otherwise would constitute "spoon-feeding." Viewed in this simple lesson delivery fashion, teaching is something any intelligent person can do. This belief can ignore professional knowledge because it is easy for teachers' lessons to have quality if they are independent of student learning. The Holmes Group rejects such simple views. It subscribes instead to a conception of fully competent professional teachers.

Interactive teaching as the hallmark of competent professionals

The Holmes Group's vision of teaching is born of both time-tested conceptions of teacher qualities and responsibilities, and of recent understandings about role requirements. Central to the vision are competent teachers empowered to make principled judgments and decisions on their students' behalf. They possess broad and deep understanding of children, the subjects they teach, the nature of learning and schooling, and the world around them. They exemplify the critical thinking they strive to develop in students, combining tough-minded instruction with a penchant for inquiry. Students admire and remember them many years after leaving school, since such competence and dedication in teaching are unfortunately not as common as they should be.

Competent teachers are careful not to bore, confuse, or demean students, pushing them instead to interact with the important knowledge and skill. Such teachers interpret the understandings students bring to and develop during lessons; they identify students' misconceptions, and question their surface responses that mask true learning.

Competent teachers have knowledge, skill, and professional commitments that avoid the problems of the "bright person" versions of the teaching-learning process. The professional knowledge these teachers possess goes beyond a strong liberal education. It is not merely common sense, nor is it learned only through trial-and-error teaching or the experience of being a student. Rather, it includes academic and clinical learning that prepares one to manage both mastery of content and the complex social relations of the classroom in a way that fosters student learning as well as an attachment to learning. As professionals, these competent teachers would never breeze into a classroom, present a prefabricated lesson and breeze out again, claiming to have taught. Such a facile approach trivializes teaching, and sends the message that learners and learning are unimportant. True professionals would never participate in such a one-way process, for they know that teaching and learning are interactive.

Professional teaching and children's learning

For competent professionals, students' learning is the *sine qua non* of teaching and schooling. They both understand and are discouraged by the nonchalant attitudes that tolerate anything less. Such professionals are deeply concerned by mounting evidence that many of this country's teachers act as educational functionaries, faithfully but mindlessly following prescriptions about what and how to teach. Conducting classes in routine, undemanding ways, far too many teachers give out directions, busywork, and fact-fact-fact lectures in ways that keep students intellectually passive, if not actually deepening their disregard for learning and schooling.

Professional teachers recognize that such teaching may *appear* harmless, but they know its insidious consequences for children. Because parents are not in the classroom, they cannot see or directly assess the damages. The consequences remain distant, abstract, and easily rationalized. These consequences are imperceptible, rarely erupting in a single dramatic event. But competent professionals know and have great empathy for the effects of mediocre teaching on children.

For many children, partial understandings of school subjects turn into hopeless confusions and obscure abstractions. Struggling to make sense of the fragile, piecemeal understandings they possess, these children fall further behind each month and year. Comparable experience across multiple subjects leads these students to generalize about their abilities; and in growing numbers they assess themselves incapable of making it through school. Many leave, joining the ever larger population of dropouts and unemployed teenagers. Many other students simply persist lethargically, learning little, but accepting it as "just the way school and learning is"—a boring, meaningless waste of time.

Truly competent teachers find it as important to discover ways of helping those who find learning difficult and frustrating as they do helping those more like themselves, who find school learning easy and rewarding. Such competent teaching becomes more important daily, as the student population shifts to include a greater portion of educationally at-risk students. Competent professionals realize that the at-risk status of many students is largely a product of economic, intellectual, and social disadvantages outside the school's purview. Although poverty, neglect, indifference, and ignorance affect learning, true professionals recognize that in-school factors also play a role. School and teacher stereotypes and expectations can narrow student opportunities for learning and displaying competence. Children's at-risk status is created and exacerbated by school and classroom enforcement of limited assumptions about their potential abilities and strengths. The expressive behaviors of children from minority cultures, children from non-English speaking homes, and children with special learning needs are routinely misinterpreted. They either receive less attention than they rightfully deserve or are assigned to inappropriate classes and denied adequate or appropriate opportunities to learn.

Competent professional teachers recognize the hidden biases of school policies and classroom practices. They do not ignore the problems students bring with them from home or assume that such problems mean inevitable failure. Rather, they recognize that the social context in which learning takes place is a critical dimension over which they have considerable control and that multiple teaching strategies can create opportunities for young people deemed as failures by others. Competent teachers are important to all students, but they are especially critical for these growing numbers of educationally at-risk children.

Today's teachers and teacher educators are aware that neither schools nor universities are now able to develop or reward the professional competence in teaching we envision. Nevertheless, many are eager to participate in changing these unacceptable conditions. Aware that our contemporary problems are rooted more in unresponsive, bureaucratic institutions than in recalcitrant individuals, competent teachers and teacher educators are prepared to participate in the reconstitution of public schooling. But the naive views that keep teaching limited to giving out information and instructions must first be overcome.

Institutions Unfit for Teacher Professionals

The traditions of recruitment, norms of preparation, and conditions of work in schools have severely hindered efforts to improve the quality of teaching. This unfortunate legacy was created by the youthful, transient, and large work force needed to staff our schools as the United States attempted to achieve universal education. These norms and traditions contributed to a flat career pattern, roundly condemned as teaching's "careerlessness," where ambition and accomplishment went unrewarded both in terms of expanded responsibilities and autonomy, and higher salaries. No longer in step with contemporary intellectual and social realities, the impact of this inheritance must be understood and changed if we are to remedy our current educational problems.

During the past century, many young adults taught school temporarily before assuming the responsibilities of their real careers. Women typically chose marriage and full-time housekeeping, although they sometimes returned to teaching. Men usually moved from teaching into higher education, educational management, or other white-collar occupations. Unless combined with a religious or single life, teaching was seldom chosen as lifetime work. The amount and quality of preparation it required did little to encourage the view that one was making a serious commitment to a long-term career. Teaching in the United States evolved as convenient, respectable, and relatively challenging employment for bright and energetic workers who were "passing through," en route to more serious life commitments. It was constructed as a job, rather than a profession; and it accommodated talented short-timers as well as those educated minorities and single women with few other choices for employment.

During the perennial shortages that have existed since the mid-nineteenth century, the nation relied upon the generous subsidy of those whose options were limited by prejudice and civic custom. Demand was handled by granting emergency credentials or inordinately weak credentials. These deceptive remedies created the illusion that all was well. They confused the public by masking the critical distinction between "covering classes" and "competent teaching."

The historical evidence is clear. When teachers grew weary of the excessive work requirements and impossible demands of teaching, most moved on. Those few who sought to make the occupation satisfying to themselves and their students for prolonged periods became increasingly dissatisfied. Naturally, there were exceptions to this pattern, and extraordinary individuals made outstanding contributions, dedicating themselves to a life of teaching. But the norms for an occupation with more than two million workers cannot be based on what can be accomplished by a small number of saints and heroines.

This evolution of teaching as a non-career went largely unnoticed by American society consumed with developing the massive enterprise of universal schooling. But for those who were attentive, the emerging "revolving door" accommodations were predictable, both for the occupation itself and its pre-service and in-service teacher education programs.

The minimal expectations and meager investments that accompany a transient work force gradually became ingrained in the occupation's structure, patterns of preparation, status, and self-image. Independent working arrangements and program flexibility accompanied the intermittent work schedules of individual teachers. Among teachers, a strong reliance on external expertise and directive management followed, and an intellectually dependent "tell-me-what-to-do" attitude became the norm. Only brief investments in teacher education made sense: Why would intelligent people pursue long and serious study if they expected to engage in such work for only a year or two? Why would people seek to excel and acquire skills when they would not be expected or permitted to use them in their work? Designed for a youthful, high-turnover job market, teaching and teacher education have never been appropriate for those who would make teaching their career. Until recently, this circumstance did not seem to be a problem for the field overall.

Over the last two decades, however, society has changed in a number of ways that profoundly affected the nation's teaching force. America's college-educated women pursued careers other than homemaking. Employment opportunities for educated women and minorities increased. And the majority of American households came to depend upon more than a single income. For the middle-class families supplying the nation's teachers, two employed adults became the norm.

The consequences of these changes for the teaching force were complex and interactive. Many women who formerly left teaching to marry or rear children retained their jobs. They soon found themselves confronted with the frustrations and negative effects long associated with prolonged work in teaching. With few opportunities for upward mobility, the same situation confronted a growing number of male teachers staying in classrooms. The difficulties encountered by their predecessors, the few who made careers of teaching, were suddenly experienced by a substantial majority of the teaching population.

Many of the most competent left, able to find alternative work. This was especially true for talented women and minorities who found attractive careers in other fields. It was also true for those teachers having marketable knowledge in math and science. Many of the less competitive teachers, however, were effectively stranded.

Growing numbers of young college graduates failed to find teaching positions as the nation's population of children declined in the 1970s and greater numbers of experienced teachers stayed on the job. The teaching force became older and more weary; many remained in body, but not in mind or spirit. They retired on the job. The institutional norms of an earlier era, counterproductive norms that relied heavily on young college graduates with limited occupational choices who would remain for only a few years, no longer fit the aging workforce and affected its quality and composition negatively.

Social and demographic trends will aggravate these consequences of earlier recruitment patterns. The size of the occupation itself poses serious difficulties for changing our recruitment strategies. Taking schooling for granted, Americans under-estimate the magnitude of human resources necessary for quality universal educa-tion. If the schooling enterprise were modest in scope and educated only a portion of the U.S. population, it would not be difficult to staff all classrooms with highly qualified teachers. If 2,000 or even 20,000 new teachers were needed annually, the situation could be managed readily.

But when estimates run as a high as 200,000 a year, the challenges associated with recruiting, preparing, and screening this many competent adults become over-whelming, especially when the working conditions and rewards for the work are inadequate or counterproductive.

Current demographic factors will make it especially difficult to obtain an ade-quate number of competent teachers in the coming decade. The pool of young col-lege graduates from which prospective teachers have been selected will be smaller than at any other time in recent history. Furthermore, this population decline in young adults occurs at the same time that the children of the "baby boomers" are growing in numbers and creating new demands for schooling. Teachers will be needed for these children at the same time that an extremely large number of practicing teachers will retire.

This unusual demographic situation is compounded by a decade of low enroll-ments in teacher education. The depressed job market for teachers, combined with the public's general awareness of problems in teaching, has discouraged qualified can-didates from entering the field. Now engaged in other productive careers, not many will relinquish pay and prestige to become teachers.

Affirmative action achievements of the past decade have also contributed to the situation. The nation's schools can no longer count on a captive market of bright, energetic minorities and women, for they now have attractive alternatives in busi-ness, industry, and other professions. Thus, the schools must not only compete in ways they never have before, they must do so at a time when the potential talent pool is decreasing, the demand for new teachers is increasing, and the reputed nature and returns of teachers' work, even given effort and success, are unattractive. For the first time, the desirability of teaching as a career will be tested in an open labor mar-ket. Contemporary circumstances and the structure of the occupation together make our response more critical than at any point in our nation's history. If we respond as we have in the past, unprecedented numbers of incompetent teachers will be hired; and contemporary social and economic circumstances will keep them in the nation's classrooms for many years to come. The level of performance and posture toward professional responsibility of these persons will shape the norms and effects of teaching well into the twenty-first century.

A Differentiated Profession

We need to change the career structure of teaching if we expect to improve the quality, engagement, and commitment of the teaching force. To attract, prepare, and retain a truly competent teaching force, intellectually capable adults must have more flexible access to classrooms. And we must counteract the confining role definition for teachers that discourages many effective practitioners from remaining in their classrooms. Improving teaching's attraction and retention powers requires a differentiated professional teaching force able to respond to the opportunities provided by a staged career that would make and reward formal distinctions about responsibilities and degrees of autonomy.

Differentiating the teaching career would be advantageous to individuals, public schools, and professional schools of education. It would make it possible for districts to go beyond limited financial incentives and to challenge and reward commitment. This is essential to encourage teachers to reinvest in their work, and earn rewards while remaining in their classrooms; it will also counterbalance the defection of talented, committed teachers into administration. Some occupational mobility and choice, so conspicuously absent from teaching today, would help to ease many of the frustrations that drive talented teachers from their classrooms.

Differentiated staffing would make it possible for communities to respond to disequilibrium in the supply of and demand for teachers. To meet past shortages, standards were lowered across the board and individuals with spurious preparation were able to achieve full professional status as teachers. The concept of differentiated staffing would permit responsible expansion and contraction of a pool of teachers, while protecting the integrity of the professional teaching force. A hierarchy of levels of responsibility corresponding to degrees of professional education, experience, and performance evaluations would make it possible to adjust to spot shortages in specific fields, or even more generalized shortages, by adding, subtracting, or shifting personnel resources in a fashion far more rational than is customary today. It would be possible to limit the autonomy of certain teachers who would work under various degrees of supervision, thereby avoiding the traditional practice of bestowing full professional prerogatives on everyone brought into the classroom, regardless of their credentials or demonstrated abilities.

A number of vital institutional goals could be accomplished through differentiated professional staffing. Remediation and the improvement of teaching, for example, would be efficiently handled through the constructive supervision that specialized, differentiated roles in schools would make possible.

Finally, since we understand the reciprocal relationship between teaching and teacher education, differentiating the career would enhance professional schools of education. Just as the knowledge, skills, and sense of professional responsibility developed in teacher education programs affect the behavior of teachers, the working conditions and career structure of teaching influence the standards, structure, and content of teacher education. Improved teacher education must accompany and be accompanied by changes in the role, function, and nature of teaching. Both schools and universities must attack the problems of teacher education and teaching simultaneously.

To create a market for professionally trained teachers with advanced graduate credentials, it is essential to provide expanded career opportunities and rewards in teaching. Otherwise, prospective teachers will have few incentives to invest in the demanding professional education essential to competent teaching.

A differentiated profession would be built upon the distinctive contributions of three groups of practitioners, as outlined in the first part of our report. The *Career Professional Teacher* would be capable of exercising authority at both the classroom level and the school level. The *Professional Teacher* would function with full autonomy, within the limits of role requirements, in the exercise of his or her classroom responsibilities. This person's purview, however, would be limited primarily to the classroom or to a particular group of students. The *Instructor* would practice only under the systematic guidance and supervision of a Career Professional Teacher. Thus, each of these individuals would have an important and distinctive role to play.

Many bright, well-educated adults could be effective teachers without making a career commitment to teaching. They may be undecided about their vocation, or they might prefer to teach children as secondary or tertiary work. They may wish to combine their work in schools with work in other settings, such as business or in the home. We will need the contributions of capable college graduates willing to make a limited investment in teaching. If qualified professional teachers oversee their work with children, our schools could accommodate them.

These novices, or *Instructors*, would not be professional teachers in the sense of committing themselves primarily to the occupation or acquiring a lengthy and professional preparation for a teaching career. Because of their limited perspective, Instructors would have their lessons structured and reviewed by professional teachers. Instructors would not participate formally in setting school policy, evaluating personnel or programs, counseling students and parents, or determining curriculum. Initially, they would be allowed to do only what their limited academic background suggests they could do—interact with others about a subject they know well. Because of their limited knowledge and demonstrated skill, Instructors would have carefully delineated rights, responsibilities, and benefits. They would not have tenure, nor autonomy and obligations afforded fully professional teachers. However, since they would know their subjects well and their instructional competence could be assured by qualified professional teachers, their full- and part-time services would be invaluable to the schools.

Obviously the teaching work force should not consist entirely of individuals who participate on a temporary or limited basis. Capable college graduates must also be encouraged to invest fully in a teaching career. Such Professional Teachers deserve working conditions that support sustained success, and they need alternatives in schools to accommodate their different aspirations.

Unlike Instructors, Professional Teachers would be certified as autonomous practitioners, entitled to exercise their classroom duties without supervision. Not only subject matter specialists, they would also be specialists in pedagogy. They would understand the core ideas in the subjects they teach, the likely learning problems children encounter at different ages, and the multiple ways by which teachers can overcome these problems. As skilled diagnosticians of children's learning needs, they would understand the physical, social, and intellectual changes that continue to occur as their students mature. They could make appropriate judgments about when to seek outside help, and when they could remediate learning problems themselves. They would be trained in techniques of motivation and classroom management and could evaluate curricular materials.

Professional Teachers would not only be effective instructors in the classroom, they would also be better prepared to serve in a very real sense as *child advocates*. They would be able to ensure that their schools and communities met the educational needs of students. They would understand enough about the role of educational "experts" (i.e., school psychologists, social workers, reading specialists) to participate as equals when discussing issues relevant to a child's future. As research has demonstrated, many classroom teachers now defer to these experts in educational decision-making, even when it may not be in the child's best interest to do so. When confronted with arcane test results, teachers—like parents—frequently feel disadvantaged in presenting their own, often more valuable, insights regarding a child's status and needs. The Professional Teacher would speak with legitimate authority on behalf of children. Thus, these practitioners would be more autonomous and responsible in making judgments about students than most teachers are today.

The vast majority of teachers spend their days in settings isolated from other adults or that provide little variety in their responsibilities for instructing children. Many outstanding teachers thrive on this intensively focused role. They are, literally, the backbone of the teaching force. They find their success in instructing children rewarding, and their training, creativity, and commitment are best directed toward their classrooms. Nothing should undermine their effective instruction in the subjects and grade levels for which they have demonstrated competence.

Other teachers, however, would appreciate and benefit from alternatives to their work with children. Interested more broadly in educational policy and improvement, they would like to collaborate with other adults on problems related to school effectiveness. Such teachers ordinarily have to stop working with children if they wish to help advance the field of education. Opportunities for educational leadership must be combined with teaching itself to keep such teachers actively committed to improving their schools.

Career Professional Teachers would possess the knowledge and skill essential to improving the educational effectiveness of other adults in schools. Specialized roles for Career Professional Teachers might include teacher education (guiding the classroom work of Instructors, for example, and providing staff development opportunities for all school-based educators), curriculum improvement, testing and measurement, strengthening home-school relationships, preparing instructional materials, and conducting action research. These Career Professionals are needed to achieve school effectiveness, but current ways of organizing educational work and rewards discourage teachers from assuming such demanding responsibilities. Although expected to constitute only twenty percent of the teaching force, Career Professionals would play a key role in revitalizing the teaching profession.

Some occupations have used differentiated staffing to make artificial and counterproductive distinctions in the workplace, to fabricate hierarchies in an effort to claim higher status and autonomy. Teaching must be careful to avoid the problems that have plagued other occupations. Large, complex organizations, nevertheless, do become hierarchical: Educational institutions have functioned that way for more than a century. The problem lies not with differentiation and hierarchy, but with illegitimate, irrational, and counterproductive organizational distinctions. Rational, differentiated professional staffing in schools that is based upon defensible differences in training, authority, and responsibilities will make it possible to respond fairly to the complexities of teaching and learning in large, diverse institutions. The question is not whether hierarchies will persist in educational organizations. The question is whether they will be based on defensible, rational distinctions, or on the flight from teaching and traditions of sexism, as they ordinarily are in the schools today.

Differentiated roles in teaching will also require differentiated forms of teacher education. Not all institutions of higher and professional education will perform the same roles. Some will concentrate on providing a coherent undergraduate liberal arts education, the sort of experience necessary to prepare Instructors. Other institutions will provide the academic and clinical graduate education needed by the vast majority of classroom teachers. Still other institutions would also provide the advanced graduate education to prepare qualified teachers for a variety of career leadership roles.

The Pitfalls of Credentialism

Recommending that America elevate teaching's status by raising standards, reforming professional education, and improving career opportunities through differentiated staffing has its potential pitfalls. Because the undertaking would be costly to individuals and institutions alike, we must do everything possible to anticipate and overcome the unintended, undesirable consequences of our proposals. One danger, for example, lies in the possible abuse of new credentials.

Earlier initiatives in education and other occupations, shaped by a similar dedication to tougher standards and professionalism, have shown that good intentions are not enough to prevent several predictable problems. Imposing new credentials has tended to exclude certain groups, particularly minorities unfamiliar with entrance and certification examinations. Ultimately, performance standards tend to decline to mediocre levels. Practitioners tend to become complacent, unwilling to experiment or entertain risks in serving the public. The knowledge and skills tested and certified by credentials tend to exclude qualities desirable in teaching such as warmth, empathy, reliability, a lack of pretentiousness or defensiveness, an alertness to human subtlety, and an ability to draw people out as well as together.

By misrepresenting what practitioners can actually do, credentialing can ultimately erode the public's trust in the quality of a profession. Credentialing problems can lead individuals to squander money, time, and energy, and can cause institutions to waste resources. Even worse, problems with the integrity of credentials can lead to outright quackery: providing services that actually harm clients.

Schools have a special relationship to the public. Because education is compulsory for all citizens, teaching and teacher education have a unique obligation to avoid the pitfalls of credentialism. Education must resist the temptation to enrich itself as other occupations have done, by offering mediocre performance behind a facade of higher credentials. We can no longer respond as we have in the past, when we tolerated the employment of underqualified teachers while appearing to raise credential standards. We can no longer pretend that raising credential standards for teachers is the same as improving teaching.

Teaching can improve its professional status only by improving its effectiveness—by raising the level of children's achievement and deepening their engagement with learning. Similarly, teacher education's professional status can be improved only by bestowing genuine credentials that reflect the highest standards and the most rigorous preparation possible.

Irresponsible credentialism

There are dangers associated with the professional privilege of granting credentials that teaching and teacher education in particular should avoid. We will examine several forms of deceptive, irresponsible credentialism. Teaching and teacher education must resist the trap of *pseudo-credentialism:* bestowing credentials regardless of demonstrated ability to perform all professional responsibilities autonomously. Pseudo-credentialism does not require professional schools to raise their standards or to improve the quality of the education that they offer. It allows them to continue what they have been doing by awarding a different credential. It does not guarantee that the credential reflects the possession of a specific body of knowledge or skills. The certification and accreditation processes establish the credential's value artificially and politically.

Pseudo-credentialism takes different forms in different professions and their professional schools. In teaching and teacher education, for example, teachers are paid according to the number of credits earned beyond their bachelor's degree, regardless of whether additional education improved their teaching. State-imposed continuing certification requirements routinely benefit teachers and teacher educators financially, with little regard to the substance of the advanced credentials invested in or awarded.

Pseudo-credentialism is a powerful weapon in the arsenal of opportunistic professionalization. As a strategy for increasing an occupation's professional status, pseudo-credentialism's popularity lies in its ability to control or restrict entry into an occupation. Pseudo-credentials can be used to exclude potential practitioners and limit access to an occupation, thereby creating an artificial scarcity, as medical and law schools have done for most of the twentieth century. But more relevant to teaching and teacher education, they can be used to ease the entry of underqualified practitioners into an occupation during a period of shortage, while appearing to maintain or even raise standards of preparation. Along with professional schools in other fields, schools of education have been guilty of manipulating the value of their credentials for some time.

Professional schools, particularly those responsible for teacher education, can no longer afford to continue the tradition of pseudo-credentialism. Teaching and teacher education must not seek professional status by distorting the value of their credentials, without regard for the quality of the training available or demonstrations of professional competence.

Teacher educators must not simply add on course requirements, or demand a fifth year of training, without rethinking the value of such changes. Nor must they endorse standardized examinations that do not reflect the range of knowledge, skills, and dispositions characteristic of competent professional practice. Teaching and teacher education cannot afford to imitate many of the professionalization strategies that other occupations have employed.

The potential abuses of pseudo-credentialism, however, should not lead us to reject professional education and certification, and replace them with the assumption that those who know something can automatically teach. Opening the entitlement to teach to the open market—one response to disenchantment with the abuse of existing credentials—would not solve the problem of teacher quality. Indeed, *deregulation* would aggravate the learning difficulties of most children.

We should recognize that rejecting professional education in favor of allowing college graduates from the academic disciplines to assume full responsibility for classroom instruction only substitutes one form of pseudo-credentialism for another. Ironically, by allowing college graduates lacking professional education to teach, as deregulation would permit, we would willingly substitute one form of educational proxy for another.

In neither case is real teaching ability being required, recognized, or developed. In one case the credential consists of doing whatever is necessary to complete a traditional teacher education program (ordinarily maintaining a minimum grade-point average and passing specified courses in order to accumulate credits). In the other case, the credential consists of whatever is necessary to earn a bachelor's degree in one of the disciplines (by similarly accumulating course credits and maintaining a specified grade-point average). Course grades and the accumulation of credits constitute the coinage of both credentials. Neither case necessarily produces good teachers. Good teaching and the improvement of children's learning are essentially irrelevant to both. Neither approach is likely to help us respond effectively to the situation we face, and neither is acceptable.

From the earlier discussion it should be obvious that competent, responsible teachers must possess far more than subject matter knowledge. Just as there is a role for higher education to play in building maturity and disciplinary knowledge in the arts and sciences, there is a role for professional education to play in strengthening prospective teachers' understanding of responsibility; developing their ability to engage students in academic learning; and cooperatively guiding their eventual induction into the classroom.

In addition to the problems of pseudo-credentialism and deregulation, teacher education must guard against the temptation of the other extreme, *blind credentialism*. We need to be cautious about forcing professionals who have already demonstrated their competence and responsibility to earn additional credentials in order to satisfy well-meaning but dysfunctional certification requirements. Endorsing professional education does not imply that real performance evaluations will not be made, or that the credentials available through the educational programs will be accepted in lieu of on-the-job assessments of teaching ability. The *issue* is how to prepare the pool of teachers who are to be allowed to be evaluated. The *problem* is how to prepare the pool of teachers who will earn the highest assessments for their instructional effectiveness.

Responsible credentialism

The Holmes Group proposes an alternative to the sort of irresponsible forms of credentialism outlined above. We endorse an approach to professional education and recruitment into teaching that will produce the most trustworthy pool of professional teachers. Professionally educated and certified teachers would possess a strong liberal arts and disciplinary background, a repertoire of imaginative teaching and coaching skills, and a commitment to the responsibility for the learning of all children.

Problems in Undergraduate Liberal Education

Improved teacher education is not possible without the concomitant reform of the nonprofessional components of the undergraduate curriculum for prospective teachers. Teachers should know their subjects thoroughly and have the intellectual qualities of educated, thoughtful, and well-informed individuals. Professional courses of study in education should meet the standards of the core disciplines from which they derive; that is, educational psychology must be sound psychology and courses in the methods of teaching mathematics must embody sound mathematics. When students come to pursue their professional studies in teaching, therefore, they must come already equipped with a sound command of the undergirding discipline. Clearly, teacher education is dependent upon the arts and sciences, consistent with the primary disciplines.

Many of the criticisms levied at high schools by *A Nation at Risk* and other recent reports are equally valid for the university. Both the Scholastic Aptitude Test and Graduate Record Examination scores have declined in the basic aptitude tests and in academic subject examinations. Like public schoolteachers, university faculty award higher grades than students earn. Most undergraduates, like their high school counterparts, are intellectually docile, indifferent, and disengaged from learning. Like all teaching positions, faculty positions are becoming less attractive. And, as in the high school, there has been an unjustifiable proliferation of elective courses and major subject areas. In general, the pressures inherent in the laudable goal of universal schooling have led institutions of higher education to compromise their standards in much the same fashion as the high schools.

The specific criticisms in the national reports about higher education tend to confirm The Holmes Group's analysis of the weaknesses in the undergraduate programs at their own institutions: a lack of curricular coherence and an avoidance of a core of enduring and fundamental ideas of the sort that the National Endowment for the Humanities cites in *To Reclaim a Legacy.* Yet the mastery of such a core is perhaps more important for teachers, especially elementary schoolteachers, than for any other professional group. All professionals use knowledge in their work, but teaching—insofar as it is not simply career counseling and social work—is actually about knowledge.

The reform of undergraduate education toward greater coherence and dedication to the historic tenets of liberal education is thus essential to improving teacher education. Teachers must lead a life of the mind. They must be reflective and thoughtful: persons who seek to understand so they may clarify for others, persons who can go to the heart of the matter.

We must address the failure of university faculty to assume corporate responsibility for the entire undergraduate program, a problem exposed by the American Association of Colleges in *Integrity in the College Curriculum.* The discipline or departmental organization, the source of so much strength in the modern university, also limits faculty attention and leadership related to issues that extend beyond the narrow boundaries of the academic major, issues that are central to a broadly and liberally educated teacher. At best, the contemporary academic major is largely a preparation for graduate study in the field or for entry-level employment. This limited focus does not provide an adequate grounding in the disciplines for professional teachers who, at all levels, must find and present the most powerful and generative ideas in a way that both preserves the integrity of disciplinary knowledge and leads students to understand the subject.

The traditional course of study in an academic major, in its premature rush to specialization and vocational preparation, often fails to elaborate the structure of the discipline, its origins and goals; and ignores criteria that cause some issues to merit deep study and others to be merely interesting or trivial. These areas, slighted in traditional programs, are of fundamental importance to education in general and to teachers in particular.

The Holmes Group agrees also with the National Institute of Education's report *Involvement in Learning,* which argued that the test of sound academic policy was whether it increased the students' active involvement in genuine learning, especially during the first two years of the baccalaureate. This engagement with learning is essential for teachers to develop a mastery of the discipline at a level that guarantees their authoritative and confident response to the inevitable and legitimate requests they will have from their pupils to "do" or "perform" the discipline, not just talk about it. In addition to content, it is the quality of engagement which characterizes a liberal education.

In sum, it is too easy for critics of current teacher education programs to say that prospective teachers need to take more courses outside of the colleges of education. As James Conant complained, such views "invariably represent a point of view so oversimplified as to be fundamentally invalid." Over two decades ago, his landmark study of teacher education revealed that the subject area courses were tedious and the general-liberal studies were in a state of disarray, even in the most prestigious colleges and universities. Conant's findings on the depth and breadth of the subject area requirements fit the situation today: "Thousands of students each year wander through survey courses with only the shallowest knowledge of the subject;" and

"One cannot assume that a holder of a bachelor's degree from an American college has necessarily pursued a recognized subject in depth, or in a coherent pattern."

But while the higher education community has recognized these problems for a long time, we have failed to develop appropriate solutions. A major concerted effort is essential, therefore, to stimulate effective reform. We must assemble the outstanding faculty scholars to grapple with the issues in ways that lead to redesigned and better taught courses and programs of study that are very different from those generally found in the modern university.

The Holmes Group leadership, however, is aware of the challenge and complexity of reforming undergraduate liberal arts education. The difficulties of shifting the reward structure in the traditional academic disciplines in order to make a coherent undergraduate liberal arts education possible will have to be confronted once again. Lengthy and costly battles have been fought over this goal. The frustrations and disappointments of academic and philanthropic leaders who failed to produce lasting change in institutions of higher education are well known. The power of prevailing incentives for exaggerated specialization, premature vocationalism, and excessive fragmentation within disciplines undermines consensus-building about content. Attracting and retaining talented scholars to teach the courses once consensus is reached are similarly difficult.

Regardless of the problems, it is essential to change the course selection patterns and class content encountered by prospective teachers during their pre-professional studies. Such a reform campaign would not only benefit prospective teachers, but would strengthen the higher education of all college students.

Inadequate Professional Education

Reforming the education of teachers depends upon engaging in the complex work of identifying the knowledge base for competent teaching, and developing the content and strategies whereby it is imparted. Although specialized professional knowledge has been under development for some time—and dramatic strides have been made during the past two decades—an amalgam of intuition, unreflective reactions, and personal dispositions still seem to ground the right to teach. Improving teaching requires teachers to act on legitimate professional knowledge, skills, and an ethos of responsibility.

To proclaim that high school teachers should have academic majors does nothing to improve teacher education in most research institutions; virtually no prospective secondary teachers now major in education. By tradition, they major in one or more subject fields and take the same disciplinary courses and general-liberal studies required of all students pursuing the baccalaureate degree. These substantial content requirements limit the opportunity of prospective secondary teachers to develop their knowledge and skills in transforming and using subject matter knowledge in teaching. Their pedagogical studies are restricted to a few university courses and a brief period of supervised practice in the schools. The well-documented lack of flexibility in high school instruction, and the preponderance of boring lectures, can be largely attributed to inadequate pedagogical training and screening for secondary teachers. Prospective elementary teachers, in contrast, take a more substantial set of offerings in pedagogy, but do so at the expense of essential knowledge in the subjects they teach. In both circumstances, the content and process of pedagogical study demand analysis and redevelopment.

Basically a "non-program" at present, professional courses are not interrelated or coherent. The curriculum is seldom reviewed for its comprehensiveness, redundancy, or its responsiveness to research and analysis. Advisement is often ineffective, leaving students to wander about, rather than progressing systematically in a cohort through their programs. Rituals and ceremonies that honor the important work of teachers are rare.

Scholarship and empirical research in education have matured, providing a solid base for an intellectually vital program of professional studies. A program of professional studies must integrate at least five components to qualify as a comprehensive plan for teacher preparation. The first is the study of teaching and schooling as an academic field with its own integrity. The second is knowledge of the pedagogy of subject matter—the capacity to translate personal knowledge into interpersonal knowledge, used for teaching. A related third component is comprised of the skills and understandings implicit in classroom teaching—creating a communal setting where various groups of students can develop and learn. The fourth consists of the dispositions, values, and ethical responsibilities that distinguish teaching from the other professions. Finally, all these aspects of professional studies must be integrated into the clinical experience where formal knowledge must be used as a guide to practical action.

Studies of education as a discipline provide a description and explanation of the phenomenon of schooling itself—its development, its purpose, and the micro and macro mechanisms that make schooling possible and sustain it. A sound study of education, whether at the graduate or undergraduate level, would provide a way of understanding schooling in the same way that the study of any discipline illuminates a set of phenomena. In this sense, education is one of the arts and sciences since it applies tested modes of inquiry to a phenomenon of universal scope and significance.

The unique educational matter, not in the domain of any affiliated discipline (namely, the behavioral sciences, history, and philosophy) is curriculum; yet this is one area about which we have little compelling information and theory. Education is the discipline of the disciplines. While the determination of the origins, purpose, and mechanisms of schooling is vital, the heart of the matter is the structure of knowledge and what knowledge is of most worth.

Until the last two decades, scholarship in education and the content of the hundreds of university courses in the subject had to rely heavily upon the findings in other disciplines, particularly the behavioral sciences. Collected in non-school settings, this information as transferred to issues of educational practice has been unsatisfying to everyone. It was unconvincing and provided only ambiguous guidance about educational practice and policy. Within the last twenty years, however, the science of education promised by Dewey, Thorndike, and others at the turn of the century has become more tangible: The behavioral sciences have been turned on the schools themselves, and not just in laboratory simulations. Studies of life in classrooms now make possible some convincing and counter-intuitive conclusions about schooling and pupil achievement. Ironically, now that the promise of science of education is about to be fulfilled, many current reform recommendations recall an older literature that demands a decrease in the time given to the study of this scholarship.

Current literature demonstrates that well-meaning, and well-educated persons will make a number of predictable pedagogical mistakes that will disproportionately harm at-risk pupils who traditionally do not do well in school, and who may be unlike their teachers in background and temperament. We can expect these well-meaning adults to teach as they have been taught by their own teachers and parents. As novice teachers, they will teach the way young children teach each other—by direct telling and demonstration of the correct information.

There will be a general failure to employ the more indirect but powerful teaching strategies, like maieutic methods, role playing, and social interaction and cooperation strategies. Such strategies require disciplined practice that typically exceeds even that offered by extraordinary teacher education programs. It takes training, for example, to wait more than a few seconds for pupils to answer a question before filling the silence with elaborative comments that disrupt the students' thinking. It takes training to increase the higher order questions a teacher asks; to decrease the preponderance of teacher talk; to provide advanced organizers, plans, and clear directions; to give teachers the cognitive resources to make pedagogical decisions and to manage productively the hundreds of distinct interactions they will have with pupils each day.

A major undertaking for research universities committed to strengthening teaching as a profession is the reformation of pedagogical study requirements. Foremost for elementary teachers is the need to restore the primacy of content knowledge and to better unify it with the methods of teaching. This goal reaffirms the complex relationship of teacher education to other academic units on campus and indicates the need for collaboration in revising and renewing both pedagogical studies and the liberal arts curriculum.

While a grounding in subject matter is not sufficient for prospective teachers, neither is the equally important broad view of the subject fields with their internal structure and commonalities with other areas of study. Professional education must develop the capacity to present and reformulate content so as to engage a variety of pupils; increase familiarity with available curricula and strengthen the critical acumen necessary to judge their value for particular settings and goals. Such pedagogical expertise is essential to build the bridge between personal understanding and the capacity to teach. Prospective teachers must also develop the capacity to establish effective tutorial relationships with their students. Students do not approach learning as empty vessels; they more likely present the teacher with initial conceptions that are incomplete, flawed, or otherwise in need of transformation. Knowing the likely universe of such preconceptions for a cohort of students, assessing their learning, interpreting errors, and discerning predominant ways of construing meaning, are all essential for helping students learn.

The common setting for imparting subject matter is the classroom. Instructing learners in groups and managing numbers of students in confined spaces call for yet another set of skills that go well beyond keeping order. An example is orchestrating the economy of the classroom, counting not only time and curriculum materials among its resources, but also the teacher's instructional efforts and those of students. In well-managed settings, they reciprocally support learning.

Creating and sustaining a communal setting respectful of individual differences and group membership, where learning is valued, engagement is nurtured, and interests are encouraged, require more than a set of identifiable skills. The successful transmission of these attitudes and values is more a function of the teacher's dispositions and beliefs that come to imbue the classroom culture.

The development of desirable professional dispositions in prospective teachers is as much of a challenge as the cultivation of valued attitudes in younger students. Didactic instruction is of limited value. More influential is the act of playing out these values in the ordinary interactions of daily classroom life. To successfully enact valued dispositions, they must be authentic, internalized by the faculty and teachers alike. Teachers cannot be disinterested, lethargic, and uncaring if they are to cultivate curiosity and engagement in their students. Although dispositions cannot be directly taught, they can be acquired in settings where they are regularly acted out, with opportunities to practice them. The overall design of professional programs must reflect the need for their cultivation.

The academic pedagogical studies available in colleges of education routinely fail to develop such essential professional knowledge, skills, and dispositions in the teachers they prepare. The clinical component of the pedagogical studies program similarly fails to strengthen the professional qualities needed to ensure competent classroom instruction.

Virtually every evaluator of the traditional teacher education program finds that the graduates attribute their success as teachers to their student teaching experience or to their first years in the classroom as teachers. Indeed, the grade the student receives in the student teaching course is one of the few academic predictors of teaching success. For these reasons many reformers believe that an extension of student teaching opportunities into other parts of the teacher education program is worthwhile.

However, there are reasons to be skeptical about widely held claims for the benefits of the traditional clinical experience. Although students value it most highly, as do their counterparts in all professional preparation programs, the teacher candidate's field experience is neither broad nor deep. Mentor teachers are often selected by school officials with little understanding of the particular learnings to be acquired, and with little appreciation for the professional knowledge of competent teachers and teacher educators. University supervision is infrequent. It is common for the practice experience to be limited to a single school, classroom, and teacher—all of whom are basically unknown to the university faculty and unfamiliar with other aspects of the teacher education program. Rarely does the experience build upon the general principles and theories emphasized in earlier university study. Almost no person fails these courses and almost all earn top marks for their efforts. Yet most student teachers quickly conform to the practices of their supervising teacher and rarely put into practice a novel technique or risk failure. Student teachers succeed because they relinquish the norms of professional colleges of education without a struggle. The typical student teaching experience is not a genuine laboratory experience because the possibilities of failure and risk are minimal. The emphasis is upon imitation of and subservience to the supervising teacher, not upon investigation, reflection, and solving novel problems.

University faculty, working with selected clinical faculty from cooperating schools, are needed to reexamine contemporary pedagogical offerings. Professional programs need to be revised by adding, deleting, or modifying courses to produce an articulate, coherent pedagogical curriculum that has intellectual integrity. Methods and content courses need to be complementary and compatible with one another and develop an ethic of inquiry and professional judgment. Clinical experiences must occur in multiple sites to provide learning opportunities with youngsters of diverse ability, motivation, and cultural background. Most importantly, we must respond to the tensions always associated with constructively relating theory and practice by drawing upon the insights and learning available to teachers in both their academic work and clinical experiences.

Lack of Demonstration Sites

Recognizing the interdependence of teaching and teacher education suggests a promising alternative to traditional sites for preparing prospective teachers. *Professional*

Development Schools, the analogue of medical education's teaching hospitals, would bring practicing teachers and administrators together with university faculty in partnerships that improve teaching and learning on the part of their respective students. Such schools would largely overcome many of the problems associated with traditional academic and clinical pedagogical studies programs. They would provide superior opportunities for teachers and administrators to influence the development of their profession, and for university faculty to increase the professional relevance of their work, through (1) mutual deliberation on problems with student learning, and their possible solutions; (2) shared teaching in the university and schools; (3) collaborative research on the problems of educational practice; and (4) cooperative supervision of prospective teachers and administrators.

The concept of Professional Development Schools assumes that improving teaching ultimately depends on providing teachers with opportunities to contribute to the development of knowledge in their profession, to form collegial relationships beyond their immediate working environment, and to grow intellectually as they mature professionally. The idea of such collaborative sites also recognizes that university-based research and instruction in education must have strong roots in the practice of teaching if they are to maintain their intellectual vitality and its credibility with the profession. Professional Development Schools, then, would provide a structured partnership for developing the teaching profession and ultimately improving students' learning.

Because the Professional Development School has a unique training role, many of its staff members would have formal responsibility for teaching prospective professionals. While continuing to practice their profession on a regular basis, this "clinical faculty" would have university appointments and be reimbursed for their contributions to the training program. The clinical faculty—comprised largely of accomplished elementary and secondary teachers—would have attained the stage of Career Professional Teacher and successfully completed advanced studies in teacher education.

The second purpose for creating exemplary school sites, broader than the first, is the development of professional knowledge and practice. Professional Development Schools would provide an opportunity to test different instructional arrangements, under different types of working conditions. In this way, they would contribute to the ongoing refinement and codification of successful teaching and schooling. While not necessarily valuing innovation for its own sake, those who work in these schools would have to maintain an open-minded and experimental attitude. It is important that they be constantly seeking ways to increase their instructional effectiveness with diverse groups of at-risk youngsters. Experimentation and sustained evaluation would become integral aspects of the ethos of the Professional Development Schools. They would be actual demonstration sites where recent scholarship could be consistently reviewed and selectively incorporated into operating policy and practice. The most innovative professional practices would be developed, demonstrated, and critically evaluated at these sites. By creating "models" of exemplary practice that could be tried out elsewhere, Professional Development Schools could make a major contribution to the development, codification, and implementation of professional knowledge.

Finally, Professional Development Schools would help to strengthen the profession by serving as models of promising and productive structural relations among Instructors, Professional Teachers, Career Professional Teachers, and administrators. Improving these relations, expanding opportunities and responsibilities, would make working conditions in schools rewarding enough to attract talented novices and to retain competent, dedicated teachers. Professional Development Schools would provide an optimally balanced program of study and experience for the neophyte under the tutelage of teacher educators and teachers working in the vanguard of practice. They would also offer talented persons who enter teaching, who love it and want to improve it, a means of advancing without leaving the classroom, physically or psychologically. Thus the senior teachers (Career Professionals) in a Professional Development School would be rewarded with the opportunity to be engaged in a variety of ways; in teaching, research, teacher education, and policy formation.

A Collective Commitment to Action

With these issues as our focus, the members of The Holmes Group and their institutions are committed to a broad strategy for reform of teacher education. We recognize that powerful forces are working against major reform. One of these forces, ironically, is the dramatic increase in demand for teachers that will occur over the next several years. If states and localities follow past practice in responding to this demand, by offering temporary certification to unqualified teachers and by allowing certified teachers to teach outside their field of competence, then efforts to reform teacher education will be substantially undermined.

Another force working against major reform of teacher education is, unfortunately, the education reform movement itself. A number of recent proposals for education reform have suggested that attracting high-quality teachers is a key component of education reform—a principle that we endorse. Reformers have recommended other principles with which we concur: attention to subject matter competence, differentiated career opportunities, clinical experience, and the like. But none of the reform proposals has addressed the central issue in the improvement of teaching—the professional stature of teachers. Until this is addressed, we will continue to attempt educational reform by telling teachers what to do, rather than empowering them to do what is necessary.

Reform advocates have never fully appreciated the fact that the problems of teacher education mirror society's failure to treat teaching as a profession. If the rewards, career patterns, working conditions, and professional responsibilities of teachers indicate a second-class occupation, then candidates for teaching and teacher education will tend to follow those expectations. Teacher education cannot be improved in isolation from the profession itself. The Holmes Group is committed not just to the improvement of teacher education but to the construction of a genuine profession of teaching.

Furthermore, policy changes recommended by many reform advocates are only the first stage of lasting reform. Past attempts at large-scale reform show that changes imposed from above, without the concurrence and collaboration of those who must implement them, have limited and unpredictable effects. Changes in the structure and content of teacher education depend, over the long term, on strong linkages among policymakers, scholars, and practitioners. The Holmes Group is committed to carrying the reform of teacher education into the classroom by establishing strong linkages with schools; into the central office and boardroom by working with local school systems; and into the state legislative chamber by working for changes in the policies that shape the teaching profession.

At the same time, we recognize that there will be many mistakes, false starts, and unanticipated problems with our proposed agenda. We also recognize that solutions which work in one setting may require adaptation to work in another setting. We foresee that we will learn much about the strengths and limits of our proposed agenda in the years ahead. Hence, The Holmes Group is committed to exploring a range of alternatives around several common themes and to sharing the wisdom of experience among ourselves and with others. As we become more confident of solutions to the problems of constructing a teaching profession, we commit ourselves as institutions of teacher education to establish accreditation standards that reflect our five major goals.

To Make the Education of Teachers Intellectually Sound

Competent teaching is a compound of three elements: subject matter knowledge, systematic knowledge of teaching, and reflective practical experience. The established professions have, over time, developed a body of specialized knowledge, codified and transmitted through professional education and clinical practice. Their claim to professional status rests on this. For the occupation of teaching, a defensible claim for such special knowledge has emerged only recently. Efforts to reform the preparation of teachers and the profession of teaching must begin, therefore, with the serious work of articulating the knowledge base of the profession and developing the means by which it can be imparted. The Holmes Group recognizes the central importance of a strong liberal arts education in the preparation of teachers. Of all professions, teaching should be grounded on a strong core of knowledge because teaching is about the development and transmission of knowledge. With this in mind, The Holmes Group commits itself to phase out the undergraduate education major in member institutions and to develop in its place a graduate professional program in teacher education.

At the same time, The Holmes Group agrees with recent criticisms of the lack of coherence and the lack of focus on enduring questions in undergraduate education. The disciplinary and departmental structure of universities is a symptom of limited faculty involvement and leadership in important issues that extend beyond the boundaries of the academic major. This structure presents major problems for the development of broadly educated people, whether they intend to be teachers or not. In addition, the structure does not encourage university faculty in the academic disciplines or intending teachers to explore systematically the special challenges of teaching academic subjects.

Reform of teacher education must be coupled to changes in undergraduate education. The Holmes Group is aware of the complexities this relationship presents. Members of the group will work with the chief academic officers and departmental colleagues in their institutions to develop strong and intellectually defensible courses in the core subjects, and to interest disciplines and departments in linking subject matter knowledge to teaching.

Providing prospective teachers with strong subject matter knowledge does not equip them with the understanding or skill necessary to teach that knowledge to someone else. The Holmes Group recognizes serious problems with the way teacher preparation is currently structured. Prospective high school teachers focus on disciplinary courses and general-liberal studies, leaving little room for systematic understanding of how to develop their knowledge and transform it for use by others. Prospective elementary teachers spend substantially more time on pedagogy, but do so at the expense of subject matter knowledge. Members of The Holmes Group commit themselves to a thorough reassessment of the pedagogical curriculum and to the development of a strong, coherent program of professional education in this area.

Clinical experience is the final element of the intellectual foundation of teaching. Despite the fact that clinical experience is almost universally praised by teachers, it presents some of the most serious problems with existing teacher education. The clinical component of teacher education must be integrated more systematically with research on professional practice, with the reconstruction of the pedagogical curriculum, and with the development of the profession. The Holmes Group is committed to developing clinical experience in a number of settings and to focusing clinical experience on the systematic development of practice, not simply on exposing prospective teachers to experienced teachers.

To Recognize Differences in Knowledge, Skill, and Commitment Among Teachers

Improved teacher education must be accompanied by changes in the structure of the profession. Raising standards of admission, increasing educational requirements, and increasing expectations of knowledge and mastery for teachers will encourage competent applicants only if the rewards of teaching and opportunities for professional advancement are commensurate with the educational requirements. Hence, a differentiated structure is a prerequisite for the construction of a profession of teaching.

The Holmes Group commits itself to the development of a differentiated structure at three levels: the Career Professional Teacher, who would be capable of assuming responsibility not only within the classroom but also at the school level; the Professional Teacher, who would be prepared as a fully autonomous professional in the classroom; and the Instructor, who would be prepared to deliver instruction under the supervision of a Career Professional Teacher. The Holmes Group also commits itself to make the changes in graduate education necessary to prepare professional teachers for this differentiated structure and to use its influence to change state and local policy.

To Create Relevant and Defensible Standards of Entry to the Profession of Teaching

The hallmark of a profession is its responsibility for the quality and competence of its members. This responsibility is twofold: responsibility to the members of the profession, for the human and financial investments they have made in their preparation must not be devalued; and responsibility to the public at large that the knowledge and skill of the profession are present in its members. The Holmes Group commits itself to develop and administer a series of Professional Teacher Examinations that provide a responsible basis for decisions on entry to the profession. Because of the limitations of standardized testing in predicting the future performance of teachers, The Holmes Group commits itself to require students to demonstrate mastery of important knowledge and skill through multiple evaluations across multiple domains of competence.

> Students admitted to teacher education will be required to demonstrate basic mastery of writing and speaking.

> Prior to a clinical internship, students will be expected to pass an examination demonstrating their mastery of the subject they will teach, their skill in lesson planning, and their instructional delivery.

> During their work in classrooms, prospective teachers will be required to observe

and evaluate a variety of teaching styles, including their own, and to present evidence of analytic skill in this area as part of their professional portfolio for advancement.

These examinations will provide a basis for evaluation not only of prospective teachers but also of the professional schools themselves.

The Holmes Group also recognizes its responsibility to help create a profession representative of the larger society. The most difficult problem in this regard is minority representation. Minority undergraduate enrollments and minority entry to teaching have been declining at the very time when the proportion of minority children in schools has been increasing. Unless this problem is addressed, we may soon have a teacher force composed overwhelmingly of people from majority backgrounds teaching students who are primarily from low-income and minority backgrounds. Holmes Group institutions commit themselves to significantly increasing the number of minorities in their teacher education programs. We will achieve this objective by increased recruitment at the pre-college level; endorsing loan forgiveness programs for minority students entering teaching; developing programs to increase retention of minority students enrolled in teacher education programs; and assuring that evaluations of professional competence minimize the influence of handicapping conditions, poverty, race, and ethnicity on entry to the profession.

To Connect Schools of Education with Schools

The improvement and professionalization of teaching depend ultimately on providing teachers with opportunities to contribute to the development of knowledge in their profession, to form collegial relationships beyond their immediate working environment, and to grow intellectually as they mature professionally. The improvement of teacher education depends on the continuing development of systematic knowledge and reflective practice. These two imperatives lead Holmes Group institutions to commit themselves to establish Professional Development Schools and working partnerships among university faculty, practicing teachers, and administrators that are designed around the systematic improvement of practice.

These Professional Development Schools, analogous to teaching hospitals in the medical profession, will bring practicing teachers and administrators together with university faculty in partnerships based on the following principles:

Reciprocity, or mutual exchange and benefit between research and practice;

Experimentation, or willingness to try new forms of practice and structure;

Systematic inquiry, or the requirement that new ideas be subject to careful study and validation; and

Student diversity, or commitment to the development of teaching strategies for a broad range of children with different backgrounds, abilities, and learning styles.

These schools will serve as settings for teaching professionals to test different instructional arrangements, for novice teachers and researchers to work under the guidance of gifted practitioners, for the exchange of professional knowledge between university faculty and practitioners, and for the development of new structures designed around the demand of a new profession.

To Make Schools Better Places for Practicing Teachers to Work and Learn

The construction of a profession, through the improvement of professional education, the development of a differentiated structure for professional opportunity, the creation of standards for entry, and the creation of settings for mutual exchange between research and practice, will have profound effects on the competence and aspirations of new teachers. The existing structure of schools, the current working conditions of teachers, and the current division of authority between administrators and teachers are all seriously out of step with the requirements of the new profession. If the construction of a genuine profession of teaching is to succeed, schools will have to change.

The Holmes Group is committed to changing the structure and working conditions within schools to make them compatible with the requirements of a new profession. Member institutions will work toward this end by developing exemplary models for new divisions of authority among teachers and administrators in Professional Development Schools, and by working within their institutions to make the professional education of administrators compatible with the requirements of the profession of teaching.

APPENDIX A

The Holmes Group as an Organization

Background and Structure of The Holmes Group

The Holmes Group grew out of a series of deliberations among education deans on the problems associated with the generally low quality of teacher preparation in the United States. Their initial discussions focused on the lax standards that have been tolerated for many decades. Weak accreditation policies and practices, and the historic disinterest in teacher preparation on the part of major research universities received special attention. Clearly these factors were not independent. The deans and academic leaders in these universities have long recognized the inadequacy of existing standards and review procedures employed by national professional and state government accrediting agencies. But the low priority assigned to teacher education in their own institutions provoked little effort to change the situation.

In the fall of 1983, the Johnson Foundation agreed to sponsor a meeting of seventeen deans who were willing to consider alternative ways of involving the major research universities in an effort to enhance the quality of teacher education. Several months later, the foundation hosted a follow-up meeting at its Wingspread Conference Center, this time attended by twenty-three deans and a number of the chief academic officers from research institutions. These leaders reviewed and approved a two-phase plan calling for the development and implementation of rigorous new standards for teacher education in the leading research universities in each of the fifty states. The goal was also set to have at least one such research university engaged in these endeavors for every 25,000 teachers across the United States. A proposal, developed and submitted for funding in the ensuing months, was reviewed positively by a number of granting agencies. Financial support for the first phase of the plan was eventually provided by the Carnegie Corporation of New York, the Ford Foundation, the Johnson Foundation, the New York Times Foundation, and the U.S. Department of Education.

Efforts to develop new standards of quality began in the fall of 1984 and continued over the next eighteen months. Many meetings were held and numerous guidelines were drafted, reviewed, criticized, and revised. The sessions were often intense. None of the organizing deans lacked opportunity for input, although none were able to have things just as they preferred. A range of views was encouraged, and principled arguments received serious attention. Selected consultants assisted with special expertise when the problems were particularly complex or controversial. The process was demanding, as the participants increasingly realized the serious nature of the task.

A first attempt at The Holmes Group report was drafted and reviewed in the spring of 1985. Substantial criticism led to major revision, with a second draft receiving almost unanimous approval at the June Wingspread meeting. At this time, it was decided to defer recommendations on special education, bilingual education, vocational education, and early childhood education until more extended consideration of the particular issues associated with those fields was undertaken. Meetings with specialists from these areas were arranged for further study.

It was also decided at this time that further review of the issues continuing to concern the several dissenting members of the group should be undertaken, since the intent was to achieve consensus if at all possible. Thus, additional time and effort was given across the summer to further understanding and problem-solving in the hope that full support would be obtained. But another critical issue surfaced. If member institutions adopted the new approaches being recommended by The Holmes Group, would they necessarily have to move away from their present teacher education practices? Could institutions continue "business as usual" for the most part, while possibly experimenting with some of the ideas proposed as worthy reforms? Or, stated yet another way, could institutions stay in The Holmes Group if they remained unconvinced of the value added by the proposed reforms? The questions were important ones, and they required further consideration and debate.

The steering committee posed this and remaining questions for decision by the full group in the fall of 1985. Meeting in Washington in November, so that one combined session could be held with the academic vice-president of the NASULGC institutions, the organizing deans made The Holmes Group official.

Articles of incorporation were signed, and a combined national-regional organizational structure was put in place. In this plan, the United States was divided into five geographical regions, with each region headed by a regional coordinator who would represent the national office in their respective regions. The regional plan was designed to increase efficiency, involvement, and exchange among school and university faculty and administrators from those participating across the regions. The regional coordinators would facilitate planning, implementation, and study among member institutions.

Each regional coordinator would serve on The Holmes Group's National Coordinating Committee, along with the president and vice-president of the Board of Directors. The National Coordinating Committee would be responsible for planning and documenting implementation activities, establishing ad hoc committees for specialized tasks, planning general membership meetings and conferences, and managing funding for the regional and national offices.

Each member of the National Coordinating Committee would sit on the Board of Directors of The Holmes Group. The Board would act as both a decision-making body and a research/study group. The chairpersons and vice-chairpersons of each standing committee would also be members of the Board, which would be responsible for recommending policy for the organization and guiding the general activities of the standing committees.

Presently, the structure includes the following four standing committees: Curriculum Development; State Planning and Policy; Testing and Evaluation; and Membership. Each standing committee would have participating members from the various regions. Bylaws describing the purpose, membership, and organizational structure of The Holmes Group have been drafted, and will be made available to charter members for examination prior to The Holmes Group's first official meeting where they will be revised as needed, and adopted.

The Character and Membership of The Holmes Group

The November gathering of all organizing members of The Holmes Group again established its character as a reform-minded body. The status quo in teacher education could no longer be accepted. After considerable discussion, they affirmed again that undergraduate students must have a strong general-liberal education, and they must major in academic subjects rather than education. And before being certified to practice with the autonomy professional teachers require, they needed to demonstrate clear mastery of the school subjects they would teach—implying the equivalent of a minor. Further, baccalaureate graduates would not be recommended for certification as teachers without a professional master's degree in education; and in particular, one that included a year of rigorous academic and clinical study, as well as a year's internship under the tutelage of Career Professional Teachers. Most of the assembled leaders assumed that these stringent requirements would necessitate more than the four years of preparation ordinarily required of prospective teachers.

The persistent problems associated with the "more than four years" issue would be handled by the accommodation of *Instructors,* who would be permitted to teach under the supervision of Career Professional Teachers for a limited period—providing they had acquired a sound liberal education, a strong undergraduate major or minor in the subject they would teach (or its equivalent), and the basics of pedagogy. This modified reform plan had the benefit of not preventing strong baccalaureate graduates from having the opportunity to instruct children; but at the same time, it promised that their movement toward becoming professional teachers—with all the rigorous study and evaluation that implied—would be assured.

The November discussion and a subsequent reconsideration by the Steering Committee in January and February was clear: Holmes Group universities would give primary emphasis to the preparation of Professional Teachers and Career Professional Teachers. And they could prepare talented Instructors if they chose, so long as the distinctions in training and responsibility between Professional Teachers and Instructors remained clear. But the central thrust of The Holmes Group would be furthering the profession of teaching through training and research—and toward this end, its member institutions would subscribe to the agenda and action commitments described in this report.

Thus, members of The Holmes Group would not only emphasize the preparation of professional teachers, but they would also work with one another and with affiliated institutions to provide leadership in improving teaching, schooling, and teacher education as here described. Those supporting quite different reform agendas, or those taking major issue with the primary goals and action commitments of The Holmes Group, would be encouraged to pursue their directions through other organizations supporting their own unique predilections.

Presently, The Holmes Group is establishing its charter membership and furthering its implementation plans. In keeping with the view that a focused effort among a reasonable number of research universities will increase the chance of successful reform, invitations for charter membership in The Holmes Group have been issued jointly to the chief academic officer and dean of education at 123 institutions. At least one leading public university in each state has been invited, and at least one institution for each 25,000 teachers in a region has been asked to join.

Institutions belonging to the American Association of Universities have been invited to become charter members of The Holmes Group, as have other institutions identified in reputational studies for the excellence of their research and development in education. Other factors taken into account include whether or not the institution offers a doctoral program in education, the past record of investment in research and development activity on the part of the institution as a whole, and the percentage of minority enrollment at the institution.

To become a charter member of The Holmes Group, the chief academic officer and the education dean at the institution must support The Holmes Group's agenda, and they must describe their general plans for encouraging development and implementation of the reform efforts at their institution. Institutional commitment to achieving Holmes Group goals would be demonstrated by the following:

- Active efforts to implement the reform agenda;
- Ongoing related research and development activities;
- Systematic documentation of implementation processes and outcomes;
- Conscious networking and shared work across institutional boundaries (within the university, between the university, elementary and secondary schools, between the university and the state department of education, and between the university and other professional institutions and organizations);
- Provision of adequate institutional support for the effort;
- Changing policies regarding the entry requirements for professional teachers, so that a quality graduate professional degree is required; and
- Payment of initial membership fee.

Once institutions have met membership requirements, continued participation in The Holmes Group will include an annual progress report, participation in the regional and national projects and activities of The Holmes Group, and payment of annual membership dues. Charter members may cease participation at any time simply by failing to submit their annual report and dues.

It is the intention of The Holmes Group leadership that just as the development of a national test for professional teachers will provide a "quality check" for individual teachers, membership and participation in The Holmes Group eventually will serve as a quality check for research universities and their graduate professional schools or colleges of education. Toward that end, once charter membership has been established and pilot programs for implementation of The Holmes Group reform effort are under way, the group's membership committee will accept applications for possible selection and participation from the deans and academic officers of other institutions wishing to affiliate with the group. It is anticipated that application for Holmes Group membership will be open to other research-intensive institutions within a three- to five-year period.

■|■|■

Contributors to the Written Report

JUDITH E. LANIER
Dean, College of Education
Michigan State University

DAVID K. COHEN
Visiting Professor, College of
Education
Michigan State University

MICHAEL W. SEDLAK
Associate Professor, College of
Education
Michigan State University

RICHARD S. PRAWAT
Professor, College of Education
Michigan State University

FRANK B. MURRAY
Dean, College of Education
University of Delaware

RICHARD ELMORE
Professor, College of Education
Michigan State University

MARIANNE AMAREL
Visiting Professor, College of
Education, Michigan State University

GARY A. GRIFFIN
Dean, College of Education
University of Illinois, Chicago

JOHN R. PALMER
Dean, School of Education,
University of Wisconsin-Madison

■|■|■

Participants in the Development of the Reform Agenda

MARIANNE AMAREL
Visiting Professor
College of Education
Michigan State University

DONALD P. ANDERSON
Dean, College of Education
Ohio State University

J. MYRON ATKIN
Dean, School of Education
Stanford University

CARL F. BERGER
Dean, College of Education
University of Michigan

CHARLES E. BIDWELL
Chair, Department of Education
University of Chicago

JACK E. BLACKBURN
Dean, School of Education
Auburn University

BURTON BLATT (deceased)
Dean, School of Education
Syracuse University

FRANK BROWN
Dean, School of Education
University of North Carolina

ROBERT BULLOUGH
Associate Professor, Graduate School
of Education
University of Utah

JOE R. BURNETT
Professor, College of Education
University of Illinois-
Champaign/Urbana

CHARLES W. CASE
Dean, College of Education
University of Iowa

NANCY S. COLE
Dean, College of Education
University of Illinois
Champaign/Urbana

JAMES COOPER
Dean, School of Education
University of Virginia

DEAN C. CORRIGAN
Dean, College of Education
Texas A & M University

JAMES I. DOI
Dean, College of Education
University of Washington

CARL J. DOLCE
Dean, School of Education
North Carolina State University

MARIO D. FANTINI
Dean, Graduate School of Education
University of Massachusetts

SHARON FEIMAN-NEMSER
Associate Professor, College of
Education
Michigan State University

WILLIAM E. GARDNER
Dean, College of Education
University of Minnesota

WILLIAM D. H. GEORGIADES
Dean, College of Education University
of Houston-University Park

BERNARD R. GIFFORD
Dean, School of Education
University of California, Berkeley

ROBERT D. GILBERTS
Dean, College of Education
University of Oregon

NAFTALY S. GLASMAN
Dean, Graduate School of Education
University of California, Santa Barbara

C. WAYNE GORDON
Professor, Graduate School of
Education, University of California
Los Angeles

PATRICIA ALBJERG GRAHAM
Dean, Graduate School of Education
Harvard University

GARY A. GRIFFIN
Dean, College of Education
University of California, Los Angeles

WILLIS D. HAWLEY
Dean, Peabody College
Vanderbilt University

HAROLD L. HERBER
Professor, School of Education
Syracuse University

LORRIN KENNAMER
Dean, College of Education
University of Texas-Austin

KAREN KEPLER-ZUMWALT
Professor, Teachers College
Columbia University

ROBERT H. KOFF
Dean, School of Education
State University of New York, Albany

JUDITH E. LANIER, Chair
Dean, College of Education
Michigan State University

HOWARD MEHLINGER
Dean, School of Education
Indiana University

CECIL G. MISKEL
Dean, School of Education
University of Utah

JOHN O. MULHERN
Dean, College of Education
University of South Carolina

FRANK B. MURRAY
Dean, College of Education
University of Delaware

RICHARD A. NAVARRO
Assistant Professor
College of Education
Michigan State University

NEL NODDINGS
Associate Professor
School of Education
Stanford University

JOHN R. PALMER, Vice-Chair
Dean, School of Education
University of Wisconsin-Madison

PENELOPE PETERSON
Professor, School of Education
University of Wisconsin-Madison

HUGH G. PETRIE
Dean, Faculty of Educational Studies
State University of New York, Buffalo

RICHARD S. PRAWAT
Professor, College of Education
Michigan State University

JAMES RATHS
Professor, College of Education
University of Illinois-
Champaign/Urbana

MARK R. SHIBLES
Dean, School of Education
University of Connecticut

LEWIS C. SOLOMON
Dean, Graduate School of Education
University of California, Los Angeles

P. MICHAEL TIMPANE
President, Teachers College
Columbia University

ALAN R. TOM
Chair, Department of Education
Washington University

RICHARD L. TURNER
Dean, School of Education
University of Colorado

FRED H. WOOD
Dean, College of Education
University of Oklahoma

SAM J. YARGER
Dean, School of Education
University of Wisconsin-Milwaukee

■|■|■

Consultants, Advisors, and Discussants

TERREL H. BELL
Secretary, U.S. Department of
Education

MARIO A. BENITEZ
Professor, College of Education
University of Texas-Austin

H. S. BROUDY
Professor Emeritus, College of
Education
University of Illinois
Champaign/Urbana

ROBERT BUSH
Professor, School of Education
Stanford University

DAVID L. CLARK
Professor, School of Education
Indiana University

GEORGE H. COPA
Professor and Chair, Department of
Vocational and Technical Education
College of Education
University of Minnesota

CINDY CURRENCE
Media Consultant & Free-lance
Writer, Williamsburg, Virginia

OLAF DAVIDSON
President, American College Testing
Program

TOM ENDERLEIN
Project Officer
Secretary's Discretionary Grant
U.S. Department of Education

RICHARD FERGUSON
Executive Vice-President
American College Testing Program

EDWIN GOLDWASSER
Vice-President for Academic Affairs
University of Illinois
Champaign/Urbana

JOHN GOODLAD
Professor, College of Education
University of Washington

MILDRED BARNES GRIGGS
Professor, College of Education
University of Illinois
Champaign/Urbana

JUDITH K. GROSENICK
Associate Dean, College of Education
University of Oregon

HENRY HALSTED
Vice-President, The Johnson
Foundation

DAN LORTIE
Professor, Department of Education
University of Chicago

EDWARD J. MEADE, JR.
Chief Program Officer, The Ford
Foundation

FRANK NEWMAN
President, Education Commission of
the States

DONALD D. O'DOWD
Executive Deputy Chancellor,
State University of New York

ROBERT M. O'NEIL
President, University of Virginia

GARY GLEN PRICE
Professor, College of Education
University of Wisconsin-Madison

MARILYN RAUTH
Executive Director, Educational Issues
Department, American Federation of
Teachers

RICHARD REMINGTON
Vice-President for Academic Affairs
University of Iowa

MAYNARD C. REYNOLDS
Professor, College of Education
University of Minnesota

SHARON ROBINSON
Director, Instruction and Professional
Development, National Education
Association

BELLA ROSENBERG
Associate Director of Public Relations
American Federation of Teachers

PHILLIP SCHLECHTY
Professor, School of Education
University of North Carolina

LEE S. SHULMAN
Professor, School of Education
Stanford University

PETER SMITH
Lieutenant Governor, State of
Vermont

IDA SANTOS STEWART
Associate Professor and Chair
Early Childhood Education
College of Education
University of Houston

HENRY T. TRUEBA
Professor, Graduate School of
Education, University of California
Santa Barbara

MARC S. TUCKER
Executive Director, Carnegie Forum
on Education and the Economy

C. L. WINDER
Vice-President for Academic Affairs
and Provost
Michigan State University

ARTHUR WISE
Director, Center for the Study of the
Teaching Profession
The Rand Corporation

■|■|■

Working Drafts of Goals for The Holmes Group Standards

General Goals

1 To change the preparation patterns and occupational structures of teaching so that highly competent people see it as a worthy investment *either* for a brief period of national service or for the long-term as a professional career.

2 To change the entrance standards for teaching so that only college graduates with established records of strong academic ability and successful records of apprenticeship with selected teachers and professors are allowed to teach in our schools.

3 To change the selection process for teaching so that talented college graduates with very modest preparation in education can work for one to five years as instructors; i.e., provided they have sound technical training in the basics on pedagogy, and quality guidance and oversight from professional teachers throughout the school year.

   (NOTE: Such an approach could be modeled after our nation's already successful Peace Corps and ROTC programs.)

4　To change the selection process and role expectations for those who would pursue teaching as a career so that only those with outstanding qualifications would fill the ranks of professional career teachers; i.e., those persons willing and able to do the following:

- Successfully pursue an in-depth course of study for professional preparation;
- Pass rigorous examinations that evidence mastery of the required knowledge and skill;
- Demonstrate four consecutive years of teaching that are evaluated regularly and judged consistently to be of truly outstanding quality and commitment; and
- Assume responsibility for helping schools be more effective through professional work with adults as well as with children.

5　To then change the reward structure for professional career teachers so that the extrinsic, as well as the intrinsic, returns for the work are comparable to that of other respected professions.

6　To change the working relationships, roles, and responsibilities within and between schools and universities so that their collaborative endeavors can assure the public of well-educated teachers for America's children.

Specific Goals

The Institutional Environment for Teacher Education

1　*The university honors its commitment to the nation's elementary and secondary schools through multiple investments in teachers and teaching.*

　　The commitment on the part of the institution of higher education to improved effectiveness in the "lower schools" is made visible in many ways. Included among these is support for recognizing excellence in teaching, both at the university and in the schools; scholarships for helping needy talented students and assuring cultural diversity among those pursuing teaching careers; the design and conduct of serious research and development aimed at the improvement of teaching and learning in the nation's schools; and multiple arrangements enabling teachers to participate readily in the continued learning opportunities available through the university.

2   *The university works with selected school districts to create exemplary school sites for student and faculty learning about teaching excellence.*

Referred to here as *Professional Development Schools,* such sites are needed if prospective and practicing professionals are to experience excellence in teaching and schooling. Here the contemporary problems associated with the teaching workplace and narrowly conceived teacher roles are remedied. Instead, working conditions are created that allow for the demonstration and evaluation of the very best in teaching practice. Unlike the laboratory schools of old, these are "real world" schools and as often as possible include pupils from disadvantaged homes. Cooperatively established and maintained with selected school districts, such sites become integral parts of the university's "learning community" in teacher education. A significant portion of the initial and continuing education of professional teaching personnel takes place here since these sites provide an appropriate environment for clinical instruction and professional socialization of teaching candidates and interns.

3   *The university fosters an interdisciplinary climate in teacher education that reflects the importance of disciplinary diversity, depth, and relatedness to teaching.*

Research-intensive universities employ faculty whose academic preparation assures disciplinary strength in the study of educational phenomena. In addition, they employ a set of teacher education faculty that includes persons with a range of relevant disciplinary expertise, cultural background. and subject matter specialization necessary to understand and improve the highly complex areas of teaching and teacher education. Overspecialization that inevitably leads to program fragmentation and overgeneralization that tends to encourage superficial study are consciously avoided. Instead, there is a valuing of collaboration among faculty with different disciplinary expertise that encourages coherent programs of professional preparation.

4   *The university expects an ethos of inquiry to permeate its teacher education programs at the university.*

The faculty and students at research-intensive universities are encouraged and supported for their propensity to question, to analyze, and to share emerging insights with others. The institution thus provides its teacher education faculty and students with the time, support, and high expectations required for excellence in scholarly inquiry and productivity. Systematic study of phenomena relating to formal education is commonplace, as is the regular exchange of new understandings with other professionals seeking to advance the art and science of teaching.

5   *The university creates significant opportunities for teacher education students to develop collegial and professional norms.*

A sense of community among the students pursuing careers in teaching is accorded through reasonably sized cohorts that enter and pursue coordinated programs of study. These classes have faculty mentors and advisors who remain with them throughout their initial preparation, helping develop personal and professional commitments to the occupation. Such advisors or mentors also facilitate program oversight and attention to the formal occasions designed to celebrate excellence in professional study and practice.

6   *The university assures equitable rights and responsibilities to the academic unit accountable for teacher education.*

The oversight and governance provisions for teacher education within a college, school, or department are comparable in concept and implementation to those of other post-baccalaureate professional schools. This assumes that the teacher education faculty, as well as the characteristics and qualities of the training program itself, undergo regular critical review by academic and clinical faculty from peer institutions. The process and results of these evaluations are made public and shared widely.

7   *The university supports regular improvement of teacher education and participation in a national consortium for ongoing research, development, and program improvement.*

Making the suggested reforms proposed here a reality calls for joint planning, shared expertise, and collaborative inquiry among the participants at research-intensive institutions, and among the collective set of such institutions across the country. To this end, intra- and inter-institutional working groups collaborate in the development of the following: (a) one or more experimental programs for career professionals; (b) curriculum materials, including a case literature to illustrate and illuminate principles of good teaching; (c) a set of examinations and assessment procedures used to evaluate candidates as they move through the stages of career development; (d) a set of inquiries related to teaching and teacher education which could be replicated across the various states and regions of the country; and (e) procedures for gathering appropriate demographic information related to teaching and formal education.

Faculty in Teacher Education

1   *The faculty responsible for preparing teachers are themselves competent and committed teachers.*

The teacher education faculty refers here to both university-based faculty and school-based faculty.

Allowing for notable exceptions, the teaching practices of these faculty emulate sound principles of pedagogy. They are evaluated by peers at least every two years for the presence of such qualities and this evaluation affects decisions regarding salary, promotion, and professional development. In addition, these faculty provide most of the formal instruction and clinical supervision required in the professional studies component of the program. Others, such as graduate students and part-time instructors, who teach in the program are only permitted to do so after a successful internship with a member of the professional faculty, and only when regularly supervised and evaluated for their teaching performance.

2   *The faculty responsible for educating teachers include both university-based and school-based faculty.*

Practicing schoolteachers are selected as clinical faculty on the basis of an exemplary record of teaching practice and attainment of professional career status in teacher education. Ordinarily, part of the professional assignment for clinical faculty is given to teaching pupils in school, while the remainder is given to work with academic faculty and students in teacher education. The school-based faculty would typically be referred to as clinical faculty, while the university faculty would be referred to as academic faculty. The clinical faculty would have special university appointments and be reimbursed for their professional contribution to the training program.

3   *The academic faculty responsible for teacher education contribute regularly to better knowledge and understanding of teaching and schooling.*

The scholarly productivity of the academic faculty in teacher education contributes to the codification of effective practice and to better understanding of aspects of education that have promise for improving teaching and learning in schools. Academic faculty members' scholarship is evaluated by peers in education and in disciplines associated with their scholarship. The evaluation affects departmental decisions regarding salary, promotion, and professional development.

4   *The teacher education faculty who demonstrate competence as strong teacher-scholars are recognized for this unique and important combination of abilities.*

To be outstanding in both professional teaching and scholarly productivity is neither easy nor common. Scholarship requires contemplative idea exchange, disciplined study, and reflective writing for an abstract audience. Teaching requires interactive people-exchange, thoughtful lessons, and sharing understandings directly with concrete groups of learners. A combination of talent in both areas is worthy of recognition. Thus, the designation "Fellow in Teacher Education" is created to celebrate excellence in scholarship and teaching among teacher education faculty nationally, and the status of "Fellow" would be recommended for a majority of the teacher education faculty in research-intensive universities. Candidates for fellowship status are full-time faculty who submit evidence to a national board attesting to their ability to meet established criteria. A Committee of Review consisting of leading educators (yet to be established) judges which of the applicants merit the status of Fellow.

Students in Teacher Education

1   *The students matriculating through the various phases of study required for career professionals are academically talented and committed to teaching.*

Students recruited for teacher education programs possess superior intellectual talent and appear capable of exerting educational leadership in their schools and communities. They are committed to continued learning and teacher accountability for deep understanding and knowledge of their pupils, subject specializations, profession, and society. Students admitted to teacher education candidacy evidence proficiency in oral and written forms of communication, with those who fail tests in either area accepted only provisionally until they remedy the deficiency. Students who rank in the lowest quartile of the college population nationally are denied admission into teacher education programs for career professionals.

2 *The student groups recruited and accepted into teacher education reflect our nation's obligation to a multicultural society.*

The preparation of minority students as career teachers is an important commitment, especially as the population of schoolchildren in the United States becomes increasingly diverse both ethnically and racially. Recruitment and retention programs are established to help meet the need for teachers who represent diversity in racial and ethnic background; specifically, the goal is to significantly increase the percentage of minority students in teacher education each year for the next ten years.

3 *Students evidence mastery of requisite content knowledge through written examination at various stages of their professional career development.*

At three points—prior to status as an intern, novice, and career teacher—students must pass required components of a Professional Teacher Examination (PTE). Developed by faculty from institutions participating in The Holmes Group consortium (liberal arts, subject area specialists, and professional educators), in cooperation with a major testing firm and practicing professionals, this examination measures achievement of knowledge and skills emphasized in the preparation program.

4 *Students, as judged by professionals, evidence appropriate ethical commitments and teaching capabilities prior to successful completion of their internship.*

During the induction year, students are required to successfully complete a half-time teaching internship. Concomitantly, they continue their academic study and work towards completion of the master's degree in teaching. As a necessary part of successful master's study in teaching, the intern teachers must be judged by the academic and clinical faculty as exemplifying both the qualities and ethical character befitting a career teacher, and the teaching performance appropriate for a novice teacher.

Curriculum in Teacher Education

1 *The curriculum for prospective career teachers does not permit a major in education during the baccalaureate years—instead, undergraduates pursue more serious general-liberal study and a standard academic subject normally taught in schools.*

Three major components in general-liberal study for prospective career teachers are recommended. These include studies of basic cultural knowledge, knowledge regarding knowledge itself, and knowledge about people. Studies of cultural knowledge include not only social, linguistic, and literary conventions, but the political, historical, scientific, and technical areas that foster "cultural literacy." Career teachers would be among the more culturally literate members of society and, as such, have sufficient background knowledge to comprehend the newspapers, magazines, and books addressed to the most literate segment of our nation's population. Career teachers would also be articulate about the sources of knowledge, how it changes over time, the multiple views that abound within disciplines, and how knowledge is evaluated and tested. They would distinguish between findings and explanations for findings, and possess the capacity for critical thinking and self-directed learning. Career teachers also acquire knowledge and experience important for professionals who work with people in complex social settings. Such knowledge would enable them to understand how social organizations function and how they influence people. They would come to describe and analyze issues of professional ethics, and the challenges and opportunities present in a society which has within it many groups that vary in culture and ethnic background. Finally, the prospective career teacher's major in an academic subject would increase understanding and appreciation for subject matter depth and mastery. The major could include study of the history of the subject, competing theories in the field, its epistemology, and primary modes of inquiry.

2   *The curriculum for prospective career teachers requires a master's degree in education and a successful year of well-supervised internship.*

In their pedagogical study, prospective career teachers acquire special knowledge enabling them to think with depth and flexibility about the enduring problems encountered in teaching. Such problems concern:

(1) our society's multiple, often conflicting expectations for schools and teachers; (2) the challenges of teaching diverse individuals in group contexts; (3) the need to select appropriate content in the face of multiple goals, changing knowledge, and finite instructional time; (4) the complexity of motivating students to learn while evaluating their progress; and (5) the responsibility of sustaining professional growth and commitment over the course of a career. Beyond knowledge of such problems and how they are illuminated by theory, students also develop the ability to identify conceptual principles of pedagogy and illustrations of

their operation in actual practice. Eventually, students develop the ability to make their own situationally appropriate decisions and take action in regard to such problems—and to study their consequences. Supervised by clinical faculty, interns teach children half of their time, and participate in teaching clinics, engage in action research, and study curriculum. The intent is to prepare teachers who can learn from teaching, not merely survive it.

3 *The curriculum for elementary career teachers would require study in multiple areas of concentration (each equivalent to a minor) in the subject fields for which teachers assume general teaching authority and responsibility.*

One or two courses in a subject (such as mathematics or science) are no longer judged adequate for the autonomy and responsibility expected of career teachers. Thus, by methodically combining baccalaureate and post-baccalaureate studies, elementary career teachers would successfully complete area studies in each of the five basic fields taught in elementary schools: language and literature, mathematics, science, social science, and the arts. The exact nature of these "area concentrations" is yet to be spelled out, but it is envisioned that each will be roughly equivalent in time commitment to a minor field of study. The student's undergraduate major, naturally, would take the place of one of the required concentrations.

4 *The curriculum for secondary career teachers would include significant graduate study in their major teaching field and area concentrations in all other subjects they would teach.*

During post-baccalaureate study and prior to being recommended for career teacher status, secondary teachers would be required to successfully complete the equivalent of an advanced specialist degree. At a minimum, such work would comprise at least one-third graduate study in the area of the teacher's major. Secondary teachers would also successfully complete a cognate area of study equivalent to a minor, but would be encouraged to continue work in this second area until it reaches the equivalent of a second major.

5 *The curriculum for all prospective career teachers would include substantial knowledge and skill regarding appropriate policy and practice in teaching students with special needs—advanced graduate study would be required for career professional roles in special education.*

All career teachers should be qualified to effectively teach students with special needs in regular classrooms. Those who would specialize in the teaching of special populations would be expected to obtain *additional* knowledge and understanding, however. Special education consultants or teachers of special populations (e.g., children with learning disabilities, bilingual, gifted, or emotionally impaired) would need to obtain the added competence as part of advanced graduate work. Thus, teachers would qualify for autonomous work with special populations only after achieving career teacher status and advanced specialized study in areas relevant to the education of such populations.

6　*The curriculum required for teacher attainment of career professional status requires advanced study appropriate for specialized work in education with other adult professionals.*

Up to now, outstanding teachers had to leave teaching if they wished to participate more extensively in the work of professional education. Now, professional career teachers build on their strong knowledge and competence in teaching youngsters and combine it with additional knowledge pertinent to this expanded educational role. Thus, advanced study to prepare career teachers as specialists in (1) curriculum development, (2) research and evaluation, (3) teacher education, (4) work with special populations, (5) school policy and management, or (6) particular subject fields, would be made available by research-intensive universities—as would assistance in working with schools to create roles for teachers that *combine outstanding teaching of children with outstanding work with adults in education.* Successful completion of such advanced study would carry recognition as a Professional Career Teacher, and could lead to a second advanced degree (e.g. an educational specialist degree or the doctorate in education).

■|■|■

PART TWO

A Report of The Holmes Group

Tomorrow's Schools

Principles for The Design of Professional Development Schools

■|■|■

The Writing Group

The voices expressing the ideas and recommendations in this report are many: innovating school and university faculty and other citizens working on the reform of education throughout the United States. Their names are listed in Appendix A. Those responsible for culling and summarizing themes from the discourse and for writing this report are:

LAUREN S. YOUNG
Assistant Professor, College of
Education, Michigan State University

GARY SYKES
Assistant Professor, College of
Education, Michigan State University

JOSEPH FEATHERSTONE
Professor, College of Education
Michigan State University

RICHARD F. ELMORE
Professor, College of Education
Michigan State University

KATHLEEN DEVANEY
Communications Specialist
The Holmes Group
Berkeley, California

■|■|■

Preface

We began this work fired with a simple concern for the quality of teacher education in America. The more we talked, the more we realized that teacher education represents a mesh in a very wide net that stretches from the universities to the schools and out to the wider society. Pull on one part of the net, and you end up tugging on all the other parts, too. The idea of a Professional Development School—a new kind of educational institution that will be a partnership between public schools and universities—reflects our fundamental commitment to teacher education; but of necessity *Tomorrow's Schools* ranges over many parts of the net.

"We" are the members of The Holmes Group, a consortium of nearly 100 American research universities committed to making our programs of teacher preparation more rigorous and connected—to liberal arts education, to research on learning and teaching, and to wise practice in the schools. Our commitment serves a deeper purpose. We incorporated in 1986 *"to enhance the quality of schooling,* through research and development and the preparation of career professionals in teaching."

The Holmes Group manifesto, *Tomorrow's Teachers,* published that spring, spelled out the specific goals we thought were necessary: "Make the education of teachers intellectually sound. Make better use of differences in knowledge, skill, and commitment among teachers. Create relevant and defensible standards of entry to the profession of teaching. Connect schools of education with schools. Help make schools better places for practicing teachers to work and learn."

We were critical of the way our universities educate teachers but optimistic about what we can do if we can create partnerships within our universities and with the schools in our communities. We recognized that schools and colleges of education cannot continue to emulate disciplinary departments in universities, largely ignoring the field of practice. Rather, a school of education must shape a separate identity as a professional school with strong roots in reflective practice and strong bonds to the public schools.

We believe these bonds between universities and schools should be a partnership among peers. Practicing teachers, administrators, teacher educators, and administrator educators should work together to make fine schools for children that will also be realistic, challenging, and supportive settings for the field studies of prospective teachers and for the rising professionalism of practicing teachers. More than that, in these schools university and school faculties should collaborate in research about the problems of teaching and learning so that exchanges of expertise can refresh and even reshape the curriculum and teaching at the university and the school.

The partnerships envisioned in *Tomorrow's Teachers* were to be formed around the following principles:

> "*Reciprocity,* or mutual exchange and benefit between research and practice;
> "*Experimentation,* or willingness to try new forms of practice and structure;
> "*Systematic inquiry,* or the requirement that new ideas be subject to careful study and validation; and
> "*Student diversity,* or commitment to the development of teaching strategies for a broad range of children with different backgrounds, abilities, and learning styles."

In 1988, with the Ford Foundation's funding, The Holmes Group began to prepare a second report based on those principles. This report, *Tomorrow's Schools,* was to argue the purposes and to outline the dimensions of the tasks of connecting a university-based education school to one or more public elementary and secondary schools so as to create a new educational institution—a "Professional Development School." This is the report you have in your hands.

The report began as a series of conversations among leading school and university faculty members from across the nation. Eighteen teachers, administrators, teacher educators, and administrator educators came together July 15–16, 1988 at Michigan State University, The Holmes Group headquarters. For two days they described and discussed the models of learning and teaching that they thought should shape schooling.

About 100 other participants took part in five similar seminars that followed between September and December, 1988. In those seminars the discussants focused on changes needed in the way teachers work and the roles they play in the school; on teaching students with different backgrounds, abilities, and learning styles with equity and efficacy; on schools' relationships with families and communities; on different styles of school leadership; and on ways to restructure the organization of schools and school districts. The names of the participants in those seminars are listed in Appendix A: "Contributors to the Report."

With detailed notes from all six seminars in hand, each of the five Holmes Group regional organizations held discussions during 1989 among faculty members active in campus Holmes Group reforms and school people they work with. In what ways would these educators question, redefine, and/or enlarge upon the ideas, issues, and controversies that arose in the six conversations in East Lansing? Similarly, representatives from business, state governments, and national education policy experts were drawn together to critique the emerging ideas and to offer their views on the future structure of schools and work of educators. In the summer and fall of 1989, a report was drafted and critiqued by a committee of The Holmes Group Executive Board and by the Tomorrow's Schools Steering Committee—a national group of school and university faculty members recognized for their ability to envision and affect educational policy and practice in the United States. Finally, the report was reviewed and endorsed, with some recommendations for changes, by representatives of Holmes Group member institutions at their annual meeting, January 27, 1990.

In this report, we are promoting an idea. Although every single practice within the ideal package is in successful operation in some form, somewhere, no single Professional Development School such as we propose here actually exists. This does not mean we are talking about something imaginary, but that we must be careful not to confuse principles and vision with some particular building. The principles we propose here have no mailing address.

We advance our vision as the beginning of a process—conversations/actions/conversations/revisions—that will take a long time. Those who want to join in should think of signing up for the duration. We believe that universities, schools of education, and public schools all over the country need to start conversations about long-term directions and prospects for cumulative change and collaborative work—among institutions that have for too long run separate courses. Our expectation is that the conversations will first begin within the schools of education that take part in The Holmes Group. This document could be the text for those faculty seminars.

Thus, if we had to choose a particular audience for this document, it would be our university colleagues and their colleagues in the schools. This is The Holmes Group talking to itself, we would say.

But we know that the audience for talk of education reform is growing wider by the day. What we have to say may be of intense interest to many in our nation awakened by the crisis of the schools and its threat to our society's future. A busy education reform movement at the state and national levels is finding it hard to maintain a sense of direction. It remains uncertain about fundamental principles. We believe that we identify, reinforce, and clarify essential principles here. We welcome all who listen in. The schools in a democracy are rightly everybody's business.

Most of the time in this volume we are talking modestly of creating a relatively small number of institutions with a special mission centering on the initial and life-long education of teachers as professionals. We would prefer this report to be read as an argument for efforts modest and particular—limited enough to accomplish, yet important enough to be worth doing. It will certainly be sufficient unto the decade if we can create a thriving network of Professional Development Schools. But our underlying purpose will be thwarted if such schools don't also begin the long march toward worthy schools for everybody's children.

One argument in this report is the decisive importance of the capacity of the local school—as a learning community—to set its own agenda. Another is the futility of the quest for one best system of educating teachers or children. Both these points reinforce our conviction—and our hope—that Professional Development Schools shaped around the principles we set forth here will flourish as a species and add great variety to the ecology of education. One reason for creating them is to promote diversity and experimentation in an educational landscape that often looks flat and monotonous. Rich variety will prove to be a source of great strength in the ensuing conversations among the network of those taking part in this work.

The idea of creating Professional Development Schools offers something vital and renewing. It also gives interested people in schools of education and school districts an opportunity to step forward and play a leading role in educational reform. We think it's time for educators to help reshape a reform movement that, for better and for worse, often has bypassed the education profession. Instead of reacting to each new hummock on the school reform landscape, we can begin shaping the contexts in which we work. We are the ones to start building tomorrow's schools—today.

■|■|■

Acknowledgments

A project such as Tomorrow's Schools, designed to advance the national discourse regarding the preparation of professional educators in exemplary settings, benefits greatly from the invaluable contributions made by several others. They deserve our mention and expressions of gratitude.

Members of the Tomorrow's Schools Project Steering Committee brought together the range of perspectives needed to develop the school-university connections so critical to better teaching and learning in America's educational institutions. This distinguished group drawn from teaching, administration, teacher education, and administrator education came from across the nation to enrich and advance our thinking about what we were hearing in the seminars, and about what was missing. As the primary advisory group to the Tomorrow's Schools project, they lent their advice throughout the eighteen-month process. Our work on these difficult issues was facilitated and strengthened by the substance and soundness of their judgment and commentary.

Sam Bacharach	Steven Bossert
Ruben Carriedo	Ivy Chan
Joseph Delaney	Lisa Delpit

Joseph Fernandez	Haven Henderson
Shirley Hill	Susan Moore Johnson
Magdalene Lampert	Deborah Meier
Phillip Schlechty	Thomas Sergiovanni
Henry Trueba	Nancy Zimpher

A core group of The Holmes Executive Board, the Liaison Committee, served in an important conceptual and connecting role. In addition to The Holmes Group President, Judith Lanier, the Liaison Committee included David Colton, Mary Harris, Cecil Miskel, Lonnie Wagstaff, and The Holmes Group's five regional vice-presidents—Donald Anderson, Dean Corrigan, Gladys Johnston, Frank Murray, and Hugh Petrie. The vice-presidents fostered broad and recurrent discussions of the seminars' major themes, enabling school and university faculty at the local and regional levels to put forth opinions and advice that helped shape the national report.

The roster of seminar participants who shared with us their ideas—in person and/or in writing—is impressive by any standard. We found our major intellectual bearings in the knowledge, experience, wisdom, and creativity of this group of the education policymakers who provided comment and critique on the major ideas and questions we synthesized from the seminars. We thank Susan Fuhrman and the Center for Policy Research in Education for hosting the policy seminar at Rutgers University.

Three individuals deserve special mention. Judith Lanier provided steadfast counsel from the conception to the publication of this report. She recognized the importance of bringing together the several communities of educators whose diverse experiences and perspectives grounded and expanded our understandings. Her leadership and commitment to improving teaching and learning for America's youngsters and their teachers provided focus to our efforts from the very beginning. Edward Meade, Jr., of the Ford Foundation gave early encouragement and counsel as we framed the project, and his acknowledgment of its likely value helped obtain the essential financial assistance from the Ford Foundation. Harry Judge, from Oxford University and Michigan State University, attended all seven seminars, concluding each with unique, questioning, good-humored commentary that made us think again.

We thank several Holmes Group and Michigan State University staff for their able and generous contributions to this project: Eric Weir, for his superb recordings and summaries of the seminar deliberations; Mary-Dean Barringer, for the teacher perspective that she brought regularly to the writing team, and for her general administrative assistance; Joan Eadie, for the planning and coordinating associated with bringing participants to the seminars; and Brad West, for his fiscal and accounting assistance, and for his help in distributing this report. Joanne DiFranco and Jeanette Minkel provided secretarial and conference coordination for the project. Lawrence Cole, graphics coordinator in Outreach Communications at Michigan State, designed the cover and text format, and coordinated the printing of the report.

Finally, we must acknowledge the time and energy given by many faculty members and administrators at Michigan State University, which hosted the seminars and meetings of the Steering and Liaison Committees and the Writing Group. The intellectual and financial resources of Michigan State contributed indispensably to this effort.

■|■|■

Why Professional
Development Schools?

The whole Holmes Group effort hinges on a complex set of reforms happening all together: liberal education—that is, deep understanding of the disciplines by teachers and their students; reconstituted, coherent education studies; and clinical studies expertly supervised in authentic, exemplary settings. Where they all come together is in the Professional Development School—in essence, a new institution.

By "Professional Development School" we do not mean just a laboratory school for university research, nor a demonstration school. Nor do we mean just a clinical setting for preparing student and intern teachers. Rather, we mean all of these together: a school for the development of novice professionals, for continuing development of experienced professionals, and *for the research and development of the teaching profession.*

We mean these schools to help the teaching profession in six ways:

- By promoting much more ambitious conceptions of teaching and learning on the part of prospective teachers in universities and students in schools;
- By adding to and reorganizing the collections of knowledge we have about teaching and learning;

- By ensuring that enterprising, relevant, responsible research and development is done in schools;
- By linking experienced teachers' efforts to renew their knowledge and advance their status with efforts to improve their schools and to prepare new teachers;
- By creating incentives for faculties in the public schools and faculties in education schools to work mutually; and
- By strengthening the relationship between schools and the broader political, social, and economic communities in which they reside.

As we began in 1988 to work out the idea of the Professional Development School, The Holmes Group was mindful of the long history of attempts to improve schools. We brought together 120 educators from schools and universities across the nation to exchange their experience and ideas in six two-day seminars on their aspirations for tomorrow's schools. (The quotations placed within this text are taken from notes of the conversations in those seminars.)

The long struggle to make teaching a respected profession inspired and sobered the seminar discourse. The participants commented on the work of thoughtful progressive educators, who insisted on studying children and pedagogy, who gave us classic examples of inspired classroom teaching, and who laid the foundations for educational psychology. Seminar participants were mindful of the movements to establish laboratory schools in universities, and other efforts to draw universities and schools together. Teacher education has its heroes and great moments, and these were recognized.

The seminar participants advised that in conceiving the Professional Development School we build on the university-based curriculum efforts of the 1960s and their attempts to bring the best minds of the university to the task of improving the curriculum of the schools. Build on the concerns that brought the revolution for racial equality to American education, they said. Draw on the best reform experience of recent decades and on the examples of teachers whose work they described or whose classrooms we had visited.

We do not flatter ourselves that we have something completely new to offer American education. The Professional Development School envisioned in this report resembles the laboratory school movement in some respects. In other ways it recalls the curriculum reforms of the mid-1960s. But it departs from the past in two directions. First, the Professional Development School is an effort to invent an institutional coalition that will bring all the required forces together—universities, schools of education, and public schools. And second, it promises to work on the problems of teaching over the long haul—as long as several generations of teachers. This combination of institutional support and a commitment to the long haul might have made a big difference for any of the earlier reform movements and ideas we have cited. All of them lacked institutional support and staying power.

In addition, we have powerful ideas—to create ambitious learning communities of teachers and students that are at the same time centers of continuing. mutual learning and inquiry by prospective teachers, experienced teachers, administrators, and education and liberal arts professors. We think our efforts to build inquiry into such coalitions and to do this over time are in fact something new under the reform sun.

Schools and wider publics

Continuing pressure for education reform is exerted by a pervasive public worry about the relationship between schools and the broader society. Corporate leaders worry about whether the schools can educate young people to succeed in jobs that will require a high level of collaborative decision-making and understanding of complex processes. Intellectuals worry about the erosion of citizen participation in basic democratic processes and whether schools are teaching students core American values and the fundamentals of our government. Parents worry about whether schools give their children a fair chance to learn what they need to get ahead and be happy.

> At the heart of democratic life is acceptance of uncertainty and the personal. The school should be an area of uncertainty. The goal is to learn to live with uncertainty, to live with it productively. And always there is a relationship with people.

These worries are expressed against the backdrop of social, economic, and cultural conditions that are radically different from the way they were when the worriers went to school. The changing structure of the family, the changing composition of our population in age, ethnicity, and income level, the changing demands on the skilled work force, the growing political and economic interdependence between the United States and other nations: All are factors that profoundly influence society's demands on and provision for public schools.

In the past, American public education has taken a mainly reactive posture toward such community concerns. Public schools almost always respond to whatever is the crisis of the moment, but in responding, they often confirm that they did not anticipate it. Professional Development Schools must be laboratories where astute people from universities and schools form alliances with the broader community to anticipate solutions to emerging social, economic, and political concerns. Just as Professional Development Schools should be places where students and teachers work at the outer edges of their expertise, so too should they be places where educators and community leaders work at the outer edges of the educational and social problems facing children.

Both university and school teachers should have an exhilarating 'whitewater' feeling of working at the edge of their knowledge, being engaged in a new kind of work.

Professional Development Schools and education reform

The conversations in our seminars shifted frequently from Professional Development Schools to the general topic of education reform. Some of what this report has to say bears on the question of school reform more generally. But this report is not urging a way of reforming all schools. The reasons are threefold. First, Professional Development Schools will assume some responsibilities—notably the preparation and induction of new teachers—that are simply not part of most schools' mission.

Second, the reform of American education—however necessary—is a broader, more ambitious enterprise than we in The Holmes Group can possibly accomplish. We are, after all, urging the creation of a relatively small number of schools designed to be the focus of professional preparation, school research, and the improvement of teaching. Third, some of the ideas that are tried in Professional Development Schools may not work. and hence shouldn't be the basis for reform of schools more generally. So one must be careful to distinguish the agenda of this report—the creation of Professional Development Schools—from the broader agenda of educational reform.

The Holmes Group doesn't have any business telling the community what kind of schools it should have, but it does have a right to say how teachers should be prepared.

Professional Development Schools are, however, related to education reform in a deeper, more systemic sense. Past efforts at school reform give little cause for optimism about the current school reform agenda. We are again in the middle of a bustling era of school reform that may vanish without a trace. "New York City has tried every single good educational idea—once," is how one seminar participant put it. Scholars have observed that school reformers have never had difficulty creating small islands of the ideal or even sustaining such small experiments for relatively long periods of time. Much of what we would like to see is happening now: in the classrooms of isolated teachers, in schools inspired by principals who are lone entrepreneurs, in universities and colleges of education where a few maverick professors always turn up. The Lone Rangers may always be with us, but we think it is time to settle the educational frontier and build communities of practice and inquiry that will endure over time. The main problem of education reform is that fundamental changes in the conditions of teaching and learning seldom take hold beyond these outposts. An irony of education reform is that during certain periods of history, "restructured schools" have been everywhere and nowhere at the same time. Public schools easily deflect or co-opt the best efforts of school reformers.

Professional Development Schools are a self-conscious attempt to solve this problem. They are an attempt to institutionalize the development of new knowledge and practice so that educators' best ideas don't end up in isolated islands of exemplary practice. Professional Development Schools will develop new visions of teaching and prepare practitioners who can implement these visions. They will represent long-term arrangements between universities and school systems, rather than isolated atolls of good practice. Over time, they should produce a more responsible way of introducing new ideas into all schools.

The discussions underscored our initial conviction that many different types of Professional Development Schools will be needed in many different settings. *Thus this report is a challenge—a call to action—rather than a template for a single conception.*

I don't want us to talk about a Professional Development School that will be one structure for the profession. That makes me nervous. I'd rather think of it being an enabling setting, a loose nest where ideas can be tried out.

What are the ideas?

In the chapters that follow, we lay out six principles as to how a Professional Development School should organize itself. We offer these principles as starting points for conversations and negotiations among university and school faculties embarked on a mutual endeavor. The principles are not heavily prescriptive; neither are they lightly held. They reflect the distilled experience of some 120 first-rate educators who thought long and seriously about what they could contribute to the invention of a new institution dedicated equally to the learning of its students, student teachers, and school and university faculty.

Principle One

Teaching and learning for understanding. All the school's students participate seriously in the kind of learning that allows you to go on learning for a lifetime. This may well require a radical revision of the school's curriculum and instruction.

Principle Two

Creating a learning community. The ambitious kind of teaching and learning we hope for will take place in a sustained way for large numbers of children only if classrooms and schools are thoughtfully organized as communities of learning.

Principle Three

Teaching and learning for understanding for everybody's children. A major commitment of the Professional Development School will be overcoming the educational and social barriers raised by an unequal society.

Principle Four

Continuing learning by teachers, teacher educators, and administrators. In the Professional Development School, adults are expected to go on learning, too.

Principle Five

Thoughtful long-term inquiry into teaching and learning. This is essential to the professional lives of teachers, administrators, and teacher educators. The Professional Development School faculty working as partners will promote reflection and research on practice as a central aspect of the school.

Principle Six

Inventing a new institution. The foregoing principles call for such profound changes that the Professional Development School will need to devise for itself a different kind of organizational structure, supported over time by enduring alliances of all the institutions with a stake in better professional preparation for school faculty.

These principles are laid out in five succeeding chapters. A conclusion suggests what Holmes Group universities should do to make a start.

■|■|■

Teaching for Understanding

In a Community of Learning

Teachers, professors, school principals, and superintendents came to East Lansing from across the nation in July, 1988 to begin the dialogue—six two-day seminars—from which this report is drawn. They reaffirmed our nation's traditional and continuing purposes for schooling—academic learning, economic progress, and active citizenship for a democracy.

They insisted, however, that if these traditional purposes are to be fulfilled in the new century, there will have to be radical changes in how children learn in school and how we teach. We can sum up a complex discussion by simply saying that all of our schools are going to have to do a better job of helping children to use their minds well. All children—not only the most privileged and most accomplished, but the most needy as well. For this to happen, our schools will have to become better communities.

So our first two principles are intertwined:

1   Lasting learning—the kind that allows students to go on learning for a lifetime—is what we call teaching for understanding.

2   Such learning will take place only in schools and classrooms that work as communities of learning.

1   Teaching and Learning for Understanding

Education's basic goal is the cultural progress of individuals and society. Good schools teach many things, including the habits of mind and character needed for making a living and making a good life. The deeper, generic task of education is teaching students how to *make* knowledge and meaning—to *enact* culture, not merely acquire it.

The critical question is not 'What does the teacher do?' It's 'What does the teacher get the kids to do?' Basically we're talking about teaching as an act of leadership. Teaching is essentially helping people get excited in a subject area, which leads them to engage in the big ideas, the cultural ideas.

By culture we mean complex things, but nothing very arcane. We mean the shared meanings developed over time by particular groups of people out of their common life and the necessity for coping with the world. Schools, of course, have a special responsibility to help students develop traditional academic culture—the organized meanings embedded over time in the great stories and the learned disciplines. We strongly support this traditional academic role of schools, with two important qualifications.

First, we want schools to help students to take an active, rather than a passive role. Curriculum needs to become a way of living and acting to make sense of experience. The richest stories of the society and the organized academic disciplines offer access to such treasures as: a familiarity with the past, the capacity to use complex symbols with purpose and power, the ability to make new meanings, the power of the imagination, and, in particular, the power of critical thought. Nowadays a good education helps students develop a view of the adequacy of the reigning visions of culture and its canon. Ultimately, education prepares students who can argue such matters and even transform the reigning ideas of culture itself. From the start, good schools help their students to become more appreciative and critical of culture in several senses beyond academic culture—to take pride in their own culture and to become critics of popular culture, for example. To reach this kind of cultural understanding—and to enact it in classrooms—teachers will need a much better education in the arts and sciences than they now are getting. Arts and sciences faculty must join in the work of educational change.

Our second qualification of the traditional task of teaching academic culture to students involves yet another sense of the word "culture." Schools need to do a much better job of building on students' own cultural capital. Teachers will have to become closer students of their own students. A pluralistic democracy whose schools are full of immigrant children and children from many peoples and races requires teachers prepared to become more thoughtful about "culture" in another sense: cherishing and building on the webs of meaning and value and community that students bring to school. We see the schools as building bridges between traditional academic culture, the culture of students, and world culture.

'Acknowledging diversity' means binding the rich mosaics all together.

The heart of teaching for understanding is the creation of learning community. By "understanding" we mean learning that equips you to go on learning for a lifetime: the complex, internalized, public and private scaffolding of information, insight, and experience in any field that can lift you to the next question, and get you started on it. Such learning emerges best from an active process of constructing public and private meaning in a community of discourse. This is the link between understanding and community. Teaching for understanding won't happen in classrooms where students sit silent and passive. Through participation in discourse, teachers help students construct more adequate meanings. They learn, for example, that not all understandings are equal: Some are more helpful than others in making yourself at home in the world, in specifiable ways. The kinds of meanings we associate with the public display of evidence and logic offer powerful ways to specify such helpfulness. Certain (not all) of the most thoughtful and worked-out meanings in human tradition are represented by the communities of discourse that have evolved over time into what we call the disciplines. To understand a subject means in effect that you have been initiated into a community of discourse—that you take part in the conversation. Ultimately the conversation spans the centuries, but for most students it first becomes real only here and now in the circle of faces in this class, third-period American history, with the radiators banging.

We use the word "conversation" here both literally and metaphorically. Literally, because learning to transact the lingo in your own voice is in fact a key aspect of understanding in any field. Metaphorically, because the "conversation" can take shape in silence or—more powerfully, sometimes—as direct experience. The student exploring the qualities of soap bubbles in a good science class is taking part in a conversation—a dialogue in the mind—even when few words are exchanged. So is the student working alone on the piece of sculpture. So is the student whose senior spring project is thoughtful work in a veterinary hospital.

The view that lasting and powerful learning involves the mastery of discourse and active participation in a community is the basis for much fine teaching. The community of discourse is the means by which good teachers turn into lifelong voices inside the heads of their students. And its absence illuminates why, lacking learning community, too many of our classrooms are going through motions—the fragmentary English exercises, for example, that bear no relation to live speech uttered and listened to for a living purpose. The transactions of significant experience—the connections made in a human community—are the roots of all powerful learning. We ignore them at the price of waste and boredom.

Conversation, experience, interpretation, criticism, engagement, voice, participation, purpose: These are some of the words we link with teaching for understanding. Recent work in cognitive psychology argues that knowledge is an active and participatory affair. Such psychology is saying what good teachers have known for a long time. It's not enough just to tell students things—though there is nothing wrong with a good lecture. They also need to learn how to interpret what they learn, and to relate it to what else they know, and whenever possible to have some experience of what is being taught. They need to take the new information and fuse it with more conscious and refined meanings.

> What we are learning from cognitive scientists is, first, that people are inveterate constructors of meaning: They're going to make sense of it in some way. Second, people make sense of the environment differently in learning different content. Third, context causes people to make different sense of things than they do in school. And fourth, within all of that, different cultures will value these things in different ways.

Learning at all levels is an active process, in which children construct and reconstruct knowledge as they go along. To know something is not only to take in the bare information but to interpret it and relate it to other knowledge. Powerful learning, then, comes about when students can develop a mental scheme in which to frame their knowledge and then go on to make fresh knowledge and an even newer mental scheme. Much current cognitive research holds that there is no way to make real use of knowledge other than creating a personal intellectual apparatus that holds information together and allows the learner to play with it. Real knowledge is purpose-built, site-built, and infused with the learner's sense of purpose.

It is a severe understatement to say that little of this view informs educational policy or practice today, although the teaching of good teachers everywhere confirms its usefulness. Conventional wisdom and much teaching practice assume the contrary: that learning is the accumulation of facts and isolated skills, and that basic skills must precede in time the exercise of more complex understandings. First the basics; then the complex literacy of discussion, interpretation, and criticism. If the examples of thoughtful practitioners and the theories of the cognitive psychologists are right, acquiring facts has to march hand in hand with deep thinking, wrestling with the facts. Concepts and facts define each other. They are the foreground and background of serious thinking, and are therefore inseparable.

Our seminar participants insisted that the separation of "basic" facts and skills from more complex and ambitious learning is a fundamental mistake. At every stage of learning, the students who enact complex meaning are those who learn the deepest kind of literacy—who can interpret a text imaginatively, for example, or adapt a given mathematical approach to a new context.

But if we say that this is cognition and this is affect, or this is basic and this is higher order, we just have the wrong model. You can't get one without the other. You don't get the basics without the advanced.

The disciplines: "clubs" students join

This view of teaching for understanding also meshes with much recent thinking on the nature of the academic disciplines themselves. Literacy can be thought of as the series of clubs we want our students to join—the science and math and writing and art clubs. In joining they take part in the long human conversation that includes the dead, as well as the living, and will go on into a future we can hardly imagine. The disciplines are the products of generations of work in the smaller conversations or learning communities—the club called mathematics, the club called science, the club called literature. We tend to think of the disciplines as products—embodied in a particular scientific advance or a textbook, for example. But it would be closer to the mark to think of them as long-running conversations. The knowledge they represent is dynamic, not static; fluid, not solid; and very much a human creation. Our students will remain passively ignorant—will not understand—if we teach them the products of these communities alone—the final codified results but not the process of inquiry, dialogue, and criticism. This is not, our participants emphasized, an argument against knowledge and content. They, too, were alarmed at the evidence that U.S. students today don't know enough simple math and science, so little American history and international geography. But the remedy for this ignorance is not memorizing lists of facts or even passages from the Great Books.

Expertise is more a matter of working at the limits of
your competence than it is spouting well-learned information. Students get a sense of 'Well, I don't understand
that,' but that's not at all a defeating notion anymore. It's
very much 'So! I'm working at the limits of my competence. And that's where experts are forever moving,
and that's how they gain new knowledge.' That's an idea
that's very powerful.

Knowledge in the disciplines is, like all other cultural understanding, imaginatively constructed, not passively acquired. Sophisticated observers of the disciplines
see them as communities of discourse in which knowledge is made and remade.
The conversation about chemistry goes on, but the field is not what it was thirty years
ago. Neither is English or mathematics. They are shifting human creations, fashioned
by communities of scholars over time. The political upheavals in our own lifetime—
the revolutions in the historic status of women and people of color, for example—
are a powerful reminder that ideas and intellectual conventions change. (Revision
in scholarship and other fields can, of course, take the shape of a return to some new
version of tradition.)

The idea is not to make graduate students out of third graders, in some parody
of the university-based curriculum reforms of the mid-1960s. But we do want to equip
third graders to live in a world in which knowledge and meaning change, as well as
remain the same. Teachers need to know how to help students learn this intellectual
balancing act. We need to educate our students to take part in the big conversations;
some endure over time and remain the same; others change with the speed of rocket
ships. Teaching for understanding has to embrace both the organized traditions that
are the product of the past and the process of imaginative meaning-making that
can remake tradition if necessary—that can make it new. Knowing how to draw on
tradition and how to make it new are the methods our students will use to stay at
home in the world.

The kind of teaching we need does not require exceptionally brilliant or creative people. What is important is
that teachers be engaged, that they observe their students, follow them closely, find out what excites them, and
then help them to do that. You will know you have been
successful if students leave school after ten or twelve years
with a passion for something.

Learning stories that matter

Teachers have long been the storytellers of the society. In one way or another, they tell important stories embodied in learned disciplines and cultural traditions. They are not successful unless students can go on to make the stories their own, sometimes telling new stories in the process. A good story in any field weaves together disparate elements into a whole that fits together. The narrative form and the logic of scientific analysis are the two fundamental methods by which the human race makes order in the world. Everyone begins with a story, an autobiography; a good education builds on this story to add many others. The challenge of "the classics" now and forever is that the young need to be helped to reread them in light of the problems of their own times and their own concerns. As Walt Whitman puts it, we need to learn to write the poem fresh as we read it.

Our story metaphor has a familiar ring in fields such as English and history and social studies. We want to apply it to math and science and the arts as well. Jaime Escalante not only teaches the logic of calculus to his Advanced Placement students in a barrio high school; he also teaches the legends and myths of mathematics—conveying the heroism of mathematical thinking. There are grand narratives embedded in math and science, too; such great stories help students to fit things into coherence.

Our students are growing up in a world awash with information. How can they sort out the important from the irrelevant? One way will be learning stories that matter—not only great fiction and poetry, but the central stories of mankind, of the nation, of science, of art. Students need a grasp of narratives that can serve as intellectual and moral frameworks. Without a scaffolding of important stories, we have no way of beginning to judge what things mean. In a blizzard of "sound bites," random news, and factoids, our students need to use stories to find meanings.

The storytelling metaphor for teaching for understanding also underscores the importance of imagination and judgment in the whole process of acquiring any kind of deep literacy. The students need to sense that the story is important; and telling any story well is an exercise in subtle valuing—interpretation, appreciation, and criticism.

A school where children learn

In a school where students are taught for understanding:

- Fifth graders may experiment with pendulums and refine contrasting hunches about timing and length into testable theories.
- The history class on the topic of Reconstruction may learn that history is

not only a record of facts, but also the complex moral and political enterprise of reinterpreting the past.

- Tenth graders can understand that there is no one best interpretation of Keats's poem "Ode to a Nightingale," but rather a multiplicity of meanings. (There is also the difficult understanding that not all interpretations are equally valid.) Geometry students can build computer models of alternative solutions to problems.
- The second-grade math class can learn that math is not only a set of algorithms to use and memorize, but a way of thinking about order itself.
- All students demonstrate that writing is a fundamental way of understanding yourself and the world, as well as language.

Students in this way learn facts, but also take part in conversations that help them make use of facts to interpret experience and think critically about it. Much learning is hard, dull work. The French verbs need to be memorized. So may the multiplication tables or the Gettysburg Address. A scaffolding of lesser learning and discipline is often necessary on the way to "the big time" of deep literacy. But students persevere by taking part in the community in question—math, science, art, language—as it wrestles with facts and concepts. This active participation is the key.

Key elements in understanding

If we follow the advice of seminar participants, teaching for understanding will have hallmarks such as these:

- A principal stimulus for learning is the student's own sense of purpose and efficacy. Teaching is not simply locating knowledge out there and trying to beam it into students' heads. It involves using students' ideas as a foundation to build on, taking what students already know and think as a point of departure for new learning.
- The "basics" are not just facts but also concepts and relationships: the webbing among ideas. Concepts and facts make up a related background and foreground.
- Students don't arrive at "higher" levels of thinking and discourse by spending years building up the "basic" skills. The separation of skills from the actual practice of literacy has produced a steady diet of splinters with no experience of wholeness and depth. Students' main work ought to be to tackle and explain complexity rather than to complete simple assigned tasks. Young children are doing this all the time, as teachers know who pay them deep attention.

- Teachers possess or pursue complex knowledge of the subjects they teach, because they need to diagnose the mistakes students make and foresee where they can get to in their understanding—and because the subjects continue to possess a vital interest for them.

- Every child makes a contribution to the classroom using his or her own experience, and learning tends to be cooperative. Students are aware of the importance of participation in discourse and conversation, and teachers help each student find a voice and add talent to the collaborative.

- School work encourages students to see the links between learning and power in a host of realms—not least their own sense of efficacy.

- School work promotes an attitude of wonder and curiosity, stirring the appetite for lifelong learning.

- Kids taste the real stuff of understanding and pleasure along with kid stuff.

- A school should embody intrinsic, as well as instrumental purposes, or students will end up missing the point of learning. Why learn to read? Too many of our students get stingy answers. Too few get the fully convincing explanation: because it will make your life rich. Deep understanding is often the result of serious play. Too many of our schools are grim places, with a philistine lack of beauty and wit and playfulness. Teachers who take part in culture themselves learn that children's play is the thread that runs true—and that the teacher's art can be the needle that guides it into the larger fabric of meanings.

Affect and cognition are not antagonistic. You can't have children working as a community of scholars and collaborators without them caring for one another, and you can't have taking charge of your own mind with the emotional aspects left outside of it.

---

2   Discourse, Community, and Democracy

Powerful learning for a purpose requires action and participation and reasoned discourse. These are essential elements of life together in a learning community. Reading programs need to become reading-and-writing-and-talking programs that embody the thick texture of uses and purposes of language in a real community of inquiry, or children will not see the point. You write to say something you want to say to an audience—which can include yourself. You read to find out something you need to know, or for pleasure, and what you learn is enhanced by sharing it with others. No matter at what level you test, you are an illiterate if you end up with nothing to say and no desire to read. You have been taught the bare skills, but not dialogue and participation; scraps of information, but not the capacity to make culture. Liberal learning for all requires that students enact their learning in a community of learning, or it won't be theirs for real.

Thus the second principle to emerge from our seminars reflects a wish to turn in a new direction of history: *The ambitious kind of teaching we hope for will take place in a sustained way only if classrooms and schools are thoughtfully organized to become communities of learning in which all students participate actively.*

In older cultures, most of the best schooling came out of the association of learning with power. When the children of the elites were well-taught, they were educated to think powerfully and for a purpose, to express themselves powerfully and for a purpose, and to make use of their learning to create and criticize new forms of community in which they were strong members. They were taught how to rule and how to make culture. The trouble, of course, was that their governments served the interests of the few, and traditional academic culture was rationed to first-class passengers.

One task of education in the new century is to democratize the best of this older, elite version of learning. A way to think about this issue is to say that we now aim to make the liberal arts available to all, in appropriate forms, at all levels. Good talk in the second grade about *Frog and Toad* is not generically different from what goes on in a good university seminar on *The Tale of Genji.* Both are, recognizably, a form of the active participation in making culture that we call the humanities.

A rising chorus of voices is arguing that all our citizens need a good education as never before. We agree. The reasons are staring us in the face: the changing character of work in a competitive world economy; the new intellectual demands on citizens in a fragile and interdependent planet threatened with nuclear and ecological ruin; the complexities of the new information order; and the possibilities of a lifetime of learning for all. All these have upped the stakes for democratic schooling.

Along with all these developments there has been a broad revival of hope for democracy in many parts of the globe—a dramatic, world-wide change in expectations about who participates in power and culture. No one knows whether new and old dreams of democracy will continue to flourish in our precarious world, but we in The Holmes Group are willing to wager on popular intelligence.

To some, the broad vision of learning set forth here may sound like a series of frills. Such a view is possible only with very short sight. Cultural progress—the well-rounded development of each citizen—is not the toy department of education. It is the bedrock of future economic, political, and cultural progress in an increasingly complex world. Short-sightedness and bastard pragmatism have not been good for

U.S. industry in recent decades. We do not think they will advance education either. We believe that education will have to play a broad role not only in equipping people for jobs, but also in educating citizens to take a hand in the decisions affecting the economic, political, and cultural evolution of a democratic society. This is why there is new urgency to Whitman's old dream of a culture for all commensurate with the political promise of democracy.

> We're trying to develop something that's never been done in an organized way, here or in the rest of the world. We have to say in a reasonable tone of voice that we are just learning how to do this. We are inventing it as we go. This is a great new ambition in the history of the world. It will be hard and take a long time.

This has not been a historic aim. It is in fact unprecedented in world history. It will take two or three generations of teachers, which is the kind of time scale we have in mind for Professional Development Schools. Although good teachers have worked in every generation to provide an education for all to match the promise of U.S. democracy, our education system at its outset assumed two tracks: a liberal education for the elites, and training for those who would work with their hands. In one form or another, these old, outworn assumptions still pervade U.S. schooling. We believe it is time to abandon them.

We look at the Professional Development School as a model of learning community that will act as a bridge in the long process of creating a democratic culture. For this to happen, teachers will have to learn to play an intellectual balancing act. On the one hand, new participants have to learn the rules of the conversation as it currently runs: its texts, its dominant concerns. On the other hand, new voices will contribute new stories and new themes in a process that will eventually transform mainstream culture. In acting as cultural bridges, schools will be wise not to neglect either end—the traditional academic culture or the new stories, especially the stories that arise from children and the life of their communities. Seminar participants argued that schools need to become bridges between the mainstream culture and the lives and cultures of their students. The cultural bridge they had in mind promotes traffic in two directions. Schools should build on the linguistic and cultural capital students bring with them, so that in the end, students can possess both mainstream meanings and the culture of their own community. In doing this schools need to act to strengthen the fragile and threatened webs of local community. Schools fail students if they deny them a passport to the mainstream; they also fail if students graduate with a sense that their own culture is worthless. We should help students see their stories as part of a wider epic that includes the entire human race—a planetary version of the humanities for the new century.

Higher standards for all students will almost surely spell higher rates of failure for the slow and the different unless our schools become more inclusive communities. A community of learning has the potential to turn rigorous notions of understanding into maps of available new experience for children, rather than a new set of hurdles.

Children with special needs

We pointed to a link between the quality of community life and realistically high expectations for all students. This link is particularly important for the students who may prove to be the biggest challenge for Professional Development Schools: children with special needs, especially those with severe needs. The legal and bureaucratic struggles for the educational rights of such kids have often created barriers to creating good learning communities for them. The reader may sense a jump if we move from celebrating the arts and sciences for all to a look at the first groping efforts at painting on the part of a girl with cerebral palsy. If our ideas about the generic qualities of learning in a community hold up, there really isn't a jump: A definition of learning as making meaning in a community can encompass the spectrum of human experience and yearning that stretches from her first, shaking sketch to more accomplished work in the slides of the art history course.

> What's in this for Jody? Jody is a composite of all my profoundly handicapped students. He is severely brain damaged, and this has resulted in profound mental retardation and some type of cerebral palsy. I want more for Jody and more for myself as Jody's teacher.

In a Professional Development School, teachers and teacher educators will work hard and inventively to stretch the conventional academic spectrum so that it includes children who are severely impaired. Their work could expand our idea of the humanities in several directions: richer possibilities for such children, and a recovery of the deeper sense of the underlying humanity of academic subjects, too. Making meanings, sharing suffering, imagining, criticizing, telling a story, and acting as a force in another person's life—these are generic human capacities. If teachers and schools could enact the belief that all humans are capable of making and sharing culture in some fashion, we would not be far from the roots of the matter—or from a radical rethinking of the whole field of special education. Our ambitious vision of learning for all should embrace children with special needs, who have a right to learn a valid version of the humanities, too, and who have much to teach the rest of us—teachers as well as children—about the deeper meaning of the humanities.

Community meshes academics, citizenship, and life

In the learning community, both words—"community" and "learning"—must have equal weight. A web of mutual respect, trust, and responsibility is as important as the intellectual content of programs. Without the life of the mind, community lacks intellectual purpose; without community, academic work lacks meaning. The fusion of both can create the "humanities" in the double sense of the word—the marriage of head and heart in human fellowship that produces true education.

Joseph Schwab used to point to a double meaning to the phrase "learning community." In one sense, all knowledge is at bottom communal, and all learning a matter of participation in a dialogue, real or imagined. You learn the musical scales to take part in the community, past and present, of those who make and appreciate music. You are part of that community, even when playing the piano alone. The ancient Greeks emphasized the communal aspect of mathematics when they called it a performance art, linking it to such fields as music and dance. Reading and writing and speaking are the passports to the kingdom of discourse itself, which always takes place in some kind of community. The second meaning Schwab saw in "learning community" is that the arts of participation are themselves habits and skills that need to be learned. Particularly where the web of community is fragile and threatened, and where children encounter too few adults, community itself is something that needs to be learned.

The link between teaching for understanding and democratic practice becomes clear: In a learning community, all children, not just a few, learn to collaborate in making knowledge and taking part in culture. They learn to be an active part of the community in many different, cross-cutting ways. What is required for academic success meshes with the requirements for good citizenship: effective participation in several sorts of dialogue and public action.

> In a collaborative classroom the students with less information drive the students with more. It's not 'Oh, I don't understand that.' It's a continual 'Could you explain that so it will be clearer to me?'

Seminar participants argued that our schools have ignored the task of character and civic education—in the mistaken belief, perhaps, that such matters get in the way of academic learning. School purpose, they said, embraces not just higher test scores and better employment opportunities, but full participation in the body politic. The ideals of democracy and teaching for understanding are intertwined: Passive learners will rarely think powerfully, nor will they make strong citizens of a free republic. You learn democracy—both democratic discipline and free expression—by living it in a community together.

Schools should be public democratic spaces where young citizens learn critical thinking and civic courage, traits of civic and intellectual and moral character that are not at all separate from each other. Knowledge has to operate in the service of values. Prospective teachers will need cultural and civic intelligence to place knowledge in context and make judgments about values. At some point students need to begin assuming responsibility for their thought and action, under adult guidance. You can't teach critical thinking and civic courage by the instructional methods Montaigne derided long ago as "thundering in children's ears."

> Schools perfectly model a democracy in the sense that you can't get kids to learn without their consent. A central, chronic problem of democracy is a problem of schools. You have to get their consent.

Our seminars emphasized the classroom and school as a community of learning, not to slight the individual—all education must balance individual and social aims—but because the participants believe that the individuality we prize so deeply in our students emerges as a result of their encounters with others—with families and peers and teachers. A powerful self is the result of a long schooling with others, one way or another. Students who can't listen while others are talking may never find their own distinctive voice. The definition of an educated person might well be someone who understands how to make better public and private meanings, and who can relate the two to make a distinctive self able to act with others.

Schools are public places where people master the discourse and habits that are essential to the development of both the private and the public person. This public quality—their quality as communities given over to learning—is part of the way that they bridge the distance from childhood to adult culture and citizenship.

> What we are really talking about is helping young people grow up to be loving adults. The way you do that is by being a loving person yourself.

Our seminar participants were frank to say that glib portraits of harmonious school communities do not sit well with the grinding realities of schooling in many parts of the U.S. We were not wrong, they said, to link the issue of learning community to the question of students' understanding. Participation is the key to both. Yet the necessary double webs of community and learning are strained in a democracy suffering from growing extremes of wealth and poverty.

People in the seminars deliberately refused to separate teaching for understanding from the creation of learning community. They also refused to make a clean break between the generic teachers' task of creating learning community and the particular role of teachers in U.S. democracy: to act as practical intellectuals, helping the people take part in reasoned discourse and the making of cultural meanings.

To us, the most important first step is agreeing that teachers need to become practical intellectuals, able to draw children into the cultural conversation. In his American classic, *The Souls of Black Folk,* W.E.B. DuBois left an indelible portrait of himself as a young teacher-intellectual reaching out to the people of the rural South. He taught Josie, a black girl aching to learn the best that had been said and thought. DuBois taught the old high culture, and his own view of culture was transformed, in turn, by what he learned from Josie and the world her folks had made for themselves between the horns of the American dilemma. The Josies of the land are still waiting.

■|■|■

Everybody's Children

Diversity, Equity, and Social Justice

In the kind of country that we are, and aspire to be, teaching and learning for understanding cannot be rationed to a few. The Professional Development School will be a place where everybody's children participate in making knowledge and meaning—where each child is a valued member of a community of learning. A very great challenge to the Professional Development School is to create such communities in a society whose families live on very unequal terms.

The third fundamental principle is, against the grain of an unequal society, to make teaching and learning for understanding available for everybody's children.

The seeds of failure for many children are sown early. Tomorrow's teachers will have responsibility for children who will not have an easy time of it. More will be raised by single parents. More will come from families strange to the mainstream culture. More will speak languages other than English. The biggest shadow falling over tomorrow's children will be the scourge of deep poverty. Seminar participants spoke of the growing desperation of poor families—comparing certain city schools of ours to ramshackle arks riding the waters of some incomprehensible catastrophe.

The workplace demands flexible workers, the polity demands knowledgeable citizens, and everyone's prospects for a satisfying life hinge increasingly on a high-quality education. Yet the dire predictions of those worried about this nation's economic and political future are starting to come true; teachers are among the first to witness the human costs of the society's wider failure.

These unprecedented changes already have two consequences for school people. First, in many schools, teachers and students do not share common cultural and social outlooks. Many teachers in schools and colleges are already baffled by the linguistic, racial, and social-class and cultural differences they face in their classrooms. How can they help students learn? Second, the challenges of teaching for understanding—not just "delivering skills"—multiply in schools where the inequalities of class, race, and gender are severe and may be growing. Teaching for understanding is a dialogue, we said, a conversation. We spoke of taking part in culture—opening up the humanities and the liberal arts to all. Yet the barriers to any conversation are rising.

> It is not enough to have the same program for all children. If you as teacher don't have the cultural knowledge to have all the kids get access to the same instructional goal, then you are failing to educate those children.

Grappling with the roots of failure

Society has many, often competing, explanations for the failures of poor children. In one view, schools themselves construct the failures of students. A second explanation cites the lack of any mesh between school and students' futures. Third, school failure is explained by the circumstances of the lives of poor families. And fourth, school failure is traced to unequal resources available to schools serving poor neighborhoods. One part of the work of a Professional Development School is to explore such explanations—perhaps to discredit some and to uncover others.

Do schools cause students' failure? Schools profess egalitarian ideals but sort students in a variety of ways over the course of their careers. The sorting begins early, legitimized by subtle and overt interpretations of students' abilities. Children are characterized as smart or slow because of color, neighborhood, quality of clothing, or understanding of English. Such judgments can be based on standardized tests of dubious validity, reflecting outmoded conceptions of human abilities. Once labeled, students sit imprisoned in the labels.

Look at the academic careers of two children beginning first grade. One child, who speaks and tests well, is placed in the top reading group, receives "enrichment" activities, moves into "gifted and talented" programs later on, and advances into the academic track in high school or to "honors" and Advanced Placement courses. This child learns intellectually rigorous material in the company of other academically minded students. She receives much encouragement, and is counseled for college entry.

Another child gets tagged early by standardized tests and classroom behavior as a "slow learner," "developmentally delayed," or any of a set of vague labels. This child encounters failure in a competitive environment early on. He is placed in the "low" reading group in first grade, falling further behind thereafter. He gets watered-down content, drill work on disconnected reading passages, and mindless math problems. In remedial classes, he simply gets more experience with filling in blanks. If he is placed in a special education category, he is then segregated for large portions of the day or week in special classes, left out of the life and learning of his friends in the regular classroom. Small wonder he becomes discouraged, bored, hostile. He starts to get into trouble, to acquire a reputation that further confirms the school's labels. He is counselled into low-skill jobs by well-meaning school people who have small knowledge or expectations of him. He ends as predicted: an academic failure.

These two stories reflect the first of our common explanations as to why poor children are failing in our schools—namely that schools in a sense construct failure. Labels, categories, and predictions take on a life of their own, fulfilling the original prophecy in the eyes of all the participants—teachers, administrators, parents, and students themselves. One task of Professional Development Schools is to question: Does our machinery invent and produce school failure? Can we create alternative ways of managing students' academic careers so that many more can be captured by the ideas and habits of real learning?

> Student diversity is only a problem because of the kind of school organization we have. When you take a bureaucratic mode of organization and put on top of it a legalistic mode of accountability, what it does is standardize further, which reduces the professional discretion to personalize services for children, which then creates more kids who don't fit. In all our good intentions we have made matters worse.

Do school and life seem disconnected? A second explanation for school failure is the absence of connection in students' minds between schooling and some plausible future. Many students are denied or deny themselves the rewards of successful schooling. No one has fired their imagination with the idea of college, or offered them the possibility of attractive, meaningful work. Though they arise early on, these problems are especially evident in middle schools and high schools. Professional Development Schools at these levels will need to explore imaginative ways to connect youth in tangible ways to better futures.

Is poverty to blame? A third explanation of school failure puts the blame on the circumstances of life in poor communities. We all have heard about these problems—high student mobility, high incidences of violence and substance abuse. Too many students walk into school hungry, without a quiet night's sleep, in poor health. No matter how humane and sensitive educators are, no matter how good the teachers, schools in such communities won't be able to succeed all alone. Schools need to become organizers of community effort—to discover new ways of working with parents and community and government agencies responding to the needs of children. Professional Development Schools in particular will need to become examples of how to reach out to bridge students' personal and school lives—creating a web of services and relationships that support learning.

We can learn to cherish the diversity of our students, but it creates an incredible tension as we try to respond to all the differences children bring as they cross the yard and come into the school. Unfortunately, the common traits that transcend students' differences tend to be alienation, low sense of efficacy, and demand for instant gratification stimulated by our consumerist culture.

Can we not afford good schools? Yet a fourth explanation for school failure is that some schools are as poor as the students they serve. They receive less money per pupil, pay lower salaries, attract less qualified teachers, have fewer learning resources and instructional materials, and downright unpleasant work environments—leaking roofs and a shortage of writing paper. To the scandal of the profession, beginning teachers are assigned to children most in need of expert teachers. Poor districts are often forced to rely on newcomers and to suffer the consequences of rapid turnover, as experienced teachers leave for better workplaces and for higher paying jobs in wealthier districts. Such gross disparities convey powerful messages to everybody about who is valued in our society. We believe that Professional Development Schools, many of which will purposely be sited in poor areas, will engage in social and political action to acquire additional resources and to press the claims for justice on the larger society. In our view, a Professional Development School cannot be simply a technical invention for the promotion of more efficient forms of instruction; it must engage in the struggle to better its students' present and future lives. In so doing, a Professional Development School is likely to encounter one or more of these interpretations of school failure. With the varied talents of its teachers, administrators, and parents, the school working as a community may be able to change these conditions in ways that individual faculty cannot.

There is an enormous disjunction now between the bland climate of teacher education and the agonizing problems of schools serving poor children. A Professional Development School by itself cannot solve the problems arising from society, any more than any other public school can; neither can it evade them under the pretext that they are beyond its grasp. Although creating socially just learning communities in the long run will involve building a more equal and democratic society, school and university faculty can do a better job of disentangling social and class inequities from learning opportunities. They can begin work on the proposition that all can be taught to understand.

There is a significant literature on the qualities of programs that successfully break the cycle of disadvantage. A summary of these qualities developed by Lisbeth Schorr in *Within Our Reach* (1988) provides a useful way of thinking about how Professional Development Schools might begin to work on this broader agenda. Such programs typically see the child in the context of family and the family in the context of its surroundings; they offer a broad spectrum of services that are coherent and easily accessible. These programs are noted by their flexibility. They find ways to adapt or circumvent traditional professional and bureaucratic boundaries to meet the needs of those they serve, and they enable professionals to redefine their roles to respond to severe but often unarticulated needs. And those who work in these programs are viewed by those they serve as people who care about them and respect them, people they can trust. All of this meshes closely with our vision of Professional Development Schools as strong learning communities able to reshape forms according to local needs.

Unlike the university's traditional laboratory school, the Professional Development School is to be a public school that presents the most demanding challenge—responding to student diversity in ways that engage learners in making their own meaning from subject matter—teaching understanding rather than rote. Such schools would encourage several practices: embracing all learners, creating opportunities for observation and study by experienced and prospective teachers and administrators, gaining understanding of different world views, contributing to the knowledge bases of education, and organizing for more equity.

Embracing all learners

Past efforts to teach understanding to students whose social or cultural background differed from that of the school often faltered. Old assumptions need to be questioned. Established approaches to teaching may need scrapping—along with standard notions of assessment and instructional method. Teachers will need to be able to take time to reflect on what they are doing, how it is working, what might be more appropriate, and try out diverse ways to reach and respond to students.

U.S. education is still preoccupied with students' shortcomings, and nowhere more so than in schools that enroll children from backgrounds unfamiliar to teachers. It is not hard to see why such students come up short. In addition to teachers' frequently negative expectations of them, schooling's traditional competitive ethos tends to reduce teachers to merely coping with cultural diversity. Seminar participants urged the creation of schools capable of celebrating it. Some offered evidence that cooperative methods greatly reduce teachers' and children's frustration and estrangement. These methods are promising because we need to educate a generation of teachers able to get beyond the initial sense of bafflement at a roomful of "strangers" and to meld them into a whole class stronger than its parts—and strong *because* of them. In such a class, students of varied backgrounds first respect, then value, then share, cooperate with, and learn from each other.

When teachers learn more about their students, they can build learning communities that embrace rather than smother cultural diversity. Students do differ. Without stereotyping or prepackaged responses, such differences can become opportunities for richer learning. A main aim of teacher preparation, then, should be to prepare novice teachers for a career in which they will be able to draw upon students' diversity to make learning dynamic and interesting—for children and for themselves.

We speak of "celebrating" diversity because we believe that the hallmark of a true learning community is its inclusiveness—where teachers take responsibility for helping each child take part to his or her fullest. The idea of a learning community has special significance in a democracy, where all must find their voice. Thus we see the positive potential in a diverse student body. It can naturally draw into the classroom the ideas, languages, and perspectives of the cultures of other countries. In tomorrow's richly diverse schools—if they are true learning communities—this nation's children will learn more easily that as adults and citizens they will be working and living with peoples of the whole world.

> I would ask that you begin to look at the assets that some of these children have—with the backgrounds and languages they know—that can be used for the transmission of knowledge. And second, that in transmitting that knowledge, you realize you're giving them a lot more than mathematics and science; you're really transferring a whole value system that is ingrained in the literacy system.

Creating opportunities for observing and studying cultures

Schools and universities have too often reflected dominant cultural attitudes that despised the cultures of students of color. We can no longer afford such attitudes. Critical and thoughtful citizens need an education that helps them validate their own experience and outlook and encourages their participation in mainstream discourse. Both are the birthrights of citizens in a democracy. Schools should work as channels allowing students and teachers to travel back and forth between mainstream and tributary cultures, altering the mainstream itself in a process analogous to the organic growth of languages and rivers.

Prospective teachers need experience in schools in which cultural pluralism is valued and where talk about racial, ethnic, and social-class diversity is a central item in faculty discussions. Student diversity has received inadequate or inappropriate attention by school and university faculty, most of whom enter education with little personal experience of people different from themselves. Little talk is devoted to racism and social-class discrimination in American public education. As matters stand, there are few opportunities at the university to explore the full meaning of cultural diversity.

Some states and schools districts have responded by mandating courses or workshops on such issues as bilingualism and multiculturalism. Typically, these do not lead to fundamental change. Like most in-service education, they lack coherence, intellectual rigor, and opportunities for follow-up and reflection on practice. Seminar participants advised that little can be gained by tinkering at the margins of the issue with courses that teach teachers simply to modify existing practices for the learner who is not typical.

A Professional Development School selected because of its staff's commitment to bridging cultural divides can provide novice practitioners with systematic occasions to study equity within diversity. Whether defined in terms of race, class, ethnicity, gender, religion, culture, or physical and mental handicap, every school brings together a diverse group of students, even those who at first glance appear alike. The key is concerted attention to differences among children that have consequences for their learning. Thus a school in inner-city Baltimore comprised entirely of African-American pupils or an all-white school in rural Utah might still be considered for a Professional Development School if its faculty share a commitment to make issues of diversity a central part of the professional discourse about curriculum, texts, pedagogy, classroom and school organization, and hiring decisions.

We believe that Professional Development Schools can develop as centers for inquiry—exploring ways to redirect our collective practice to integrate student cultural, linguistic, and gender diversity as central features of communities of learning. In such settings, teams of professors and teachers might together develop and evaluate curriculum units that break out of cultural standardization and present a more inclusive view of the humanities. For example, they might develop curricula that represent perspectives other than those of white males; that tell other stories from and in other languages; that teach children of color their history; and that broaden the history that their classmates learn. School and university faculty can embrace worldwide views of the liberal arts and sciences, to help rectify past distortions and exclusions, including those of women's roles and voices, and to prepare students to be effective participants in the global community. They can help every student begin to hear and tell the stories that have been treated as marginal. Such multicultural experience can be part of the next generation's liberal arts—the humanities for a new, global era.

> What may prepare young teachers to participate in this way is requirements in the school of ed for more course work in liberal arts. We tend to build the base of our profession on psychology largely, and give far too little attention to sociology, political science, anthropology, literature, and philosophy.

Education faculty might develop pre-service sequences of courses, seminars, and practica that have as common threads the application of research and theory to the whole spectrum of diversity among students—race, culture, language, academic ability, gender, and physical ability. From their university course work and from their immersion in the Professional Development School, teacher education students should come to understand how to think about subject matter, pedagogy, and learners from the viewpoint of children's different cultural backgrounds.

They should learn how to enter a different culture, how to look for multiple explanations for problems that emerge in the classroom, including those of cultural dissonance. They should learn how to learn from adults in their school communities and about building good relationships among children, parents, and school staff. Above all, prospective teachers should be helped to see and try a range of activities that teach from learners' strengths. In this way, the novice teacher would come to expect that a classroom of children would be diverse and that he could successfully play from the strength of the mix.

In the Professional Development School, we might see experienced teachers working together with university faculty to better understand the range of learners and styles of learning in their schools. We might see teachers testing curriculum modified for their own school's diverse students and explaining the results of their inquiry to their colleagues. We might see school and university faculty collecting and interpreting the practical knowledge of teachers for the purpose of establishing a case literature. We might see successful teachers writing and speaking about how they create a good learning community in their diverse schools. We might see teachers asking parents questions about culture and language, and using the answers to design programs for students in school and non-school settings. We might see staff development activities spanning several years, all devoted to diversity in relation to curriculum, to instructional materials, to student grouping, to testing and assessment, to home-school relationships, and to developing coalitions with other community agencies and institutions.

> Somehow students' current experiences in schools do not alter the meanings they carry around with them. That's exactly the case with experienced and pre-service teachers in dealing with diversity and equity. Knowledge doesn't come in isolated chunks. You don't break it up, and you don't teach it in abstractions. You embed it in a real problem—minority children and how they learn— that needs to be solved.

Gaining understanding of different world views

Greater knowledge alone will not be sufficient. It is difficult for people to see beyond their own cultural walls until they encounter situations where their cultural references no longer serve them. Knowledge of different world views and meanings grows from personal exchanges with those who hold other perspectives. These truths argue for a clinical experience that serves a diverse array of youth and that involves parents and other adults from the children's communities. They also underscore the importance of recruiting and involving school and university faculty of color.

A Professional Development School can be the place where university faculty and novice teachers learn from the experiences that many teachers bring to successful work with diverse learners. Professional Development Schools can also learn from schools that have involved parents in key and significant ways. At the same time, we should bring into both university and public school teaching more faculty from America's rainbow of nations and peoples. To do so would help to diminish the powerful negative messages—about justice and fairness, about authority and power, about inclusion and participation—that are implicit in the prevailing monochrome of our nation's teaching cadre. To do so will allow different voices to be heard and different outlooks to be shared. Schools and universities are developing a number of promising strategies to attract and retain people of color in the teaching ranks and professoriate, and to extend the participation of women in math, science, and leadership positions—but these may not be sufficient. The current situation calls for radical action by universities, colleges of education, and school systems—by Professional Development Schools.

Contributing to the knowledge bases of education

The Professional Development School is needed to contribute to education's knowledge bases about instruction for groups of diverse children. Good experienced teachers affirm the findings of cognitive researchers: Children learn in remarkably different ways. Skilled teachers take these differences into account in developing instruction. There need be no dichotomy between pursuing excellence and equity. But from social science researchers—and from parents—we know that frequently groups of children are barred access to rigorous teaching and hard learning because of their race, gender, ethnicity, or social class. As schools currently operate, they often are unable to recognize talent in students who are considered different. A rift opens between excellence and equity when one method or style becomes the norm for teaching and learning, or when student differences extend beyond the teacher's familiarity and comfort. Students with different ways of learning get cut off from the powerful ideas of the disciplines and from close relationships with more conventionally able classmates.

> 'Giftedness' is a label we use widely, a politically defined and socially constructed notion. The ninety-eight percent who have another label, 'not gifted,' have a great deal to gain from equitable democratic schooling practices. There's this myth that if you're a mainstream, middle-class kid, you're getting a good education. I believe that's just not true.

Much of the basic knowledge necessary for better teaching and learning in classrooms with widely diverse students is not yet part of the essential core of education studies. Along with their subject matter, teachers need to become students of their students—their cultural metaphors, languages and linguistic understandings, learning styles—to recognize them as resources for learning. Similarly, teachers need to study themselves, to revisit their own experiences as learners and to gain greater understanding of the cultural assumptions they bring to their students. The Professional

Development School can provide such opportunities. It can be a setting in which university faculty with expertise in culture and in cognition, in its infinite varieties, learn together with teachers who are determined to create schools where cultural diversity is embraced.

> Teachers must understand the crossroads between language, culture, and cognition. In a world changing so rapidly, where so many kids are moved without having anything to say about it from one linguistic culture to another, everything seems to be mixed up. What they thought they understood about the world has changed. What happens then? How do we reorganize the world order, the values, for these kids to learn?

Organizing for more equity

The bureaucratic organization of schools creates classifications that stereotype and segregate children. They also isolate teachers in their classrooms and administrators in their offices. This top-down organization of schools, combined with constraints imposed by lack of knowledge and experience, makes it difficult for school people to serve a varied student body. The result is a block on the energy, creativity, and skill of teachers. Thus many teachers feel powerless and unable to do what they believe is best for children. We see Professional Development School faculty confronting the conventional forms of school organization and beginning to develop new ways to organize the staff, assign children to classrooms, schedule the school day, and apportion teachers' work time, tasks, and responsibility.

> A real key is 'Why do we do things the way we do?' As long as teachers are in this little eggcrate school and isolated in their classrooms with no time to talk, there is little access to information that would be empowering. We need to begin a process where those things are up for grabs in the faculty room, as a legitimate part of the school day.

Seminar participants urged sweeping organizational changes in schools. They advised that Professional Development School faculty should investigate a variety of grouping practices, with students of different ages and abilities learning together. They recognized the difficult challenge in offering Advanced Placement calculus to some students without compromising the feeling of community throughout the school. They spoke of the strengths of learning communities developed over time, where teams of teachers and groups of pupils work together for more than one year. They argued that children's academic careers are better served when conceptions of good teaching and learning drive the organization and structure of schools. They saw Professional Development Schools evolving into something new—uniquely fashioned for their own faculty, resources, students, and community.

America's cultural diversity—a people of peoples—is one of its national treasures, providing opportunities for democratic communities of learning not available to many other nations. Teaching and learning for everybody's children is clearly an ambitious agenda. There is a small but emerging literature to guide our efforts. Holmes Group institutions will build on that base. We also hope to build on the work of many good teachers and administrators in schools across the country, who can tell stories of their struggles and successes. The challenge to the Professional Development School is to show how masses of public schools can follow their lead.

Teaching Adults as Well as Children

So far we have set forth three principles for the design of a Professional Development School. They suggest the kind of learning environment for children that we think should profoundly influence both teacher educators and prospective teachers. Now we ask, What should the learning be like for the adults in that school—not just the student and novice teachers, but the experienced practicing teachers, the school administrators, and the faculty from the university?

The fourth principle for the design of a Professional Development School is that in this school adults—teachers, teacher educators, and administrators—are expected to go on learning, too.

The Professional Development School should be a regular school where school and university faculties collaborate in giving prospective teachers practical experiences of schools and teaching. Here students preparing to become teachers observe teachers and students at work in classrooms, tutor students, work with small groups, help prepare curriculum, and help conduct research. Students come to a Professional Development School for short-term projects and assignments, as well as for extended practice teaching and for formal internships associated either with the culmination of their university education studies or with a formal, supervised induction program in the first year of teaching.

All of these experiences should be integrated with—and integral to—both the professional course of study established by the university and the ongoing life of the school. In all of these experiences, members of the faculty of the university—education professors and arts and sciences faculty—and of the school should collaborate as colleagues, meeting regularly and intensively on the whole range of tasks.

Four beliefs underlie this principle that the school is purpose-built for adults, too, to learn:

- A school dedicated to the education of teachers will be a better place for children to learn.
- Sustained experiences in a real school that takes responsibility for the learning of prospective teachers as well as for its own students will help the novice teachers to integrate what they're taught about teaching with what they see, do, and feel in classrooms.
- University courses in the disciplines, foundations, methods, and curriculum will be strengthened through connection to good practice and to problems of schooling experienced in a particular school.
- The education of school administrators can be improved through their greater attention to teaching and learning and to issues of forming a learning community.

Better for children

In a Professional Development School, the school's teachers will be challenged to be more explicit about the teaching and learning they promote; and this will sharpen and deepen their own practice. They will be asked to cultivate a heightened sense of professionalism around the mission of inducting novices, developing standards and norms of practice, and doing their own analyses of their teaching. Experienced teachers can renew themselves in the process of educating a new generation of teachers. They can recreate the intellectual base of their practice. Among other things, a Professional Development School may help persuade new and experienced teachers that a life in teaching can be rewarding and fun. As teachers begin to work as colleagues with university faculty—who bring new ideas and knowledge and who contribute time to the school's organizational planning, staff development, curriculum, and instruction—working in a Professional Development School should be intense and exciting. Such a tone would be one hallmark of success.

How would I want the work of teachers to be? I go for transparency: How are teachers' conceptions of the work with students and with one another made explicit and public and accessible among teachers? What choices are being made with children and why? I want the quality of risk taking, a seminal quality that would lead to greater variety, moments of high, fast learning; engagement and excitement.

Better for student teachers

Theoretical knowledge is expressed abstractly and generally. Personal, practical knowledge is acquired concretely through experience, and expressed anecdotally. The problem of relating these two kinds of knowledge haunts professional education in all fields; but it is especially acute in education. The aim of college preparation for any would-be professional must be to impart not only the liberal arts disciplines and technical skill, but knowledge in the form of principles, concepts, and understanding that are on tap to reliably guide technique.

Teacher education has not been organized to encourage the application of principles to practical experience in classrooms; nor to provide the systematic trial teaching followed by critique that is necessary to improve skills; nor to convey the value commitments inherent in the work of teaching. This has been both an intellectual and an organizational problem: Educators have been unable to reach consensus on a course of study that draws on and integrates the disciplines and the practical wisdom possessed by expert teachers. And colleges of education have seldom created connections to schools that encourage the emergence of shared understandings among university and school faculty. Consequently, teacher preparation usually lacks both intellectual and organizational articulation between college and school classrooms. Prospective teachers are left alone to integrate knowledge, to puzzle through applications, and to resolve contradictions, ambiguities, and tensions.

Professional Development Schools are essential to The Holmes Group goal of creating an extended, integrated program of teacher education that will join the liberal, professional, and clinical bases for practice in a comprehensive program of study and experience. We envision that as Holmes Group universities continue to develop professional studies programs that extend teacher education beyond its current, limited undergraduate niche, the Professional Development School will be one setting for field experiences that may begin in the undergraduate years, then extend into more intensive internships coordinated with continuing professional study. *A primary aim of Professional Development Schools will be to contribute to intellectually solid programs of teacher education that intertwine the wisdom of theory and practice; that encourage shared conceptions among university and school faculty; that assist novices in evaluating, integrating, and using knowledge from multiple sources; that convey the moral basis of teaching; and that recruit and keep imaginative and interesting teachers in the profession.*

A prerequisite for teaching for understanding is the teacher's knowledge of the subject. At one level, Professional Development Schools will try to connect to improved teaching in the arts and sciences in the colleges. They will work on making the knowledge students get in first-rate college courses "pedagogically available" to them in their new role as teachers. How this is to be done is a nice problem— and just the sort of thing that a program with a base in both university and school classrooms might be equipped to study.

The Holmes Group would like to see a bold and sweeping transformation of undergraduate teaching so that all secondary and elementary teachers emerge from college with clear comprehension of their subject and a broad grasp of the humanities. As we are critical of much teacher education, so we are also concerned about the passive and superficial quality of much undergraduate learning.

Teaching well requires active understanding in one or another discipline. But what should teachers know? Should they know more and more in one field, or is the best teaching essentially the work of generalists? These are issues a Professional Development School could tackle. It may be that the ways the disciplines are presently organized in universities and in the curriculum of the schools are not necessarily the best ways of carving up the world and converting it into human knowledge for students.

Some thoughtful critics argue that today's academic curriculum is more or less a relic of the disciplinary specializations of the late nineteenth century, a set of museum pieces from intellectual history rather than powerfully compelling intellectual constructs. English and other languages, math, social studies, and science are not fixed and eternal categories of truth. A thoughtful and rigorous academic curriculum in a high school might well blend science and math, for example, or English and another language and history and geography. In the academic world the nineteenth-century reformers left us, art and music are off to the side—not necessarily where they should be; theatre, which could be a powerful focus for integrating studies, is a frill. It's hard, some critics say, to teach deep content and the power of self-expression when the curriculum is chopped up in this fashion. How do would-be teachers construe knowledge and learning? Professional Development Schools may or may not come to agree with the critics. But they will be shirking their duty if they do not actively involve student teachers in exploring the implications of such debates for classroom teaching.

Many Professional Development Schools will be located in communities now poorly served by public education. The social ideals animating the Professional Development School should stress service and an ethic of caring and social justice. Seminar participants were emphatic and eloquent: Such a school would educate new teachers not only in knowledge and technique but also in conscience and vision, instilling a commitment to the learning of the poor and the marginal.

Young teachers can be challenged to take up difficult problems of practice because they will do so with the help of wise, veteran teachers. They can learn how to reach the children who are not succeeding in today's schools.

Better for education school faculty and experienced teachers

Two criticisms commonly leveled against the university are that the faculty who teach teachers are too far removed from the realities of schooling to provide knowledge that is usable; and that research on teaching and learning is too seldom based on actual contexts of schooling. A Professional Development School can ground the practice of university faculty—including both the education of teachers and the conduct of research—in the realities of schooling.

In using the term "university faculty" throughout this report, we mean to include both arts and sciences professors and education school professors. On a modest scale, liberal arts faculty from the university have always been involved in the schools, but a Professional Development School should increase their opportunities to teach younger students and to work with teachers on curriculum, new forms of instruction, teacher preparation, and research. This principle of broad involvement encompasses the full range of professionals as well, including school counselors, psychologists, nurses, social workers, and their counterparts among university faculty. Seminar participants envisioned a Professional Development School as a setting welcoming such broad participation and giving university faculty avenues to extend their interests into the schools.

Of equal importance is the continuing education of Professional Development School teachers, pursued through their own inquiries and through the ambience of the school itself. Because the Professional Development School will be a partnership between the public schools and the university, some school faculty will be formally integrated into the teacher preparation program. This could take the form of schoolteachers teaching courses at the university, participating in the development of the teacher education curriculum, and generally taking part in the work of the education school as it manages the liberal and professional education of prospective educators.

A Professional Development School must not become a colony settled by the university in the public schools. Rather, it should be an opportunity to join the strengths of the two institutions in pursuit of common purposes, and to combine their intellectual and material resources to more powerfully pursue those purposes. Seminar participants anticipate a two-way traffic between the school and the university. This traffic should directly contribute to the ongoing professional education of experienced teachers.

> To become an accomplished professional teacher requires not only systematic training and formal socialization but updating your knowledge of the subjects you teach, attending more closely to the students you teach, developing new methods for your repertoire, and extending your influence beyond the bounds of your own classroom. Knowledgeable and practical university faculty should be your colleagues in all these endeavors.

No one can begin to master the complexities of schoolteaching in the brief space of an initial preparation program. Continuing learning is a necessity. Many fine teachers engage in such learning, through reflection on their individual trials and errors, and in interaction with colleagues. But, seminar participants emphasized, most schools are not organized to capitalize on teacher learning—even though this is the key to the creation of excellent schools.

Better for school administrators

Professional Development Schools will serve also as sites for learning the art and craft of school administration. Well-formed ideas about teaching and learning worked out in the company of diverse educators and community members: These are the wellsprings of educational administration. If an administrator is to be more than caretaker of a building, then he or she must develop a powerful set of educational convictions, and an approach to putting these convictions into practice. A university is a useful place for exploring and acquiring convictions and theory; practice is best learned on site, in real schools.

It follows, then, that the proper education of administrators, as for teachers, takes place in a setting that combines the advantages of the university and the schools. Some outstanding teachers eventually seek administrative positions. "They have the craft knowledge," claimed one university educator, "but they come to us looking for something else." They need to learn the essential administrative art: nurturing a school from a collection of individual students and teachers into a learning community.

Useful knowledge exists bearing on such practice; but this knowledge is best gained in such forms of theory—practice as case analysis, internships and practica linked with university course work, and seminars that are taught by practicing administrators and administrator educators.

The processes of recruiting, selecting, training, and socializing administrators in the U.S. have failed to promote serious engagement with the core activities of schooling—teaching and learning and cultivating community. Yet one hallmark of excellent administrators is their well-articulated beliefs about teaching, learning, and school community. Professional education for administrators, then, must convey such knowledge and encourage such convictions.

What's good for students and teachers, we believe, will prove good for administrators. A Professional Development School should encourage outstanding administrators to join with university faculty in the conduct of administrator education. Together they can explore problems of practice in real settings, join inquiry to administrative practice, and attend to the ongoing learning of administrators through formal and informal staff development.

> I have a self-renewing thing. I got it at the university, from the kind of rigorous study in the disciplines that can only be gotten in the university. Then there was my K-12 experience, which gave me an understanding of how one thing builds on another. I have experience in schools with a range of ethnic diversity. I have learned that culture—what communities want—makes a big difference. And then there is my central district experience, which helped me understand how to get things done, how to run interference. But what really drives me is a strong personal agenda. For me that is helping minority students achieve.

Administrators also will gain from joining with teachers in the school's self-study and the staff's continuing professional education. These will often involve teams learning together, sharing their expertise and perspectives. For example, a seminar on approaches to science teaching might draw experienced teachers, teacher educators, and administrators together with pre-service teachers and novice administrators. The seminar might set forth the underlying theory of teaching a particular science, analyze case problems that emerge, and lead on to opportunities to try out such teaching. Simultaneously and in parallel, the seminar would take up questions of how to organize such instruction, exploring the management issues involved in efforts to systematically transform instruction schoolwide.

Joint learning opportunities of this sort have many advantages. They help to develop shared conceptions of teaching and to shape convictions about standards that prevail in the school. This kind of staff development can alert teachers to the school-wide milieu of their work and to the wider issue of the total learning careers of students. Such seminars for administrators and teachers can be a means for coordinating instruction because it will arise out of shared technical and social norms. A learning community is built from such work.

An understanding of teaching, learning, and community forms an essential ground for the art and craft of educational administration. Professional Development Schools will be good places to cultivate such understanding, and to reconstruct the education of administrators.

Center for Reflection and Inquiry

The work we have described for teachers, administrators, and teacher educators is complicated and difficult, and it calls for not just one fresh beginning but for continual reassessment, relearning, and redesign. This approach to work may seem foreign to schooling, but the most successful businesses and industries in the world regard it as essential and commonplace. They rethink, retool, research, and re-educate all the time. They do it to stay on top of the demands of new times and new markets, and to capitalize on the discoveries of formal research and invention and on the practical insights arising from their workers' experience. Schooling—on which our social order, government, culture, and economy increasingly depend—must do no less.

Participants in the Tomorrow's Schools seminars were unanimous that teaching for understanding in learning communities for everybody's children will be possible only in a school where purposeful preparation, mindful practice, critical reflection, mutual discourse, and continuing inquiry are normal ways of working, not exceptional events. All schools should do more to encourage such reflective and inventive teaching and learning.

Schools that prepare new teachers must do something more. From the time student teachers first begin seriously to hone their skills and to assume their professional attitudes, the habits of reflecting, questioning, and trying out and evaluating new ways of teaching—by themselves and with colleagues—should become embedded in their professional identity.

Thus the fifth principle for a Professional Development School is that it make reflection and inquiry a central feature of the school and a visible, well-organized presence in the school district.

In a Professional Development School, we're not talking about ordinary student teaching. We don't see the education of teachers as a short-term matter. The lifelong learning of teachers is our major point. The main reason for inquiry in a Professional Development School is to teach teachers to do it.

The universities that comprise The Holmes Group are among this nation's major research institutions, where tradition and practice center on creating new knowledge and ideas. The work of the few faculty who see themselves as teacher educators—responsible for preparing future school practitioners—often has little in common with those who see their major responsibility as the study of schooling and the education of those who will become teachers of teachers. That tension is reflected in their different expectations.

A similar disconnection between research and practice occurs *across* education institutions. The common view is that universities produce knowledge, and schools are supposed to implement their findings. Research is something produced by university faculty with specialized skills in research design and methodology. Teachers often provide the raw material for such research—they are the data—and are sometimes recipients of its findings, through in-service or technical assistance, but they are usually not active agents in shaping research questions, interpreting results, or connecting results with their teaching. Students of teaching in colleges and universities spend most of their time in college classrooms listening to lectures delivered from textbooks based on research that is weakly connected to life as a practicing teacher.

This style of education research—which has been dominant for about eighty years—has had some constructive effects. It has raised the level of critical thought and discourse about teaching. It has questioned conventional wisdom about teaching and given empirical support to new conceptions of teaching and learning. And it has introduced a higher level of discipline to the study of teaching and learning. In securing these advantages, though, this university-based style of education research has widened the gulf between researchers and practitioners in ways that tend to disable both.

The problems of this kind of educational research run deeper than a simple lack of relevance to practice. They stem from the strong grip of traditional disciplinary research on education, from the lack of a vital intellectual tradition linking issues of teaching practice with serious inquiry and writing, and from the limitations of traditional research methods in disclosing important problems of teaching and learning.

Early in its history, The Holmes Group recognized these tensions. In *Tomorrow's Teachers,* The Holmes Group proposed two imperatives:

The improvement and professionalization of teaching depend ultimately on providing teachers with opportunities to contribute to the development of knowledge in their profession, to form collegial relationships beyond their immediate working environment, and to grow intellectually as they mature professionally.

The improvement of teacher education depends on the continuing development of systematic knowledge and reflective practice.

I have yet to find a place to work that values any sort of intellectual activity on the part of teachers. Thinking is a pretty risky business. Who's going to say that inquiry is a major part of teachers' work? If you're devoting a large part of your time to thinking, you're not a teacher.

Seminar participants saw the Professional Development School as an important juncture of research and practice, where the strengths of the research tradition of Holmes Group institutions can be forged with the experiences, concerns, and interests of school people. This new institution, fostering closer connections between schools of education and schools, is fundamental to improving teaching and teacher education.

Inquiry as a mutual task

Inquiry should be defined as the common task of both university and school faculty. The agenda of inquiry might include formal research within established traditions of social science. Certainly it would include informal but systematic inquiry about the school's instruction, as well as the development of new curriculum materials and teaching methods, and experiments with different ways of organizing the school's classes, classrooms, schedules, staffing, and budget.

For example, university faculty—teacher educators as well as liberal arts professors—interested in a specific subject might collaborate with school faculty in varying the teaching content and methods and then evaluating how well students understand concepts. School and university faculty might work together to explore how technology can enable them to invent better curriculum and instruction for their schools' students. Teachers in a school could help teacher educators generate case studies for use with student teachers in their education courses. Administrators might devise and start up new management practices or new staffing patterns, and systematically document how they work.

The idea of research growing out of the daily work of teachers and students in schools is foreign to most schools. But a few schools have managed to make inquiry a central part of their work. The 1988 issue of the *Harvard Education Letter Digest* describes a number of instances of teacher-directed inquiry. A ninth-grade teacher from Alabama collaborates with a linguistics scholar from Stanford University to design a project in which she and her students conduct research on the uses of reading and writing in their own community. A group of colleagues in a Philadelphia school advise each other, using a carefully developed framework, about how they should teach specific students, based on data collected and organized around the child's emotional state, social relationships, expressive work, interests, and academic performance. A teacher in New York City keeps a detailed journal of observations of the children in her classroom. She uses the journal as a basis for planning classroom activities, parent conferences, and journal articles she writes about teaching. A group of teachers in a large eastern city conducts a study of the experiences facing first-year teachers. The results are presented to the district administration and they provoke a reconsideration of the district's methods for inducting new teachers. These kinds of inquiry can have a powerful effect not just on our knowledge of teaching and learning but on the work lives of teachers—and on our vision of teaching itself. They increase our understanding of teaching, and provide new ideas and occasions for collaboration with colleagues.

The task of agreeing on a common agenda of inquiry in the Professional Development School is not simply one of capitalizing on the existing specialized knowledge of individual university and school faculty—although the special strengths of each member are important points of departure. Rather, a common agenda requires a strategy for distributing knowledge and competence in ways that allow individuals to go beyond the bounds of their specialized knowledge, to learn new things, and to work productively as a group.

Professional Development Schools will not work well as communities of inquiry if they are simply collections of individuals doing things they are already good at. They will grow and expand if people see them as places where they can work at the outer edges of their existing knowledge, develop new capacities, and work with others on a variety of new and interesting problems.

Teachers have to learn that this is what the profession
is like. We are not looking for the final answer. Rather,

this is a search in which we will always have to be engaged.

For teachers, participation in inquiry will be a form of professional development whose rewards are both tangible—recognition, variety in work, access to additional resources—and intangible—the intellectual engagement and discovery, the opportunity to be creative and to work with others on important problems.

Inquiry in the Professional Development School should be a way for teachers, administrators, and professors to come together on equal footing. It should help forge a shared professional identity in schools and universities. And it should serve as a professional norm around which collaboration can take place, bringing together the many parties who are concerned about improving schools.

> The Professional Development School is not a laboratory school. What is needed is not just a working coalition of schools and universities as they are, but a powerful synthesis of knowledge to help us find out what the schools of tomorrow might be like. To make this happen, universities will have to take schools seriously and treat them with respect, and they will have to take a close look at their own behavior and values.

Diverse strategies and topics for inquiry

A common response by education researchers to the complexity of teaching and learning has been to focus on a few "behaviors" of teachers and students and to study their effects on a few indicators of student learning. The word "behaviors" is a tip-off to the fundamental process of over-simplification at work. This kind of research on teaching has led, either inadvertently or intentionally, to simplistic conceptions of teaching and learning and to reforms that treat teachers as passive implementers of prescribed programs.

As school and university faculty work together in schools, strategies of inquiry will begin to match the complexity and variety of good teaching and learning. Research will become more responsive to the school. In the past, researchers have used schools merely as settings for experiments. In contrast, in a Professional Development School, research will arise from issues important to the school, be conducted collegially, and will enliven children's and teachers' work.

For example, Professional Development School faculty might be engaged in a project on teaching reading to students from diverse cultural backgrounds. One concern of this faculty might be that students from certain cultural backgrounds respond more readily to teachers' questions than others. These teachers might want to develop an observational scheme to understand differing patterns of classroom interaction. There is a research literature on this subject. There are even observational instruments that might be adapted for this purpose. But the purpose of the inquiry, from the perspective of Professional Development School faculty, is not simply to replicate other research but to use collegial observation as a way to improve and refine teachers' responsiveness to student differences. Hence, the kind of instrument, the kind of observation, the nature of the results, and the nature of interaction around the results would be quite different from inquiry conducted by an outside researcher collecting data on the same subject.

Inquiry that grows out of the school faculty's concerns about their teaching and their students' learning will be more diverse than that arising from conventional canons of competent educational research. The discipline of inquiry will grow from the commitment of colleagues to understand and improve their own practice and to influence the incipient practice of student teachers, rather than from conventional rules and methods of research.

Teachers are often required to take training designed to change the way they teach. In most instances this training is brief—four or five days a year. Often it is conducted by outside consultants. Usually it is the product of district-wide priorities rather than concerns of a school faculty. Thus it is seldom connected to the problems that teachers see as most urgent. Training rarely entails sufficient follow-up in the classroom to determine whether it has influenced the way teachers teach. And the subject of training shifts from one topic to another with frequency, with little continuity from one year to the next. Yet training is a vast educational industry in the U.S.

A Professional Development School will be a center of inquiry where people can seek to improve their practice in ways that are more diverse, subtle, substantive, broad-gauged, and ongoing than training. The school's faculty will be engaged in inquiry about such matters as organization, curriculum, and methods of teaching. We don't necessarily expect Professional Development Schools to make huge new breakthroughs, but they will be able to wrestle with these big ideas persistently, in detail, to explore them over time. A certain amount of groping, improvisation, and serendipity should be part of any organization that is experimenting with new responses to complex problems. Thoughtful replication of and generalizations about promising innovations will be needed. These needn't undermine spontaneity. They should be a way of holding a focus on a common agenda of inquiry long enough so that real changes in teaching practice can occur and spread.

Inquiry and disciplined replication
as bases for school reform

The continuing education and improving practice of Professional Development School faculty can emerge from an agenda of inquiry rather than from external prescriptions designed around the education innovation of the moment. In a Professional Development School, the faculty can create a new basis for school reform.

In the past twenty years or so, school reform has become less the province of practicing educators and more the province of policymakers and experts with little grounding in practice. The reasons for this shift are complex, but at least two stand out. First, the public in general and education policymakers in particular are increasingly distrustful of the expertise of teachers and principals—increasingly willing to question their judgments. Second, as education interest groups such as teachers' and administrators' associations and school boards have become more organized and politically active, policymakers perceive them to be carrying self-interested political objectives. Consequently, policymakers look for other, more "neutral" sources of advice about school reform. The result is that the last generation of school reform, beginning in the late 1970s and extending into the present, was largely done to, rather than done with, professional educators.

> In our school we are trying to figure out something, and we are doing it using the people who do the teaching. We find that to do this we need more teachers and they need more time for reflection and deliberation. Schools, in order to be good schools, always have to be engaged in research. The work of the Professional Development School can't just be a matter of 'We figure it out, then we tell you how to do it.' In the end, everybody has to do the research for themselves, even though others have prepared the way with their work.

Professional Development Schools can provide a new institutional base for "restructuring" schools if they develop reputations as places where teachers engage in the serious work of improving teaching and learning. Seminar participants spoke of several conditions necessary in order for a Professional Development School to be an example of restructuring.

- Teachers need to learn to deal with questions that don't have ready answers, to be able to reflect and inquire about their work.

- Teachers and administrators need to know parents and the community.
- Parents should want more for their children than just getting good grades, and should know what is going on in the school and be part of the school's decision-making.
- Politicians and business people need to understand that the work of the Professional Development School is a long-term, developmental process, with no models that can be quickly installed.

Professional Development Schools can also supply a much-needed alternative perspective on the effects of school reform. They can serve, for example, as places where a limited set of reform ideas is pilot-tested before being generalized to policy. For schools trying to change, Professional Development Schools can serve as sources of information about new practices. And they can serve as sites where policymakers see for themselves, in a real school, what particular approaches to teaching and learning look like.

From "islands of excellence" to professional networks

Seminar participants noted several schools that embody the attributes we would like to see in Professional Development Schools. The historical literature on school reform is persuasive: Successful schools in which faculty study their own practice are not a novel occurrence. University laboratory schools, the progressive schools, the child study movement, the American "open education" or informal and non-graded elementary schools inspired by the British infant schools, the relatively new Coalition of Essential Schools—all manifest some of the qualities that we would like to see in Professional Development Schools. Important as these examples are in shaping our ideas about schooling, however, they have not had a broad or sustained effect on the preparation of teachers or on the practice of teaching.

School reformers have often succeeded at creating "islands of excellence"—single schools or small groups of schools with a serious commitment to improving teaching and learning. To date, however, educators have not succeeded at creating an institutional network of exemplary schools that make a broad impact on American education generally. Islands of excellence, while providing inspiration to generations of reformers, have been relatively easy for mainstream educators to ignore. They are typically dismissed as "special" schools, involving "special" children of "special" parents, pursuing precious ideas that are impossible to implement in the "real world" of public education. Otherwise powerful and important ideas about teaching and learning get discredited.

In urging its members to create Professional Development Schools, The Holmes Group takes up this challenge. Holmes Group Professional Development Schools will be focused on the pursuit of new ways to teach, in settings that have credibility with other educators and with the public at large. More importantly, the feature that will distinguish Holmes Group Professional Development Schools from islands of excellence will be their connection to each other through professional networks that will pick up and amplify successful visions, approaches, and experiments emanating from the different network members.

Professional Development Schools will have the opportunity to construct a variety of networks. One network can be the teachers who have received their initial clinical preparation in Professional Development Schools. These alumni can be a valuable source of external support and an audience for new ideas about practice, but they must be mobilized to be helpful. Another network might be a group of Professional Development Schools organized around a given university. The faculty of these organizations can serve as contacts for each other and for other teachers in their school systems for new ideas about practice. Some school districts will make formal use of this network; in others, their effects will be felt informally.

The broadest network will be the collection of all Holmes Group Professional Development Schools, calling national attention to the research and improved practice they are developing. The construction and use of these networks is, in the long run, what will distinguish Professional Development Schools from past examples of individual school reform that have failed to have a broader influence.

New forms of evaluation and rewards

In proposing that a Professional Development School become a center for reflection and inquiry, we are not suggesting that conventional research on teaching and learning be completely displaced. We are suggesting, rather, that a new kind of inquiry be given equal standing with conventional research. We also are suggesting that the development of this new kind of inquiry will require fundamental changes in the relationships now common between university and school faculties.

Professional Development Schools will need to use systems for evaluating and rewarding school and university faculty that stress involvement in a common enterprise. University faculty are presently evaluated and rewarded on their teaching within the university, on their contribution to research for an academic audience, and on their service to the community. School faculty are presently evaluated and rewarded on their teaching of specific content or grade levels and on their contribution to the schools in which they work. If these two reward systems are left unchanged in Professional Development Schools, school and university faculty will tend to pull apart, whatever their initial commitment to a common agenda of inquiry.

University faculty will be pulled away from the school by their university teaching commitments and by their professional research audiences. School faculty will be pulled toward specific issues of their schools and toward the immediate problems of teaching particular content to particular students. Thus Professional Development Schools—universities, colleges of education, and schools, alike—will need to evolve new ways of thinking about the work of their faculty, and new systems of evaluation and rewards based upon those conceptions of work.

Parity in rank between some senior schoolteachers and some university educators could help inquiry in Professional Development Schools for at least two reasons. First, parity could be one source of glue holding Professional Development Schools together as organizations rather than as collections of solo performers. Second, parity in rank could provide a mechanism for continuous growth and improvement for individuals and for the group.

What is essential is the unique view of the Professional Development School not simply as a clinical or laboratory setting at the service of a university but as a center of inquiry with its own agenda, drawing the sustained attention of collaborating school and university faculty to the school's own critical questions of practice. This agenda needs to be supported by a set of norms and incentives that keep school and university engaged in a common enterprise. That enterprise needs to be linked to a broader network of institutions sustained and supported by The Holmes Group. The Holmes Group Professional Development Schools network will provide a new basis for sustained inquiry about teaching and learning, directly related to practice, and an alternative basis for school reform for the future.

■|■|■

Inventing a New Organization

In creating a Professional Development School, typical aspects of a school's organizational structure may need to be changed wholesale:

- Work roles and assignments of the school's faculty and of the university's professors will change as the definitions of teaching, inquiry, and service are diversified and broadened. They will also change as some school and university faculty exchange roles in the education of student teachers.
- Teachers will need time to plan the school; revise the curriculum; teach and supervise student teachers; reflect on, experiment with, and evaluate their own teaching; join in research; meet with parents and with community agencies; and design staff development that's relevant to all this.
- Scheduling of classes will have to be adapted to enact principles of teaching and learning for understanding for all children, of the school as a learning community, and of ensuring equity within diversity. Curricular, grade level, and departmental organization probably will be changed.
- Ways in which faculty meet and work will need to be more direct, open, participatory, collegial—and yet expeditious and to the point.
- Leadership and relations with the central office of the school district will

allow for more decisions to be made at the school and for new work norms and expectations to take shape there.

Thus the sixth principle for the design of a Professional Development School is that the school's management, leadership, and faculty—including colleagues from the university—work together to invent a new organizational structure in line with the school's new purposes and principles about teaching and learning.

This restructuring will not be innovation for its own sake; it will be anchored in the faculty's notions of good teaching and learning. The school surely will not be the same as it was before, nor will it look like other schools in the district or other Professional Development Schools. The inventiveness and attentiveness to context with which faculties apply Professional Development School principles will produce many different organizational forms, and Professional Development Schools can be expected to look very different from one another. We think they will look alike in two respects, though: They will be fashioning new roles for their teachers, and they will be creating strong new connections with the community around the school.

The teacher's role: complexity and flexibility

Seminar participants deplored the present tendency for specialization in teaching to cause fragmentation of instruction, isolation of pupils, lack of coordination between regular and special teachers, and a subtle diffusion of responsibility for the welfare of individual students, breaking the webs of the learning community. Systems now are entrenched that codify specialist credentials, training programs, regulations, funding mechanisms, and patterns of practice.

Problems arising from specialization are only the most recent reason for rigidity in the teacher's role. Long ago, traditional patterns of school organization caused teaching jobs to be circumscribed according to grade level, subject area, and curricular placement (for instance, Business English and Honors English). In elementary and middle schools, age grading and teacher specialization by level disrupt the continuity of education over time, as students are conveyed from grade to grade, teacher to teacher. In high schools also, the narrow organization of subject matter too frequently prevents students from making vital connections to their own understanding, interests, and experiences and from bringing knowledge to bear in genuine inquiries and intellectual projects. Equally, the organization of students by tracks, special categories, and the like denies access to knowledge for many.

In a Professional Development School committed to teaching for understanding in learning communities, the principle that mainly defines the teachers' roles should not be specializations of one sort or another but rather each student's whole *career* in the school—the quality of learning looked at over a long period of time. Using this yardstick may prompt a Professional Development School faculty to design alternative ways of organizing subjects and staff—interdisciplinary studies, for instance—and grouping students by characteristics other than age and measures of ability. Such actions are likely to require flexible rather than specialist staffing. The teacher's job description then will flow from the changing needs of the school, rather than from decisions in the central office.

> People have taken for granted that a good teacher must be able to 'manage' 150 kids every day and that even good teachers will be able to 'reach' only a few of their students. This is not good enough. Now people are saying that all students should learn. Teachers know they can't meet such a standard within the current constraints. The definition has changed but the conditions of work have not.

Schools and the wider community

Many schools are swamped by the stresses and circumstances of their students—poverty, drugs, homelessness, hunger, gangs, youth employment and unemployment, and the shifting patterns of family life. Teachers' and administrators' primary responsibility is instruction, but as a practical and moral matter they cannot ignore the social and psychological.

> A greater sense of professionalism on the part of teachers should never distance them from parents and others in the community surrounding the school.

The Professional Development School needs to create constructive ways for prospective teachers to meet with parents and to integrate their knowledge into classroom life. Parents and community are vital resources. Parents can be important as tutors, storytellers, models, and interpreters of language and of cultural and community knowledge. We expect that some Professional Development Schools will explore new forms of governance in which parents and local community members play important roles. Social foundations courses might send teacher education students to meetings of community organizations, school board sessions, and the like.

Future teachers need to observe children in settings outside school—boys' and girls' clubs, day care centers, and playgrounds. Every aspiring teacher should get to know one or two families well.

Some guidelines for a school staff in taking on responsibilities adjacent to teaching were suggested by seminar participants:

- The personal well-being of children and their ability to learn are interwoven: Children inhabit one world. But the school is limited in time and competence to deal with children's out-of-school problems. Social agencies, churches, community organizations, and the business community should be recruited as active partners in the school community.
- The school's central teaching and learning functions must provide the rationale for any involvement with other kinds of concerns. Teachers and administrators must be firm and articulate about that rationale when asked to take on other responsibilities. It's obvious, for example, that hungry children won't learn well.
- The school should engage the community in dialogue on the school's educational purposes and programs, especially when issues of values divide the school from the community. All children learn best when parents and teachers share similar visions. The imperative to engage in dialogue with community is complicated, however, by the fact that in most schools "community" consists of disparate groups, sending children from far-flung areas because of busing, consolidation of rural schools, and programs that provide parents with choice of school.

Some seminar participants also advocated creating stronger connections between schooling and the outside world, since so many students now see no future payoff in school. More and more, high school teachers' best efforts do not persuade students to learn and work hard. For some, a real opportunity to attend college would be a compelling motive. For others, stronger school and work connections, and the knowledge that rewarding jobs are available for successful graduates would be powerful incentives. Teachers in some Professional Development Schools might engage with students on grounds broader than academic participation, for example, in partnerships with businesses and agencies in the work sector, or becoming partners in local and regional economic development.

Schools don't just exist to provide people for the job market. They exist to reshape the way young people think about work and their future. That's a piece of social justice.

Our seminars shared a growing consensus that the principle of a learning community could be more easily enacted in a smaller school. Bigness plagues American education. Too many swollen institutions are processing students rather than educating them. Genuine learning communities require places where people know each other and are known. Teachers and students thrive in settings where the threads of connection overlap to form a complex and thick-textured fabric of common life. Big schools, people said, ought to be divided up into humanly manageable sub-units. In a smaller school—or small units in a big school—children and teachers can wear many hats.

Five Guideposts for the New Organizational Structure

First, we advocate an organizational structure keyed to the coordination of instruction and services. As we suggested, the unit of analysis ought to be the individual student's educational career. This requires paying attention not so much to course requirements and short-term evaluations like tests, but to the variety and vitality of the student's formal and informal learning experiences, and to the ways that the student participates in the school and community and learns to shape purposes over time. Too few children today get chances for sustained, open-ended interaction and dialogue with adults. Children are more hungry than ever for adult attention, and the adults in their school have become even more crucial in their development.

> Teachers have the task of picking up the marbles for the rest of society. They will not be able to succeed by themselves alone. Teachers will need allies and coalitions outside the schools.

Not only social welfare agencies but any community agency that can link children to older, more experienced people—to older children, for example—can be an immense ally for the school. Neighborhood youth organizations provide opportunities for sustained, open-ended learning for students that may be missing in families. School learning can be given meaning by integrating study in a number of academic studies—math, science, and writing, for instance—into activities in such organizations and in the community. If such activities focus on issues of importance to the community and if the students' participation highlights the use of their school skills, the students can develop the invaluable sense of competence to deal with the worlds inside and outside the school.

Informal specialization, rotating assignments

Second, we favor flexible staffing arrangements that emerge from the needs of the local school. Our seminar participants encouraged the informal specialization that draws on the natural strengths, inclinations, and leadership of teachers. One third-grade teacher is especially strong in science, another in language arts, yet another in working with special needs children. Each assumes primary responsibility for her specialty, developing curricular materials and instructing colleagues in their use with students.

Such arrangements make sense in any school. In a school with additional missions for teacher education and inquiry, some further specialization and differentiated staffing may be essential. The design task will be to capitalize on teachers' expertise and energies, while avoiding a rigid hierarchy and divisive competition for scarce positions and resources. No single teacher is expected to master all the roles and responsibilities that students and student teachers need, nor to struggle in silence over the tasks she can't handle. The faculty works toward the collective provision of the needed knowledge and skills, drawing on university colleagues and on local resources inside and outside of the school.

Participants in the seminars also recommended development of temporary and rotating assignments. University and school faculty may be wary of long-term obligations but be willing to undertake shorter assignments, to share positions and tasks with others, and to fill permanent positions on a rotating basis. Such an approach can convey several benefits. Expertise can be identified, cultivated, and rewarded broadly among a faculty, including its extended members from the university. Variety can flavor the work. Time with youngsters, and the love of subject—good teachers' most powerful incentives—can be provided for all.

A school working along these lines will differ distinctly from the traditional professional model, in which hierarchies command and control and a collection of credentialed specialists progressively narrow their concerns for students. Professional Development Schools need to be flexible, innovative organizations with the capacity to try out alternatives, to reject or modify what does not work, and to continue experimenting. This goes not only for teaching but also for organization and management.

The flexible staffing patterns that Professional Development Schools will need are consonant with The Holmes Group goal that called for "recognizing differences in teachers' knowledge, skill, and commitment, in their education, certification, and work." In a Professional Development School these positions might in effect—formally or informally—include senior teachers (what *Tomorrow's Teachers* called "career professional teachers"), who take leadership in instructional planning, curriculum, research, and teaching teachers; experienced teachers, who teach in classrooms, mentor student teachers, and participate in all the professional tasks of the school; and classroom teachers, who work under supervision because they have not met the full requirements for professional licensure.

A number of Holmes Group universities have preparation programs for such positions. Many states have legislated both "alternate route" teacher preparation programs that allow people to teach under supervision while studying for licensure, and various "career ladder" structures that introduce advanced positions into the teaching ranks.

It may be possible to capitalize on these policy innovations in the process of creating new structures and positions in a Professional Development School. Whether positions are established with official titles, descriptions, and perks is less important than two principles: Forms should flow from the needs of the local learning community, and schools should learn to make use of the wisdom of the best practitioners.

Public forms of accountability

A third guidepost for organizing the Professional Development School is to prepare to shift from the present forms of accountability to new forms of professional responsibility.

The "prove it" environment that teachers work in has gradually intensified in recent years with the growing sophistication of the testing industry and the centralization of authority over schools. Among school systems in the world, ours is notable for its reliance on a range of accountability measures that include standardized tests administered from the national, state, and district levels, together with the collection and public display of information on other aspects of school processes, outcomes, and conditions.

The increasingly complex accountability framework in the U.S. has exacted costs. Valid and reliable information on student learning is necessary to direct the work of educators at all levels, to gauge progress toward goals, to inform a range of educational policy decisions, and to enable the public to engage in responsible oversight of the schools it pays for. But seminar participants insisted that the systems that have taken shape have also had unfortunate consequences for teaching. The range of what is taught is increasingly narrowed to what is measured—just when we are starting to develop more ambitious conceptions of learning. Bureaucratic control stifles the spirit of learning in teachers and students alike. The search for new ways to teach for understanding is inhibited by fear of looking bad on the tests. Aggregate modes of testing don't really benefit classroom teachers or individual students. Paper and pencil quantitative tests do not get at many of the wider goals of schooling.

The development of alternative means of assessment of student learning can become a natural source of school-university collaboration, joining the expertise of university scholars to the wisdom of classroom teachers. Researchers have pioneered many innovative assessment procedures to study the nature of learning, but few have found their way into use by teachers. Conversely, teachers have always engaged in informal methods for assessing learning that have not been carefully studied or widely shared. Expert teachers are superb diagnosticians. Furthermore, there are traditions to consult, including the child study movement and the efforts to document children's work as a source of insight about their learning. Contemporary experiments also are under way to try out innovative forms of large-scale assessment, using complex cognitive tasks, group problem-solving exercises, holistically scored written assignments, computer simulations, reliance on portfolios of student materials, and other means. A quiet renaissance is gathering momentum across the country that Professional Development Schools can draw on and contribute to.

We believe the time is ripe for such experimentation. Psychometric experts are uneasy about the evident problems with standardized tests. Teachers are unhappy over the increase in testing that does not help them with instruction. And the public is willing to accept professional leadership that seeks to "build a better mousetrap." Traditional notions that regarded basic skills as the necessary foundation for advanced learning are giving way to more ambitious teaching goals and methods for all children. Teaching for understanding no longer appears as an advanced goal for a select few but as the basic aim of education for all. Consequently, as teachers work to develop new teaching methods and curricular conceptions, they also must experiment with consonant forms of assessment. We need Professional Development Schools as sites for such experiments.

Professional forms of responsibility: standards setting

In our society we have come to rely on professional authority and responsibility across a range of vital human services. Underlying professional authority is both a claim and a compact. The claim is that specialized knowledge acquired through years of formal training and experience is necessary to effective practice. The compact—between the public and the profession—is that a measure of autonomy will be given in exchange for the obligation to set and enforce standards of practice. The ethical touchstone of those standards is the client's welfare.

As a sole mode of organizing and conferring authority, professionalism is open to abuse. But in practices such as teaching, professionalism is a necessary complement to public, external forms of authority that operate through regulation and law, bureaucratic procedures, or client choice.

There is an irreducible kernel of professional discretion in teaching that must be cultivated, not constrained. Teachers must have a free hand in the key decisions that go into making a classroom a learning community. Good schools ought to enjoy a parallel autonomy. Teachers as a profession and as school faculties must engage in standards-setting efforts that direct their work and build public confidence.

What's critical is to paint a vision of alternating responsibility and accountability. It is crucial to suggest (I) not all professionals are held accountable in the way teachers are, but (2) all professionals must strike a bargain with society. Professional Development Schools are potential sites for exploring new kinds of the bargain.

Measurement of results alone cannot provide adequate direction for practice nor information to the public. We need Professional Development Schools to begin developing professional standards based on practice that, together with assessments based on test results, more faithfully reflect our aims.

Most professions develop some assessment procedures based on "outcomes"—hospital-based chart reviews and audits in medicine, for example—but they do not rely exclusively on such evidence to evaluate practice. Rather, knowledge that informs practice is represented in standards that provide the best available guidance. In complex kinds of practice such as teaching, outcomes alone are an insufficient guide because outcomes are multiple, they trade off in complex ways, they unfold slowly, and many of the most important are not measurable. Further, professionals do not control all the factors affecting outcomes; and the state of knowledge is imperfect and cannot guarantee success in all cases.

Educators have not worked out ways and means to articulate principles that represent professional consensus on best practice. That is one reason why outcome measures such as quantitative tests dominate and distort public discourse on education. In medicine, the outcome, "The operation was a success, but the patient died," is not necessarily deemed outrageous. Standards exist by which it can be ascertained that (1) the decision to operate was justified, and (2) all due skill was exercised in the operation itself. In education, too, standards should be grounded not only in review of results but in judgments made about practice.

Further, the standards-setting task must be joined with the mission of educating teachers. Standards are communicated through the ways a profession socializes its new members. In teaching, however, entry to the work does not go through stages, it is not selective, and it is lacking in the powerful initiation ceremonies, rituals, and ordeals that commit novices to professionalism. Furthermore, because everyone in our society has spent literally thousands of hours observing conventional teaching, beliefs about teaching are exceptionally resistant to change. The conservative bias built into the entering teacher tends to perpetuate conventional patterns of practice.

Teacher educators have long recognized that they must help teacher education students break out of their conventions about teaching as part of the effort to improve teaching and learning. While this process can begin in the university, it must be carried through in practice. The novice's first years in teaching should expose her to norms of conduct and standards of practice. Professional Development Schools should be places where such standards are consciously developed and conveyed to new teachers.

> We're trying to inculcate teachers with a new set of social ideals. And more: Give them more experience in how you live these out. That has implications for how you organize teacher education's courses and credits.

Some participants at our seminars stressed the value of setting standards through local school deliberations. For example, standards may rise out of consideration of local problems and issues of teaching within particular schools. As school faculties engage in problem-setting and problem-solving, in the observation of teaching, and in the study of student learning, they will begin to articulate standards and principles.

The range of practice for which standards might be established is extremely broad. Standards might refer to technical-practices principles for teaching writing in the elementary grades, for infusing inquiry into science teaching, for assessing student learning across the curriculum, for encouraging multiple approaches to the teaching of reading. Or standards might be set for social aspects of instruction—grouping practices within and between classrooms, equity in distributing opportunities to learn, ways to integrate special-needs children into regular classrooms, ways to capitalize on students' cultural pluralism. Also, standards might be established relating to professional responsibilities—norms for involving parents, for assuming school-wide duties, for staying abreast of new approaches to instruction.

Other participants in our seminars suggested another source of professional standards. They argued that teachers should develop networks that supply connections across schools and that allow teachers to form broad professional identities and to gain information and perspectives outside their immediate work environment. For example, many dedicated teachers participate actively in a variety of professional associations, including those associated with the disciplines. These issue authoritative guidance on educational aims and objectives, curriculum, assessment, and standards for good teaching, and they take stands on social and moral issues in education. Standards might also be profession-wide, articulated by associations that represent best practice in such areas as science and mathematics teaching, language arts, social studies, and other fields.

These are valuable complementary perspectives—inquiry and reflection on a school's own practice, and professional associations transcending the school. We would expect faculty in a Professional Development School to participate in networks and associations that promote high standards and that provide authoritative guidance. And we would expect them to bring these outside resources to bear on the particular problems and opportunities they encounter in their school.

Cultivating collaboration

A fourth guidepost around which to invent a Professional Development School's organization is to balance individual work with collaborative work. The very definition of a Professional Development School as a site where educators learn and inquire presumes a high degree of collaboration. Master teachers spend time observing novices teach and confer regularly with them. Novices closely observe veterans. Staff development becomes a regular, ongoing feature in the life of the school, rather than an infrequent add-on, so school faculties work together to provide mutual learning opportunities. Research is conducted in joint projects among university and school faculty. Common standards get forged out of sustained dialogue. A Professional Development School pursues its distinctive mission by organizing to ensure teamwork.

Translating this into practice is the most difficult challenge for organizational design. Teamwork is likely to disrupt traditional patterns of schooling and to violate well-established routines and the norm of teacher privacy. Many of our best teachers are jealous of their time and autonomy. They will need to be persuaded that the rewards for participating in creating true learning communities outweigh the burdens of collective responsibility.

I'm not interested in collegiality for its own sake. Rather, whom do you put teachers in touch with so they get better at their work? The traditional pattern of isolated work has not served teaching well. Teacher expertise remains tacit and hidden behind the classroom door. Teachers have to wrestle privately with the many dilemmas they confront daily. Standards of practice cannot emerge because there are few opportunities to articulate and to ground them in the close, shared observation of teaching and learning. And novices receive only brief, limited opportunities to observe and be observed as part of their preparation.

This lamentable pattern persists because it seems a necessary response to a job that daily requires a small number of adults to manage a large number of students, not all of whom desire to be in school. Past efforts at formal collaborative arrangements have achieved only modest success. Some elementary schools rely on team teaching. Some middle schools have created interdisciplinary units that coordinate curriculum, student assignments, and teaching methods. But most teachers tolerate the bargain that exchanges isolation for the limited autonomy of the classroom.

Further, the brute fact of the clock—simply finding time for teachers to work together—is a big problem. Keeping school in the traditional manner absorbs all the time. Adding time has meant increasing school budgets to pay for work in the summer, on weekends, and after school. The requirement to allot more time for collegial work must be implemented as rearranging tasks and redefining roles so as to add time together to pursue shared purposes and activities. Unfortunately, new teaching positions introduced in the name of professionalism and collegiality often have produced more isolated work, not more teamwork, as "master" or "mentor" teachers have produced their own projects rather than working with other teachers. We must avoid simply adding new layers to the educational coral reef.

Seminar participants acknowledged that these are powerful, persistent tendencies that will be difficult to change. They suggested that individual schools cultivate collaboration in a variety of ways:

- Through changes in scheduling;
- By forming teams and workgroups;
- By creating teacher/leader positions designed to organize collaboration;
- By rewarding collaborative work in teacher evaluation systems;
- By using time-saving technologies for managerial and instructional tasks;
- By augmenting the faculty with people from outside the school, including university faculty and staff, community volunteers, and parents; and
- By setting aside work time for thoughtful dialogue.

Reciprocity between the university and the school

Vital to the new organizational structure of the Professional Development School will be its partnership with the university. The university will bring human and material resources to the school. But the creation of real reciprocity is problematic.

If the university regards the Professional Development School only as another clinical setting or one more special project defined by the availability of external funds, the school will be unable to do its job. The Professional Development School needs to be seen as the major focus for the university's threefold mission of preparing teachers and administrators, serving as the research and development arm of the profession, and providing direct services to the schools; just as teaching hospitals assist in the training of physicians, conduct medical research, and provide high-quality patient care. There are many dissimilarities between medicine and education, but the medical example—medical school faculty and hospital staff overlapping and interacting in many ways—is suggestive for Professional Development Schools.

We need the Professional Development School and the parity relationship because the university needs expe-

> rienced, wise teachers to help us revise the curriculum
> of education studies. If we don't do that, the Professional
> Development School is only a clinical setting.

If there are difficulties in expanding the roles and responsibilities for schoolteachers, there are equal difficulties in engaging university faculty in working in the Professional Development School. As we have noted, status, rank, and money in modern research universities derive from research activities, not from sustained work in schools. In education schools, this means that the supervision of practice teachers is often relegated to graduate students and non-tenured staff.

The university will have to change existing rules, roles, relationships, and reward systems for faculty who want to collaborate in the Professional Development School. This will be one aspect of a broad organizational change process that will ultimately reconfigure the university school of education.

Every box on the Professional Development School's organization chart should be drawn so as to create a permanent, long-term relationship with the university. Indicators of such a relationship would include the following:

- Stable governance arrangements that all parties have agreed upon;
- Permanent budget allocations;
- New positions that span institutional boundaries;
- Thorough integration of faculty and staff between the university and the schools—university faculty working in the Professional Development School and schoolteachers and administrators teaching in the school of education;
- Planning processes that set progress toward goals;
- Creation of new reward and incentive structures in the university that encourage participation in Professional Development School activities; and
- Recruitment of both school and university faculty who are committed to collaborative work.

Leadership and management in Professional Development Schools

This ambitious agenda underscores the importance of leadership. An unfortunate tendency has arisen within the current school reform movement. Moves to expand teacher roles and responsibilities are perceived as threatening administrators.

> Talking about teachers and administrators as separate
> parties is self-destructive. Professional Development

> Schools need to have the strength of their conviction in
> the way they organize themselves. Their strongest con-
> ceptions of teaching and learning must drive the school
> structure.

Seminar participants stressed that administrators are indispensable to the creation of Professional Development Schools and that first and foremost they, too, are
educators, broadly responsible for the conduct of teaching and learning. Participants
further agreed that the concept of leadership may be significantly redefined within
the Professional Development School. No single model emerged.

On the one hand, many seminar participants expressed skepticism at "strong leader"
imagery, arguing instead that leadership is a complex function diffused throughout
an effective school. In this view, teachers are the leaders, and the aim of an able
administrator is to encourage the emergence of many kinds of leadership on the
part of many participants within the learning community. This "enabler" conception, they noted, demands great skill and wisdom on the part of those charged with
formal management responsibilities.

On the other hand, some participants advocated vesting authority in an administrator who works to secure and mobilize resources, to run interference politically
for the school, to coordinate activities, and to manage the whole process of change.
This second description sounds more like the traditional school principal. These
two alternative notions are not necessarily incompatible, nor does either assume a
particular organizational model. Rather, they speak to the range of functions, roles,
and responsibilities that must be present in some form within a successful school.

> Sharing is difficult. If it fails everyone will say, 'We tried it,
> and it didn't work.' We still need strong leaders, people
> who are moral, who have integrity, who care—people who
> won't let it fail. That is what empowerment means—help-
> ing people succeed.

The widespread dissatisfaction with traditional, bureaucratic forms of organization and management produced agreement among seminar participants that
Professional Development Schools must be inventive and not bound by the past. As
teachers must experiment with new forms of instruction, so must administrators experiment with new forms of organization, new approaches to leadership in support of
ambitious teaching and learning. Here, as with learning and with inquiry, parallel
processes come into play, beckoning teachers and administrators to invent freely.

■|■|■

Getting From Here to There

We argue for Professional Development Schools in a spirit of idealism about possibilities and realism about problems. We conclude this report in the same spirit, with some reflections about the process of getting from here to there. We cannot be specific or definitive. Starting a Professional Development School is not just a design process; it's also a negotiation process. It's a back-and-forth dialogue between people in a university and people in a school district; and between principles and actions.

DEFINITION: How can we design Professional Development Schools if we've never seen one?

You can translate the six principles into shared ideas about what you want in your place and then assess what (and whom) you've got to work with. We have set forth six principles not as a blueprint but as stimuli for local thought, dialogue, negotiation, and actions. We have in mind that implementation will be a process of "small tries" directed at cumulative effects over time.

One way to start would be for a group of school and university faculty to set up a schedule of regular meetings, classroom observations, and workshops to work through the implications of one or two principles. For instance: "How would we capitalize on the talents of teachers in Martin Luther King, Jr., Elementary School and Metropolitan State University to teach middle-grades reading and math for deep understanding? How would we capitalize on the knowledge that students bring from their community to make that learning more engaging? How would we involve university teacher preparation students in our experiments and our findings?" Small tries, concrete problems, shared values, high ambitions: This is the stuff of a Professional Development School.

If such efforts are sustained and faithful to the principles, those tries will result in a new and unique institution. Those local actions multiplied will produce a wide diversity of Professional Development Schools across the country.

Many questions will be answered only by experience. Hence it is important not only to start Professional Development Schools but also to open up local, regional, and national networks in which people begin talking together about what they're doing.

Around The Holmes Group consortium, there are powerful insights on the matters embedded in the six principles. We can point to several schools committed to the principles of teaching for understanding in a learning community. We possess research on which to base inside-out transformation of conventional school instruction. But we need to hear each other's similar insights and examples of school practice, and to study the results of inquiry on our experiments.

The spread of these schools and the definition of their practice will hinge on the development of a broad, firmly grounded body of knowledge and experience that can be shared among people with a common interest in the simultaneous restructuring of schools and recasting of teacher education. Professional Development Schools will test new course and clinical work in the education of teachers, new school curriculum, new teaching practices, new research partnerships, and new formats for school administration, organization, and personnel relationships. In all of the above, the constructive uses of students' cultural diversity will be the defining characteristic—what gives the school its color and flavor.

INITIATIVE: Who should initiate Professional Development Schools?

The Professional Development Schools will work only if there is true reciprocity between school and university educators. If one party dominates, these schools may be successful in other respects, but they will fail to marry inquiry and practice. As long as a spirit of true reciprocity holds, Professional Development Schools can emerge at the initiative of a school, of a school district, of a university, or of a third party.

We expect some schools and school districts already active in school reform to link up with local universities. In other cases, universities are starting conversations with schools and school districts. Elsewhere, political leaders—governors, legislators, school board members, and community leaders—may act as brokers between schools and universities. And in still other cases, parents and community groups will lobby for new schools and make matches between schools and universities. Other good prospects for collaboration include the American Federation of Teachers' "Professional Practice Schools," the National Education Association's "Mastery in Learning" network schools, and members of the Coalition of Essential Schools. All of these efforts parallel ours in most respects, and we are eager to work with them.

We reiterate that our principles are intended to lead to something entirely different—not the conventional, familiar forms of school-university involvement. Schools and school systems are asked regularly to accept student teachers, to take part in university research projects, and to serve as sites where new models of instruction are tested. Likewise, university faculty are often asked to help in schools. Professional Development Schools should not simply formalize these existing arrangements. These ad hoc arrangements are often productive, but they lack the coherence and duration necessary to have a sustained effect on teaching and learning. In many ways they add to the fragmentation of U.S. education. This is why we stress the importance of learning community and duration over time. Universities and schools should enter Professional Development School marriages only if both parties are committed to a long-term relationship.

Starting a Professional Development School is no small project. It projects big, ambitious goals on a number of fronts: rigorous conceptions of teaching and learning, relationships of parity among universities and schools, links between schools and their communities, new structures and methods of educating teachers and administrators, and new purposes and methods for school-based research. Doing all this will require hard-headed political calculation and skill in coalition-building. New ideas will meet a multitude of reasons why they can't be done. Overcoming the inherent inertia of established institutions will require patience and determination—as well as a broad base of political support.

No matter who extends the first invitation to plan a Professional Development School together, it seems important that eventually the coalition that develops around a Professional Development School should be broadly based: business, policymakers, community organizations, social services agencies, and the like will need to be part of the action.

ARTS & SCIENCES: How can schools of education mobilize the commitment of other university faculty to Professional Development Schools?

The strongest incentive for collaboration occurs when faculty find problems they regard as intrinsically interesting and significant. It is fashionable, for example, for university faculty to complain about the level of preparation of students entering higher education. These complaints seldom are transformed into comprehensive, sustained efforts to discover what kind of preparation students need and how it might be given in elementary and secondary schools, even though individual faculty from the arts and sciences have often found the problems of learning in elementary and secondary schools intriguing and rewarding. A Professional Development School can increase the attractiveness of these problems to arts and sciences faculty by offering a focused opportunity in a setting committed to serious inquiry.

Many of the problems associated with learning academic content in elementary and secondary schools are similar to those in colleges and universities. Engaging an English professor in the experience of how elementary students understand poetry, for example, could have important payoffs in that professor's teaching of undergraduate students. Engaging a physics professor in observing how young students form their basic conceptions of matter and energy could improve that professor's ability to communicate to college students.

REGULATIONS: How can we develop new practices in the face of regulatory, statutory, contractual, and procedural constraints?

Much of what Professional Development Schools undertake will be at odds with the apparatus of federal and state regulation—as well as with collective bargaining contracts and administrative rules of local districts. The designers of a Professional Development School need to be open about these potential conflicts from the beginning. And they need to be firm about the basic rules that no public school can violate: the well-being and physical safety of students; the basic civil rights of parents, students, and staff; and the due process guarantees that apply to any public organization.

Beyond these conditions, we hope Professional Development Schools will be able to start from scratch and build the best possible learning communities consistent with the principles outlined here. We anticipate two broad strategies for confronting the inevitable conflicts with existing laws, regulations, and contracts. The first strategy is rule-by-rule waivers, in which a Professional Development School asks for explicit waivers from existing statutes, regulations, and contracts when they conflict with sound instructional practice. States and localities might give a Professional Development School preference in granting waivers, but the preference must be earned by thoughtful justification and good performance.

A second, more ambitious approach is to treat a Professional Development School as a "regulatory free zone," in which all but the elemental guarantees of health, safety, due process, and civil rights are suspended and the school is free to create an alternative set of structures. This regulation-free strategy requires bold vision on the part of local school officials and extensive cooperation among state, local, and federal officials. It requires the development of alternative mechanisms for resolving collective bargaining issues, such as the "education trust agreements" that some school districts and teachers' associations are adopting. It also requires a commitment on the part of school and university faculty to develop broad-based community support and involvement, so that freedom from legal and contractual constraints is balanced by responsibility to the public.

Several examples of both strategies are already being tried at the state and local levels. There is high interest in many localities, some states, and among many federal policymakers in experiments with deregulation of schools. Professional Development Schools should capitalize on this interest and offer themselves as experimental sites for responsible deregulation.

COSTS: How much will it cost, and where will we find the money to initiate and sustain a Professional Development School?

A Professional Development School will require extra resources both for start-up costs—planning, staff development, new technology, capital improvements—and operating costs, primarily additional teachers. For example, a Professional Development School may want to involve curriculum and instruction faculty—those with expertise in subject matter disciplines—on a weekly basis. From time to time, they might want to involve others, perhaps faculty with a specialty in child development, in counseling, or in school organization. For an elementary Professional Development School of roughly 400 students and fifteen teachers, these university involvements might reasonably add as many as two FTE faculty members—part-time assignments for several university professors. In a high school, more would be needed.

Some of these costs can be met by reallocating resources within the university and the school district. For instance, existing state and local expenditures for staff development can be used to advance the Professional Development School faculty's priorities. The school of education can allocate portions of some faculty members' time to work in the Professional Development School. One university that has started several Professional Development Schools puts into an elementary school six faculty participants one-third time on a regular basis. In a high school, the university would also contribute in-school participation by arts and sciences faculty.

A substantial share of the additional costs will have to be raised from external sources. Some states already have made financial commitments to school-university partnerships of various kinds. Businesses and philanthropic organizations are showing increasing interest in these kinds of arrangements. If universities and schools show evidence of a strong and detailed commitment to these partnerships, additional resources may be available. The burden for making this case lies, at least initially, with educators.

Professional Development Schools will provide environments for teachers and students that are richer in resources than many other schools in the same districts. These resource disparities will grow out of necessary investments in new curriculum, additional staff, building modifications, and the like. Recognizing their greater resources, faculty in a Professional Development School should consider that theirs is a school for the development of professionalism among all the teachers in the district, and that they have a responsibility to help spread what they learn to other schools, using all the formal and informal communication channels of the district.

A number of strategies can be used. Faculty can work with district curriculum and professional development staff or a teacher's center to extend new curriculum ideas to other schools. Teachers from other schools could receive some portion of their staff development activities in Professional Development Schools. Professional Development Schools can act as magnets for recruitment into districts for aspiring teachers from high-quality university programs. It is possible, in other words, to use the resources of Professional Development Schools to benefit schools more broadly.

CHOICE: Should a Professional Development School experiment with parent, student, and teacher choice?

Throughout our discussions in the Tomorrow's Schools seminars, there was a running dialogue on the issue of parent and teacher choice. One side of this dialogue said that students learn best, parents are more satisfied, and teachers teach to their maximum potential when they can voluntarily choose schools. Choice builds strong learning communities, proponents say. Others argue that introducing choice to a Professional Development School will exclude students, parents, and teachers who lack the knowledge, influence, or resources to choose to their advantage. For instance, a single, working parent without a car may be unable to take advantage of a school on the other side of town. In systems based on choice, the rich get richer and the poor get poorer, say the critics. There is a growing research literature around these arguments that is too complex to summarize here.

Our conclusion from observation, reading this literature, and discussing the issue with seminar participants, is that if designers of a Professional Development School want to deal with the issue of choice, they should do so experimentally. A Professional Development School could actively incorporate choice into its design, and carefully monitor the relationship to the operation and effects of the instructional program. A Professional Development School offering choice will have the burden of demonstrating whether choice is compatible with equity—which will mean getting involved with setting district-wide policy. Other Professional Development Schools—preferably in the same locales as those experimenting with choice—could attempt to operate within the constraints of existing pupil and teacher assignment systems. Then, as experience accumulates, there could be an overall assessment of the issue of choice among practitioners and policymakers involved in Professional Development Schools.

MODEL? Will the Professional Development School experience generalize to other school settings?

Our intention is to develop and demonstrate practices that can be adapted to schools with students representing a broad range of backgrounds. In this sense, the experience of a Professional Development School should "generalize" to other public schools, although its practices may well challenge their outer limits.

In other respects, however, a Professional Development School will be different from regular public schools in ways that won't generalize. A Professional Development School will, for example, have research and clinical education components not present in regular schools. Experimentation will sometimes require start-up funds or venture capital not available to other schools. As we noted, a Professional Development School may have to operate under different legal and procedural requirements. In these respects, and possibly others, Professional Development Schools will have to be different from other schools.

On the other hand, designers and faculty in a Professional Development School must think and talk routinely about the general significance of their work, to avoid becoming—and being perceived as—a hothouse of little relevance to ordinary teachers. Close working relationships between a Professional Development School and other schools could extend some practices of the Professional Development School into others and propagate new approaches in widening circles. A Professional Development School could be a center of a district-wide network for the improvement of teaching and learning.

Further, some Professional Development School faculty can become actively involved in state- and local-level policymaking; they might give advice, make the school open to school board members, legislators, and community leaders, and participate in broader district and state discussions of curriculum standards, testing practices, certification requirements, and the like. Their voices would help shape policy and practice in other schools. Without such efforts, Professional Development Schools run the risk of losing touch with the schools they are created to influence.

BURNOUT: How will the Professional Development School prevent overloaded teachers from burning out and quitting?

A Professional Development School will be based on new, ambitious conceptions of teaching and learning that are not yet fully understood. Teaching and learning for understanding implies (1) that teachers and teacher educators are deeply immersed in their subject matter; (2) that they understand and explore alternative conceptions of content and pedagogy; (3) that they shape each other's conceptions of good practice through inquiry and supervision; (4) that they operate at the "outer envelope" of knowledge, exploring the new rather than practicing the relatively safe; and (5) that their responsibilities are broadened to include inquiry, participation in professional development activities, and clinical supervision of novices.

A Professional Development School will also be based on more ambitious conceptions of the role that schools can play in the lives of children and the broader community. It will capitalize more systematically on the resources of the community. Especially a school that serves a high proportion of poor students will develop strong working relationships with community service agencies. The school may be called upon to perform a number of tasks—child care, health screening, etc.—as conditions of families and the community change.

If the net effect of these new conceptions for Professional Development Schools is simply to make the work of teaching more stressful than it already is, then they will certainly fail. One of the main reasons that serious educational innovations in the past have had little impact on practice is that they have relied largely on the energy of a few heroic educators.

Professional Development Schools will become a long-term force for the improvement of teaching and learning to the extent that they release and focus the talent, energy, and enthusiasm of excellent, ambitious teachers, teacher educators, and administrators. To accomplish these ends, our principles of design have called for:

- Innovation and flexibility in the teacher's job definition;
- New ways of organizing and allocating responsibility among teachers, administrators, and university educators;
- New ways of allocating budgets and new sources of funds;
- More efficient use of existing resources, including administrative overhead, to support instruction;
- More time for reflective professional conversation;
- New formats for assessing students and evaluating teachers; and
- Encouragement, resources, and collaboration with school and university colleagues to think through, work out, test, and revise *teachers'* own best ideas about teaching and to solve their most frustrating problems.

CAPACITY: How can a university build enough Professional Development Schools to provide all their student teachers with this superior clinical experience?

In the very short term, few universities will be able to accommodate all their teacher preparation students in a Professional Development School. We have stressed the need to develop high-quality settings and to focus the time and energy necessary to create an environment of community, inquiry, and professionalism. We think that the issues of quality must be addressed first in a setting of whatever scale is manageable for the university-school partners.

In the longer term, we believe it is possible for every new teacher to be exposed to a sustained period of supervised clinical practice in a Professional Development School in much the same way that every person preparing to be a physician is required to perform an internship and residency in a teaching hospital. As school and university faculty learn how to invent these new institutions, Professional Development School partnerships can gradually phase in enough additional sites to accommodate all the students in large programs. It will take time to develop these settings for supervised practice and to make them financially and politically viable. The effort will justify itself as the quality of teaching and learning improves.

For the long haul

There ought to be an essential continuity between good learning from preschool through graduate school. Our aim is not to turn grade school into a university seminar. The aim is to give all children the power to talk and act in the world, to be shapers of powerful meanings here and now, as well as in the future. These are traits of mind and habits of heart, qualities of intellect and character that mark the effective citizen as well as the scholar. They will not be learned well unless we learn how to make schools successful democratic learning communities—places in which all children participate.

Creating such communities is the essential task. It will take a long time. That is why we in The Holmes Group are in for the long haul. And it can only be done, in the main, by teachers, administrators, and teacher educators—although, as matters stand, they will need a great deal of help. Any single item on our agenda will be very difficult to accomplish. Taken together, the complete package we propose is formidable indeed. But the sense that we are moving in the right direction will sustain us in the struggle. The key to success will be the quality and endurance of the local coalitions.

A true learning community is always a site-built, intensely local affair. It can't be engineered from without. The dialogue that matters most is not in the texts, as essential as they are; it's what comes alive in the classroom community. Teachers mediate between the larger worlds of the disciplines and the lives of their students. They make the essential conversation. No wonder The Holmes Group is determined that they become truly educated.

Teaching for understanding for everybody's children therefore requires:

1   A transformation of teaching, so that teachers become practical intellectuals, able to help all students make knowledge and meaning in a community of learning.

2   A transformation of schools so that teachers and administrators get support to create learning communities.

3   A broadening of educational research to include partnerships of professors, administrators, and teachers investigating questions that are vital for the improvement of teaching and learning in particular schools.

4   A transformation of professional education so that school and university faculty learn how to take part in, criticize, and create learning communities for all students.

Plainly these changes are all intertwined. This, among other reasons we set forth in this volume, is why we urge a new institutional invention, sustained over time: the Professional Development School.

■|■|■

Contributors to the Report

Tomorrow's Schools Project Steering Committee

SAM BACHARACH
New York State School of Industrial
and Labor Relations, Cornell
University, Ithaca, New York

RUBEN CARRIEDO
Assistant to the Superintendent for
Planning, Research, & Evaluation
San Diego City Schools
San Diego, California

JOSEPH DELANEY
Principal, Spartanburg High School
Spartanburg, South Carolina

JOSEPH FERNANDEZ
Chancellor, New York City Board of
Education, Brooklyn. New York

SHIRLEY HILL
School of Education
University of Missouri
Kansas City. Missouri

STEVEN BOSSERT
Graduate School of Education
University of Utah
Salt Lake City. Utah

IVY H. CHAN
Special Education Teacher
Garfield Elementary School
Olympia, Washington

LISA D. DELPIT
The Institute for Urban Research
Morgan State University
Baltimore, Maryland

HAVEN HENDERSON
Director of Special Projects, Central
Park East Secondary School
New York, New York

SUSAN MOORE JOHNSON
Graduate School of Education
Harvard University
Cambridge, Massachusetts

MAGDALENE LAMPERT
College of Education, Michigan State
University, East Lansing, Michigan

PHILLIP SCHLECHTY
The Center for Leadership & School
Reform, Gheens Professional
Development Academy
Louisville, Kentucky

HENRY TRUEBA
Director, Division of Education
University of California
Davis, California

DEBORAH MEIER
Principal
Central Park East Secondary School
New York, New York

THOMAS SERGIOVANNI
Department of Education, Trinity
College, San Antonio, Texas

NANCY ZIMPHER
Department of Educational Policy &
Leadership, Ohio State University
Columbus, Ohio

Holmes Group Executive
Board Liaison Committee

DONALD ANDERSON
Dean [Coordinator, Midwest Region

Holmes Group], College of Education
Ohio State University
Columbus, Ohio

DEAN CORRIGAN
Dean (Retired), [Coordinator, South
Central Region, Holmes Group]
College of Education
Texas A & M University
College Station, Texas

GLADYS JOHNSTON
Dean [Coordinator, Far West Region
Holmes Group], College of Education
Arizona State University
Tempe, Arizona

CECIL MISKEL
Dean, School of Education
University of Michigan
Ann Arbor, Michigan

DAVID COLTON
Dean, College of Education
University of New Mexico
Albuquerque, New Mexico

MARY HARRIS
Dean, Center for Teaching and
Learning, University of North Dakota
Grand Forks, North Dakota

JUDITH LANIER
Dean/President, The Holmes Group
College of Education, Michigan State
University, East Lansing, Michigan

FRANK MURRAY
Dean [Coordinator
Southeast Region, Holmes Group]
College of Education, University of
Delaware, Newark, Delaware

ANN L. BROWN
Center for the Study of Reading

University of Illinois
Champaign, Illinois

HUGH PETRIE,
Dean [Coordinator, Northeast
Region, Holmes Group]
Faculty of Educational Studies
SUNY Buffalo, Buffalo, NY

LONNIE WAGSTAFF
Dean, College of Education
University of Cincinnati
Cincinnati, Ohio

Seminar Contributors

Seminar I: Models of Learning,
Models of Schooling, July 15–16, 1988
East Lansing, Michigan
IRIS CARL
Elementary Teacher and Math
Specialist, Houston Independent
School District, Houston, Texas

DAVID COHEN
College of Education, Michigan State
University, East Lansing, Michigan

JOSEPH D. DELANEY
Principal, Spartanburg High School
Spartanburg, South Carolina

RICHARD ELMORE
Seminar Co-Chair, College of
Education, Michigan State University
East Lansing, Michigan

JOSEPH FEATHERSTONE
College of Education, Michigan State
University, East Lansing, Michigan

JOSEPH A. FERNANDEZ

Chancellor, New York City Board of
Education, Brooklyn, New York

LILY WONG FILLMORE
Graduate School of Education
University of California
Berkeley, California

JESSIE J. FRY
Principal, Spartan Village Elementary
School, East Lansing, Michigan

EDMUND W. GORDON
Departments of Psychology and
African & Afro American Studies
Yale University
New Haven, Connecticut

WALT HANEY
School of Education, Boston College
Chestnut Hill, Massachusetts

DAVID F. LABAREE
College of Education, Michigan State
University, East Lansing, Michigan

DONALD LEMON
[National Association of Elementary
School Principals], Center for
Teaching and Learning
University of North Dakota
Grand Forks, North Dakota

SUSAN M. LLOYD
Secondary History and Music Teacher
Phillips Academy
Andover, Massachusetts

TOM MOONEY
President, Cincinnati Federation of
Teachers, Cincinnati, Ohio

REBECCA PALACIOS
Bilingual Pre-kindergarten Teacher
Zavala Special Emphasis School

Corpus Christi, Texas

THOMAS W. PAYZANT
Superintendent, San Diego City
Schools, San Diego. California

LAUREN B. RESNICK
Learning Research and Development
Center, University of Pittsburgh
Pittsburgh, Pennsylvania

MARLENE SCARDAMALIA
Centre for Applied Cognitive Science
The Ontario Institute for Studies in
Education, Toronto, Ontario

PHILLIP SCHLECHTY
The Center for Leadership & School
Reform, Gheens Professional
Development Academy
Louisville, Kentucky

LEE SHULMAN
School of Education, Stanford
University, Palo Alto, California

GARY SYKES
College of Education, Michigan State
University, East Lansing, Michigan

LAUREN YOUNG,
Seminar Co-Chair, College of
Education, Michigan State University
East Lansing, Michigan

*Seminar 2: Conceptions of Teachers'
Work and the Organization of Schools
September 22–23, 1988, East Lansing
Michigan*

ROLAND S. BARTH
Graduate School of Education
Harvard University

Cambridge. Massachusetts

DAVID C. BERLINER
College of Education, Arizona State
University, Tempe, Arizona

WILLIAM LOWE BOYD
Pennsylvania State University
University Park, Pennsylvania

RICHARD ELMORE.
Seminar Co-Chair, College of
Education, Michigan State University
East Lansing, Michigan

CORA LEE FIVE
Elementary School Teacher
Edgewood Elementary School
Scarsdale, New York

MICHAEL HUBERMAN
Faculte de Psychologie et des Sciences
de l'Education, Universite de Geneve
Geneva, Switzerland

ARTHUR JEFFERSON
Former Superintendent, Detroit
Public Schools, Detroit, Michigan

SUSAN MOORE JOHNSON
Graduate School of Education
Harvard University
Cambridge, Massachusetts

ANN LIEBERMAN
College of Education, University of
Washington, Seattle, Washington

JUDITH WARREN LITTLE
Graduate School of Education
University of California
Berkeley, California

DAN LORTIE
Department of Education, University

of Chicago, Chicago, Illinois

LUCY MATOS
Director, Central Park East One
Elementary School
New York, New York

MILBREY McLAUGHLIN
School of Education, Stanford
University, Palo Alto, California

CHARLES D. MOODY, SR.
Vice-Provost, Office of Minority
Affairs, University of Michigan
Ann Arbor, Michigan

WILLIAM P. MORRIS
[American Association of School
Administrators], Superintendent
Monroe County Intermediate
School District, Monroe, Michigan

THOMAS SERGIOVANNI
Department of Education, Trinity
College, San Antonio, Texas

GARY SYKES
College of Education, Michigan State
University, East Lansing, Michigan

SAUL M. YANOFSKY
Assistant Superintendent, White
Plains Public Schools
White Plains, New York

LAUREN YOUNG,
Seminar Co-Chair, College of
Education, Michigan State University
East Lansing, Michigan

*Seminar 3: Diversity, Equity, and the
Organization of Schools, September
25–26, 1988, East Lansing, Michigan*

MARY-DEAN BARRINGER
Resource/Demonstration Teacher
Wayne County Public Schools
Wayne, Michigan

ANN BASTIAN
New World Foundation
New York, New York

HARRIET BILLOPS
Elementary School Teacher
Christiana-Salem Elementary School
Newark, Delaware

LISA D. DELPIT
Institute for Urban Research, Morgan
State University, Baltimore, Maryland

RICHARD ELMORE,
Seminar Co-Chair, College of
Education, Michigan State University
East Lansing, Michigan

CECILIA ESTRADA
Principal, Sherman Elementary
School, San Diego, California

BARBARA B. LAWS
Art Teacher, Norfolk Public Schools
Norfolk, Virginia

HENRY M. LEVIN
School of Education, Stanford
University, Stanford, California

HARRIET P. MCADOO
School of Social Work, Howard
University, Washington, D.C.

RICHARD NAVARRO
College of Education, Michigan State
University, East Lansing, Michigan

JEANNIE OAKES
Senior Behavioral Scientist, The

RAND Corporation
Santa Monica, California

DORIS D. ROETTGER
Coordinator of Reading,
Heartland Area Education Agency #1
Johnston, Iowa

TOM SKRTIC
School of Education, University of
Kansas, Lawrence, Kansas

ROBERT ST. CLAIR
Principal, Hopkins West Junior High
School, Hopkins, Minnesota

HENRY TRUEBA
Director, Division of Education
University of California
Davis, California

CHARLES V. WILLIE
Graduate School of Education
Harvard University
Cambridge, Massachusetts

LAUREN YOUNG
Seminar Co-Chair, College of
Education, Michigan State University
East Lansing, Michigan

*Seminar 4: Family, Community, and
Schooling, October 21–22, 1988, East
Lansing, Michigan*

SUSAN BOLITZER
Family-School Coordinator, Central
Park East Secondary School
New York, New York

MARTHA DEMIENTIEFF
Teacher, Iditarod Area School District
Holy Cross, Alaska

MARTHA DOLFI
Elementary School Language Arts
Teacher, Pittsburgh Public Schools
Pittsburgh, Pennsylvania

RICHARD ELMORE,
Seminar Co-Chair, College of
Education, Michigan State University
East Lansing, Michigan

JOSEPH FEATHERSTONE
College of Education, Michigan State
University, East Lansing, Michigan

MICHELLE FINE
School of Education
University of Pennsylvania
Philadelphia, Pennsylvania

SUSAN FLORIO-RUANE
College of Education, Michigan State
University, East Lansing, Michigan

SHIRLEY BRICE HEATH
English Department, Stanford
University, Palo Alto, California

ELAINE LIFTIN
Executive Director, Bureau of
Professionalization, Programs, and
Operations, Dade County Public
Schools, North Miami Beach, Florida

JULIA MILIER
Dean, College of Human Ecology
Michigan State University
East Lansing, Michigan

EDWARD NAKANO
District Superintendent, Leeward
Oahu School District, State
Department of Education, Waipahu,
Hawaii

DAVID T. PETERSON
Principal, Wells High School
Academy, Chicago, Illinois

BOB PETERSON
Program Implementor, Milwaukee
Public Schools, Milwaukee, Wisconsin

LAWRENCE SCHWEINHART
Director, "Voices for Children" Project
High/Scope Educational Research
Foundation, Ypsilanti, Michigan

PEGGY SWOGER
Teacher, Mountain Brook Junior High
School, Birmingham, Alabama

JUANITA WAGSTAFF
Educational Program Director, Texas
Education Agency, Austin, Texas

LAUREN YOUNG
Seminar Co-Chair, College of
Education, Michigan State University
East Lansing, Michigan

*Seminar 5: Conceptions of Restructured
Schools, November 18–19, 1988, East
Lansing, Michigan*

PETER BUCHOLTZ
Principal, Palmetto Senior High
School, Miami. Florida

DAVID COHEN
College of Education, Michigan State
University, East Lansing, Michigan

RICHARD ELMORE
Seminar Co-Chair, College of
Education, Michigan State University
East Lansing, Michigan

SUSAN MOORE JOHNSON
Graduate School of Education,
Harvard University
Cambridge, Massachusetts

MAGDALENE LAMPERT
College of Education, Michigan State
University, East Lansing, Michigan

DENNIS LITTKY
Principal, Thayer High School
Winchester, New Hampshire

LINDA M. MCNEIL
Department of Education, Rice
University, Houston, Texas

DEBORAH MEIER
Principal, Central Park East Secondary
School, New York, New York

MARY HAYWOOD METZ
Department of Educational Policy
Studies, University of Wisconsin
Madison, Wisconsin

ARTHUR POWELL
Senior Research Associate, National
Association of Independent Schools
Boston, Massachusetts

MAYNARD C. REYNOLDS
College of Education, University of
Minnesota, Minneapolis, Minnesota

ALICE SELETSKY
Teacher, Central Park East Elementary
School, New York, New York

THEODORE SIZER
Department of Education, Brown
University, Providence, Rhode Island

LEONARD J. SOLO
Principal, Graham & Parks Alternative
Public School

Cambridge, Massachusetts

SUSAN STITHAM
Teacher, Lathrop High School
Fairbanks. Alaska

RICHARD WALLACE
Superintendent, Pittsburgh Public
Schools, Pittsburgh, Pennsylvania

PATRICIA YEAGER
Counselor, Edwards Middle School
Conyers, Georgia

LAUREN YOUNG
Seminar Co-Chair, College of
Education, Michigan State University
East Lansing, Michigan

*Seminar 6: New Models for the Role
and Training of the Leadership for
Tomorrow's Schools, December 9–10,
1988, East Lansing, Michigan*

BARBARA AGOR
Rochester Teacher Center
Rochester, New York

SAM BACHARACH
New York State School, Industrial &
Labor Relations, Cornell University
Ithaca, New York

STEVEN T. BOSSERT
Graduate School of Education
University of Utah
Salt Lake City, Utah

MIMI CECIL
Teacher, Hannah Middle School
East Lansing, Michigan

DAVID L. CLARK
Curry School of Education

University of Virginia
Charlottesville, Virginia

RUBY CREMASCHI-
SCHWIMMER
Principal, Lincoln Preparatory High
School, San Diego, California

LAVAUN DENNETT
Principal, Mont Lake Elementary
School, Seattle, Washington

RICHARD ELMORE
Seminar Co-Chair, College of
Education, Michigan State University
East Lansing, Michigan

LAWRENCE FELDMAN
Principal, Palmetto Elementary
School, Miami, Florida

LORETTA FODRIE
Teacher, Bruns Avenue Elementary
School, Charlotte, North Carolina

ERNESTINA FUENTES
Teacher, C.E., Rose Elementary School
Tucson, Arizona

JAMES A. KELLY
President, National Board for
Professional Teaching Standards
Detroit, Michigan

DEBORAH MEIER
Principal, Central Park East
Secondary School
New York, New York

BRAD L. MITCHELL
Department of Educational Policy
& Leadership, Ohio State University
Columbus, Ohio

THOMAS A. MULKEEN

School of Education, Fordham
University, Lincoln Center, New York

FLORA IDA ORTIZ
School of Education, University of
California, Riverside, California

CLAIRE L. PELTON
Director of Curriculum and Testing
San Jose Unified School District
San Jose, California

MARY ANNE RAYWID
School of Education, Hofstra
University, Hempstead, New York

THOMAS SERGIOVANNI
Department of Education, Trinity
University, San Antonio, Texas

ARTHUR WISE
Director, Center for the Study of the
Teaching Profession, The RAND
Corporation, Washington, D.C.

LAUREN YOUNG
Seminar Co-Chair, College of
Education, Michigan State University
East Lansing, Michigan

*Policy Perspectives on School Reform
April 14–15, 1989, Rutgers University
Graduate School of Education, New
Brunswick, New Jersey*

JOANN BARTOLETTI
Principal, West Windsor
Plainsboro High School
Princeton Junction, New Jersey

ROSEANN BENTLEY
President, National Association of
State Boards of Education
Jefferson City, Missouri

BRIAN BENZEL
Superintendent, Edmonds School
District, Lynnwood, Washington

ROSS BREWER
Director, Planning and Policy
Development, Vermont Department
of Education, Montpelier, Vermont

GLORIA CABE
General Liaison for Education
Governor's Office
Little Rock, Arkansas

HELEN CAFFREY
Executive Director, Senate Education
Committee, Harrisburg, Pennsylvania

RICHARD ELMORE
Seminar Co-Chair, College of
Education, Michigan State University
East Lansing, Michigan

SUZANNE FORTUNE
Program Development Specialist
Florida Education Association United
Tallahassee, Florida

SUSAN FUHRMAN
Seminar Co-Chair, Member
Westfield Board of Education
Director, Center for Policy Research
in Education, Eagleton Institute of
Politics, New Brunswick, New Jersey

DON GILMER
Representative, House of
Representatives, Michigan State
Legislature, Lansing, Michigan

SAM HALPERIN
Study Director, William T. Grant
Foundation, Washington, D.C.

HARRY JUDGE
Department of Educational Studies

University of Oxford, Oxford, United Kingdom

STEPHEN KAAGAN
Former Commissioner of Education
Vermont, Brattleboro, Vermont

STEPHEN KAFOURY
Member, Portland Public Schools
Board of Education, Portland, Oregon

THOMAS KEAN
Governor, State of New Jersey
Trenton, New Jersey

JAMES KELLY
President, National Board for
Professional Teaching Standards
Detroit, Michigan

JUDITH E. LANIER
President, The Holmes Group
Dean, College of Education
Michigan State University, East
Lansing, Michigan

AI MACKINNON
Coordinator, Federal Education
Legislation, New York State Education
Department, Albany, New York

ANNETTE MORGAN
Representative, Missouri House of
Representatives, Jefferson City,
Missouri

EDWARD ORTIZ
Superintendent, Santa Fe Public
Schools, Santa Fe, New Mexico

STEPHEN PRESTON
Director, Division of Personnel
Development, Georgia State
Department of Education
Atlanta, Georgia

LARS RYDELL
Office of Legislative Assistants, State
House, Augusta, Maine

CAROLYN SCHMITT
President, Kansas-National Education
Association, Topeka, Kansas

PHIL SWAIN
Member, Washington State Board of
Education, Seattle, Washington

MARLA UCELLI
Special Assistant to Governor Kean
Governor's Office, Trenton, New
Jersey

LAUREN YOUNG
College of Education, Michigan State
University, East Lansing, Michigan

■|■|■

Institutional Members of The Holmes Group

University of Alabama
University of Alaska
Arizona State University
University of Arkansas
Auburn University
Bank Street College of Education
Baylor University
University of California-Berkeley
University of California-Davis
Catholic University of America
University of Chicago
University of Cincinnati
Clark University
University of Colorado
Colorado State University
University of Connecticut
University of Delaware

Duke University
Emory University
Fordham University
George Mason University
Georgia State University
Hampton University
Harvard University
University of Hawaii
University of Houston
Howard University
University of Idaho
University of Illinois-Chicago
University of Illinois-Champaign/Urbana
University of Iowa
Iowa State University
University of Kansas
Kansas State University

Kent State University
University of Kentucky
Lehigh University
Louisiana State University
University of Louisville
University of Maine
University of Maryland
University of Massachusetts-Amherst
University of Michigan
Michigan State University
University of Minnesota
University of Mississippi
Mississippi State University
University of Missouri-Columbia
University of Missouri-Kansas City
University of Missouri-St. Louis
University of Nebraska
University of Nevada
University of New Hampshire
New Mexico State University
University of New Mexico
New York University
University of North Carolina A&T
University of North Carolina-Chapel Hill
University of North Dakota
University of Ohio
Ohio State University
University of Oklahoma
Oklahoma State University
Oregon State University
University of Oregon
University of Pennsylvania
University of Pittsburgh
Prairie View A&M University
Purdue University
University of Rhode Island

University of Rochester
Rutgers University
University of South Carolina
University of South Dakota
University of South Florida
University of Southern California
Stanford University
SUNY-Albany
SUNY-Buffalo
Syracuse University
Teachers College, Columbia University
Temple University
University of Tennessee
Texas A&M University
Texas Tech University
University of Texas-Austin
Trinity University
University of Utah
University of Vermont
University of Virginia
Virginia Commonwealth University
Virginia Polytechnic & State
University
University of Washington
Wayne State University
West Virginia University
University of Wisconsin-Madison
University of Wisconsin-Milwaukee
University of Wyoming

The Executive Board of The Holmes Group, as of January 1990, consisted *of* those persons whose names appear on the signatory page.

■|■|■

PART THREE

A Report of The Holmes Group

Tomorrow's Schools
of Education

■|■|■

Authors of the report

JUDITH TAACK LANIER
President, The Holmes Group
Distinguished Professor, Michigan
State University

CARLTON E. BROWN
Dean, School of Liberal Arts &
Education, Hampton University

FRANK B. MURRAY
Dean, College of Education
University of Delaware

HARRY JUDGE
Fellow of Brasenose College
University of Oxford

GENE I. MAEROFF
Education Consultant
The Holmes Group

GARY SYKES
Professor, College of Education
Michigan State University

HENRIETTA BARNES
Professor, College of Education
Michigan State University

LONNIE WAGSTAFF
M.K. Hage Centennial Professor
College of Education
University of Texas-Austin

■|■|■

Kathleen Devaney 1928–1994

Edward J. Meade, Jr. 1930–1994

We dedicate this report to two seminal contributors to The Holmes Group—Kathleen Devaney and Edward J. Meade, Jr.

Kathy joined The Holmes Group early on as its first full-time staffperson. Her primary responsibility was production of The Holmes Group's quarterly journal, *The Forum*. As chief editor and writer, Kathy composed each issue, either developing and writing the features herself, or editing the work of others, or soliciting stories and articles directly for publication. In pursuit of leads, Kathy attended many regional and most national meetings, visited many campuses, and got to know many of the deans and faculty on Holmes Group campuses. Behind the scenes she served as wise counsel to The Holmes Group leadership and Board of Directors, participating in all their deliberations, producing reports of and input for meetings. She contributed to the writing of many other Holmes reports, assisted in planning many Holmes Group events, and generally served as the connection among the national, regional, and campus activities. In all these capacities she came to know more about the actual working of The Holmes Group at all levels than anyone else.

Ed served from the outset as one of The Holmes Group's chief champions. First, as senior officer of the Ford Foundation, he made the initial grants that helped launch The Holmes Group, participating in the early deliberations that led to its creation. Then as private consultant he established the Accountability Review Panel that provided external evaluation and guidance to the group. Ed regularly attended Holmes Group meetings and acted as senior consultant on a wide range of matters, from organization and management to strategic planning to goal setting and vision-building. He helped connect The Holmes Group to powerful external constituencies in the foundation, corporate, association, and government worlds.

Kathy and Ed represented the best of The Holmes Group; they embodied our central hopes and aspirations. To The Holmes Group Kathy brought the instincts and experiences of a networker. She long believed that good ideas and practices in education spring up all over, that education is of necessity an intensely local affair, drawing on the hearts and minds of individuals working in particular contexts. Yet she also recognized the necessity for outside support and resources, and for methods of sharing and spreading good work from one locale to another. Her genius lay in identifying and making known what others were doing, then putting them in touch with each other. Kathy saw the potential of The Holmes Group as a network of learners, as a kind of nationwide professional development project that linked teacher educators to one another around an exciting but difficult and complex agenda for reform. Without Kathy, this potential, founded in respect for the far-flung work of many, never would have materialized. She was the voice of The Holmes Group, the source of courage to us all.

Ed supplied a bracing, tough-minded critique of our efforts, together with an unflagging faith in our mission. In a time of deep skepticism about university professional education, he insisted on its importance. And, he believed we were on the right track with the principles we espoused. Yet Ed also pressed us continually to stay true to our ideals and to examine honestly the progress we were making, the troubles we were encountering. Every reform effort worth its name requires a loving critic who both believes in the endeavor but is willing to challenge the effort, staying alert to any backsliding and weakening of resolve. Ed was the conscience of The Holmes Group, calling it to account on behalf of its founding ideals.

Kathy and Ed were indispensable colleagues and helpmates in the work accomplished. We will continue to miss them terribly in the work ahead.

■|■|■

Preface

The Holmes Group grew out of a series of meetings and deliberations a decade ago of a small group of education deans on the enduring problems associated with the generally low quality of teacher preparation in the United States. Their initial discussions focused on the lax standards that continue to be tolerated. Weak accreditation policies and practices and the historic indifference to teach preparation on the part of the major research universities received special attention. Weak accreditation arrangements and the low priority assigned to teacher education at major universities were part of the equation, and, in the end, this connection became the focus of the group's initial work.

Over a three-year period, the deans, in consultation with many others, saw that problems they faced were so great and complicated that their solution would require a long-term commitment of like-minded institutions to a reform agenda. Thus, a plan was proposed for a consortium, The Holmes Group, and a set of goals emerged. The consortium wished to see nothing less than the transformation of teaching from an occupation into a genuine profession that would serve the educational needs of children. To this end, the deans sought to align themselves with other organizations, agencies, and institutions that supported their goals and general directions.

The consortium sought to provide the nation with teachers and other educational specialists who have all the attributes of genuine professionals—the knowledge, prestige, autonomy, and earnings that accrue to competent people who are engaged in important matters that are beyond the talent or training of the ordinary person. Those educated at Holmes Group universities should be entrusted fully with the education of their pupils and students. They would be persons who, by talent and training, could be fully responsive to immediate demands of the classroom. They would make significant pedagogical and educational policy decisions because they would be competent to make them and because no other person would be more qualified or in a better position to make them.

Thus, the consortium became organized around twin goals: the simultaneous reform of the education of educators and the reform of schooling. It assumed that these reforms would prosper if the nation's colleges and universities were committed to the education of professionals who work in the schools. It assumed also, and somewhat rashly perhaps, that teacher education programs would be different in Holmes institutions for all the reasons that make these institutions so academically powerful in every other respect. They are institutions that attract more than their share of academically talented students; they have the faculty who, on the whole, are the nation's most authoritative sources of information in their fields; they command substantial resources; and in the case of education, they are the institutions that have educated and will continue to educate large numbers of university faculty for the professoriate in education. A consortium of institutions that educate teacher educators was needed, if only to ensure that the teachers of teachers could do their graduate work in institutions with exemplary teacher education programs.

Bearing these points in mind, the deans recognized that powerful forces worked against major reform years ago and now. One of these forces was the dramatic increase in the demand for teachers that occurred over the decade. If states and localities responded to this demand as they had in the past by giving certification to unqualified persons and allowing certified teachers to teach outside their fields of competence, then efforts to reform teacher education would be substantially undermined once again.

Another force that countered a major reform of teacher education was, ironically, the education reform movement itself. The proposals for education reform suggested that attracting higher quality persons to teaching was a key component—a recommendation the deans endorsed as well. Reformers recommended in addition that attention be given to stronger preparation in the liberal arts, increased subject matter competence, better testing and assessment, increased clinical experience, extended programs, differentiated career opportunities, raising salaries, and the like. But until recently few of the reformers had seen that these issues were interrelated and more complex than each by itself would suggest, because each by itself could become a superficial and symbolic reform that could actually worsen the problems it was meant to solve. The reform proposals would fail, as they had in the past, because they attempt education reform by simply telling teachers and everyone else what to do, rather than by empowering them to do what must be done. And they would fail because the reforms amounted to little more than slogans that could be interpreted in ways that require little actual change in the way schooling is conducted. Few molds were broken and the key features of American education—universal compulsion and group instruction—remain in place in the nation's 18,000 school districts.

The quality of teachers, of course, is tied to the quality of their education, and the deans could not improve teacher education very much by changing colleges of education without changing, as well, the universities, the credentialing systems, and the schools themselves. Almost everything had to change: the rewards and career opportunities for teachers; the standards, nature, and substance of professional education; the quality and coherence of the liberal arts and subject matter fields; and the professional certification and licensing apparatus. They must be changed in mutually supportive ways that in fact will yield the kind of educators we envision.

The policy changes recommended by reformers are only the first stage of lasting reform. Regrettably, reform efforts often end with the publication of a report. Past attempts at large-scale reform show that changes imposed from above, without the concurrence and collaboration of those who must implement them, have limited and unpredictable effects. Changes in the structure and content of teacher education depend upon long-term and genuine reform efforts by policymakers, scholars, and practitioners, and for this reason, The Holmes Group incorporated itself as a long-term regional and national organization.

Members of The Holmes Group recognized that there would be many mistakes, false starts, and unanticipated problems with their proposed agenda. They also recognized that solutions that work in one setting inevitably require adaptation to work in another setting, and for this reason, each member's plan for achieving the group's goals would be different. They foresaw that in the years ahead they would learn much from each other about the strengths and limits of the proposed agenda. Hence, The Holmes Group was born committed to exploring a range of alternative solutions organized around five themes and to sharing the outcomes of their experiments with themselves and with others.

In May 1986, The Holmes Group published *Tomorrow's Teachers*, which set forth their vision of good teaching, analyzed the obstacles to attaining it, and recommended an agenda of actions. They issued invitations to over 100 research universities to join a national not-for-profit consortium that would support members in long-term work to enact the agenda. More than ninety universities accepted and the consortium was formed at a constituting conference in Washington, D.C., in January 1987.

What did Holmes Group universities commit themselves to do?

Resolving to work in their own institutions for the professionalization of teaching, Holmes Group members joined in implementing the five goals set forth in the Group's manifesto, *Tomorrow's Teachers:*

1 Make teaching intellectually sound.

Require that prospective teachers gain a broad, coherent liberal arts foundation that incorporates enduring, multicultural values and forms of inquiry, and that is taught to a depth of understanding that enables them so to teach.

Require that prospective teachers study the subjects they will teach in depth and earn a bachelor's degree in at least one academic subject. Place that subject in a broad context of knowledge and culture. Teach that content so that undergraduate students learn to inquire about it on their own and to connect it with related subjects and issues of value.

Present the study and practice of teaching in a coherent sequence of courses that integrate research findings about learning and teaching and that demonstrate how to select and shape particular content knowledge into clear, challenging lessons for children and adolescents.

Prepare teacher candidates—through their liberal arts, education studies, and clinical experiences—to work with culturally and socio-economically diverse students.

Give teacher candidates realistic, demanding, well-coached assignments in classrooms. These should be long enough, complex enough, and varied enough to prepare them to demonstrate success with students who are different from themselves and for whom school learning is difficult.

The Holmes Group does not prescribe that the start of professional studies must be delayed until graduate school. In fact, many Holmes members have designed new education programs that students enter as sophomores or juniors and continue in post-baccalaureate studies and supervised internships. Nor does the consortium propose that new teachers must have a master's degree before being recommended for a teaching license.

Holmes Group institutions commit themselves not to a prescribed structure for teacher education, but to making professional programs for school educators— initial preparation through continuing education—a central mission of the school of education. This entails critical rethinking of the existing content of professional preparation programs. It means working with liberal arts professors and with practicing teachers and administrators to devise programs that are academically and professionally solid and integrated. That combination of academic and field experiences must be conceived to encourage a life of learning for educators and quality learning opportunities for students.

In the education studies curricula, all Holmes institutions emphasize the knowledge that has been gained in recent research on learning and teaching, and personal application of that knowledge in carefully studied circumstances in the schools. The structures of the programs vary, however, within and among Holmes institutions. Preparation programs accommodate both young and older, career-changing candidates, recognizing their differing backgrounds and professional aims.

2 Recognize difference in teachers' knowledge, skill, and commitment.

Structure internships and induction-year experiences so that beginner teachers receive the assistance and supervision they need. Bring talented and experienced teachers into partnership with the university to tap their expertise and wisdom in helping to teach professional courses, to supervise student and first-year teachers' classroom work, and to participate in research at schools.

Prepare experienced teachers for advancement in their careers through leadership roles in the schools where they teach. For instance, teacher leaders may assist their fellow teachers to reflect on or reorganize or enrich their teaching, to teach in teams or interdisciplinary groups, and to participate in making the school's instructional decisions.

3 Create relevant and intellectually defensible standards of entry into teaching.

Develop multiple evaluation instruments, measuring diverse kinds of competence, for use at several stages: admittance to teacher education, admittance to student teaching and to internship in a school, and recommendation for a teaching license.

Work to prevent testing from discouraging or excluding minority candidates from teaching. We take three tacks: (1) Develop more comprehensive measures of proficiency in teaching. (2) Mount extraordinary efforts to identify, prepare for college, and recruit students of color who would make good teachers, and then finance and sustain them throughout their teacher preparation. (3) Mount similar efforts to make faculties of education more representative of minority populations.

Work for the replacement of standardized tests as licensing exams. These minimalist tests, in use in many states, have little value in predicting the future performance of beginning teachers. They do not guarantee the public of a teacher's capability to teach, nor do these exams indicate how well a teacher education program prepares teachers.

4 Connect schools of education to the schools.

Create Professional Development Schools and working partnerships among university faculty, practicing teachers, and administrators that are designed around the systematic improvement of practice.

These Professional Development Schools, analogous to teaching hospitals in the medical profession, will bring practicing teachers and administrators together with university faculty in partnerships based on the following principles:

- **Reciprocity**, or mutual exchange and benefit between research and practice;
- **Experimentation**, or willingness to try new forms of practice and structure;
- **Systematic inquiry**, or the requirement that new ideas be subject to careful study and validation; and
- **Student diversity**, or commitment to the development of teaching strategies for a broad range of children with different backgrounds, abilities, and learning styles.

These schools will serve as setting for teaching professionals to test different instructional arrangements, for novice teachers and researchers to work under the guidance of gifted practitioners, for the exchange of professional knowledge between university faculty and practitioners, and for the development of new structures designed around the demand of a new profession.

5 Make schools better places for practicing teachers to work and learn.

Make partnerships with the teachers and administrators in particular schools. Develop these as Professional Development Schools—regular but ambitious public elementary and secondary schools where novice teachers learn to teach and where university and school faculty members together investigate questions of teaching and learning that arise in the school.

Revise the professional education of school administrators and other professionals who work in schools so that they can recognize and enhance professionalism in teachers and work in partnership with university faculty to inquire into and invent new methods and structures for their schools.

What's different about a Professional Development School?

The term is meant to convey a school devoted to the development of both novice and experienced professionals. In such schools, experienced teachers, conscious of membership in a profession, help teach and induct new members. Also, by pulling together and demonstrating their know-how, by questioning their assumptions and routines, by taking part in research and development projects, they keep on learning to teach. They contribute their experience and wisdom to the profession's systematic fund of knowledge.

The term implies a realistic setting conducive to long-term research and development aimed at the improvement of all schooling. Ideal principles to guide the design of a Professional Development School are set forth in The Holmes Group's 1990 report, *Tomorrow's Schools.*

Teaching and learning for understanding

All the school's students participate seriously in the kind of learning that allows one to go on learning for a lifetime. This may well require major revisions in the school's curriculum and instruction.

Creating a learning community

The ambitious kind of teaching and learning we hope for will take place in a sustained way for large numbers of children only when classrooms and schools are thoughtfully organized as communities of learning.

Teaching and learning for understanding for everybody's children

A major commitment of the Professional Development School will be overcoming the educational and social barriers raised by an unequal society.

Continuing learning by teachers, teacher educators, and administrators

In the Professional Development School, adults are expected to go on learning, too.

Thoughtful, long-term inquiry into teaching and learning by school and university faculty working as partners

This is essential to the professional lives of teachers, administrators, and teacher educators. The Professional Development School faculty working as partners will promote reflection and research on practice as a central aspect of the school.

Inventing a new institution

The foregoing principles call for such profound changes that the Professional Development School will need to devise for itself a different kind of organizational structure, supported over time by enduring alliances of all the institutions with a stake in better professional education.

In the five years since the publication of *Tomorrow's Schools*, The Holmes Group has been struggling with the implications of its founding goals and principles about the nation's teachers and schools for itself. How does our vision of tomorrow's teachers and schools affect the design and operation of university-based colleges and schools of education? What follows is our analysis of how university-based schools of education need to change if they are to deliver on the promises made in *Tomorrow's Teachers* and *Tomorrow's Schools*.

■|■|■

Acknowledgments

Several years of study and consensus-building deliberations culminate in this third report of the Holmes' trilogy on quality professional education for educators. The school and university faculty from over ninety leading schools of education have participated in the deliberations leading to this report, and we benefited greatly from their invaluable contributions. But from among the many who made this work possible, a number deserve our special mention.

In addition to the particular contributions of Kathy Devaney and Ed Meade, to whom we have dedicated this report, we also wish to publicly acknowledge and thank Hugh Price—formerly with the Rockefeller Foundation but now President of the National Urban League. Hugh not only encouraged our work, but helped bring together the three foundations that collaboratively funded the deliberative and empirical activities that undergird the work. Mildred Hudson of the DeWitt Wallace-Reader's Digest Fund was also very helpful and supportive, as was Marla Ucelli of the Rockefeller Foundation, and Alison Bernstein of the Ford Foundation. Their patience and continued support of our work during times of controversy and doubt were especially critical during difficult times. We owe them our sincere gratitude.

Anne Dowling and Sue Bratone at the Philip Morris Corporation deserve our thanks for helping secure funds for distribution and dissemination of our work. And once again, many faculty, staff, and students at Michigan State University warrant our appreciation for their continued help with the complexities and communications associated with these intensely collaborative efforts. Gail Nutter and Brad West continued to help with the financial challenges inherent in facilitating work among multiple foundations and a great many universities, as they did for *Tomorrow's Teachers* and *Tomorrow's Schools*. Joan Eadie took the lead in managing the people and communications around our many meetings throughout the United States, with able help from Joanne DiFranco and Elva Hernandez. Dawn Gregus, Tiffany Jackson, Erin Rooney, and Michelle Topp were among the wonderful students who helped with the many office tasks, errands, and phone-fax-&-email messages exchanged during the course of our work. But no one deserves more special recognition for her steadfast contribution to this effort than Helen Geiger. As the administrative assistant to The Holmes Group, Helen never ceased to contribute her many talents, loyal advice, and consistent help to all of the project staff, institutional members, guest advisors, reporters, and other interested parties concerned with this report. She picked up added responsibilities when other staff were unable to come through, and always did so with integrity and sincere commitment to her professional ideals. The Holmes Group Board of Directors and our membership are grateful.

■|■|■

Foreword

Tomorrow's Schools of Education describes our hopes and expectations for greatly improved professional schools for educators. These new professional schools, "TSEs" as we call them in this day of acronyms, are the kinds of university-based education schools America needs in a time of greatly increased demand for better learning. Students today must know and do more than their parents ever did in school—and today's schools must meet higher standards than their predecessors. Educators must be better equipped to meet these increased challenges. They need better knowledge and know-how for a changing world of work in schools—and they need the modern technologies that enable them to work more efficiently and more effectively in the interests of the young.

Over 1,200 institutions of higher education and a growing number of non-profit corporations now educate teachers for work in America's schools. Some offer excellent preparation for those who teach. Others provide shoddy preparation that angers and embarrasses those who care deeply about the minds and welfare of America's young. Quality control over the programs that educate and screen educators remains notoriously bad and almost anyone is allowed to prepare and screen those who teach our nation's children. The voices of youngsters go unheard while adults who should act on their behalf duck the inevitable controversies that must be faced to ensure quality educators in every classroom of every public school in America. When unqualified or incompetent teachers oversee children's learning, the children never fully recover.

These circumstances prompt two questions. Why do so many institutions want to prepare teachers and other educators? Why do professional educators and reputable professional schools allow those of ill-repute to continue? The answer to the first question is easy. Many people besides the quality-conscious mount teacher education programs because they are profitable. The education of teachers and other educators is big business in a nation that employs over three million educators. Dollar signs flash in the eyes of those looking for good market opportunities. Where else can you produce something, or offer services, and not have to be accountable for the quality of the product or services? In what other fields can you ignore effects on clients or customers and pay no consequences? The reasons why the education profession and the nation's good education schools allow those of questionable integrity to continue are more complicated.

This report tackles head-on the problem of uneven quality in the education and screening of educators—and proposes what might be done to correct it. The report does not pretend, of course, to solve the problem, but it launches a first offensive. It takes on the nation's leading universities that prepare teachers and the most influential education leaders in America. Most of these institutions are permitted to offer advanced graduate training, thereby supposedly ensuring competence at the edge of the nation's most trustworthy educational knowledge and expertise.

Our group is made up of about 250 institutions, or about one-fifth of the total that prepare and screen educators. Located in many of the nation's most powerful universities, these schools of education prepare teachers and other leaders to serve the nation's schools and to become faculty in America's schools, colleges, and departments of education. It is this one-fifth of the universities that we write about here and challenge to be TSEs.

Tomorrow's Schools of Education speaks directly to and about these 250 institutions, challenging them to become consumed with a conscience and commitment to quality, first in universities like their own and then in others throughout the nation. The universities in which these education schools reside have a tremendous effect on the remaining thousand places that educate educators in America. They develop the knowledge base for the field of education. They have great influence over the education policy that gets set in the nation. They prepare and credential—for good or ill—the nation's most influential leaders in the education field, those in schools, education schools, and state departments of education.

This report challenges these institutions to raise their standards of quality and to make important changes in all four of the education common places in their ed schools—in their curriculum, faculty, location of much of their work, and in the student body. The proposals suggest that education students have for too long been learning too little of the right things in the wrong place at the wrong time. To correct these problems, a number of universities are already taking steps to:

Design A New Curriculum: Here studies focus on the learning needs of the young and the development of educators across their careers—replacing studies less focused on youngsters' learning and development, organized by segregated roles for educators, and centered on initial credentialing.

Develop A New Faculty: Now a clear minority, the numbers of university faculty who are as at home working in the public schools as on the university campus will come to comprise the majority of the education school faculty. Board-certified teachers and other qualified practitioners will join these faculty as colleagues in conducting important research and in better educating the nation's educators.

Recruit A New Student Body: Before the next generation of educators retires, almost half of the nation's youngsters (forty-six percent) will be from one or another minority group. The nation's education workforce—teachers, administrators, counselors, and those who educate educators—must be more diverse than today. Programs must be mounted to actively recruit, retain, and graduate highly diverse groups of education leaders at initial and advanced levels.

Create New Locations for Much of Their Work: Instead of working predominantly on campus and occasionally in schools across the American landscape, the faculty and students will do much of their work in Professional Development Schools. These are real public schools selected and joined in partnership with the university for their innovative spirit and serious intent to improve the quality of learning for educators and students.

Build A New Set of Connections To Those They Serve: Long too remote from the professionals and public they serve, the education schools will together form an interconnecting set of networks at local, state, regional, and national levels—to ensure better work and accountability.

Working through the leadership in their education schools, the institutions organizing this report call for a nationwide effort to reexamine and step up the universities' contributions to the schools. The universities that develop education knowledge, influence education policy, and prepare teachers and other leaders for our nation's schools and education schools must overcome "business as usual" to meet the challenge of these truly unusual times in education. The indisputable link between the quality of elementary and secondary schools and the quality of the education schools must be acknowledged—and we must respond.

■|■|■

A New Beginning

America worries deeply about its elementary and secondary schools, a concern that ultimately must reflect on the institutions that prepare teachers, administrators, counselors, and others who work in those schools. Much like the nation's automobile industry, university-based education schools long took their markets for granted—in turn, giving insufficient attention to quality, costs, and innovation. And so we expect that universities cannot help but squirm as they ponder the implications of this report, detailing how they have gone awry and what they should do to reconstitute themselves.

No one dons the hair shirt of self-criticism for reasons of comfort. In effect, The Holmes Group, a consortium of universities doing educational research and educator preparation, acknowledges by publishing this report that its member institutions, despite hard-won improvements, need to make further strides. This concession, however, should come as no revelation. The ills of American education are cited from the rooftops. The record of more than a decade of education reform leaves the public deeply concerned about its elementary and secondary schools. People have little confidence in the questionable remedies grasped by those who think almost anything will be better than what exists.

The sense of desperation is fueled by the mood of a frustrated public who believe that the nation will pay dearly if the schools don't improve. They read reports telling them that American students compare unfavorably with peers in other countries. They realize that only limited numbers of low-skill jobs are available for students who leave high schools because of failure, boredom, or economic need. They know that tens of thousands of students who were processed through high schools must take remedial courses in college. They hear about a high-tech future for which they worry that their children are not being adequately prepared. They wonder about the ability of the public schools to accommodate the needs of poor children, minority children, gifted and talented students, pupils with disabilities, and children of limited English proficiency. Repeated urgent calls for education reform have convinced Americans that a challenge of unprecedented proportions confronts the schools.

Universities must share the blame for the perils, real and imagined, facing the public schools. Like the auto industry before them, universities will have to restructure and make drastic adjustments. They will have to change the ways in which they educate professionals for work in the public schools. One may argue, of course, over the degree of culpability that higher education bears for the ills of schooling, for certainly the schoolhouses of America are not solely the dominion of educators. Society itself casts a powerful and pervasive spell over the classroom, and educators must struggle mightily to overcome the most negative of societal influences. But no amount of excusatory rhetoric can exonerate the universities from a share of the responsibility for the shortcomings of public education. Realistically, discussions of how to improve the schools must take account of the people who make their livelihoods in the schools—as well as those at the university whose careers involve educating school professionals for that work.

The United States, after all, devotes a substantial portion of its higher education programs to studies that result in the awarding of academic credentials for educators. Education schools contribute to some ten percent of all bachelor's degrees, twenty-five percent of all master's degrees, and twenty percent of all doctoral degrees—degrees that go to people who work in the nation's schools, universities, social and governmental agencies, and a variety of institutions. And in a good number of cases, universities allocate insufficient resources to programs preparing these people even though the resulting credentials produce employment and increased pay for educators. It is unclear, though, how this arrangement leads to better schooling and better learning in America's elementary and secondary classrooms.

We begin this brief with a radical premise: Institutions preparing educators should either adopt reforms that link their educational contributions closely with improved schooling for America's young—along many of the lines proposed in these pages— or surrender their franchise. More of the same on the part of universities and their education schools cannot be tolerated and will only exacerbate the problems of public education. Schools of education, after all, accepted responsibility for the preparation of school professionals early in this century and are partners in a social contract that they must abrogate if they are unable to fulfill their end of the bargain. Society relies on education schools to help improve the schooling of children, but of what value are education schools if they prove unable to contribute significantly to enhancing the quality and social responsiveness of elementary and secondary education?

We assume this drastic stance precisely because we believe that the country needs university-based education schools and that they can make a difference in the teaching and learning of children. In fact, some institutions already have stirred the winds of change and are now making such a difference. But most others have yet to demonstrate a commitment beyond the appearance of change. Schools of education that reexamine their societal contribution to each new generation of young citizens and refocus their mission accordingly can, indeed, help solve the problems that afflict the public schools. This means not only proclaiming worthy goals, but also developing sensible strategies, making sound contributions, and setting standards of accountability. The Holmes Group commits itself as an organization to being part of this response. For if we don't join others in answering the challenge, we fear for America's ability to lift the fortunes and improve the learning circumstances of the young.

The United States has been awash with education reports and proposals for change since the nation declared itself educationally at risk in 1983. Spending for elementary and secondary education during the intervening years swelled by more than forty percent in inflation-adjusted dollars and, while some promising signs of progress are apparent, the "rising tide of mediocrity" still threatens our schools. Most of what happens in many schools today remains caught in the undertow of the status quo. Changes, by and large, flitter at the margins, touching only the edges of teaching and learning.

Action must replace inertia. The education school should cease to act as a silent agent in the preservation of the status quo. By offering courses and awarding degrees to educators in the absence of demonstrated evidence of ability and without a commitment to apply what we currently know from research and theory, the university tacitly affirms current practices. As a preparation ground for professionals, the education school must act as a partner with innovating schools to prepare and screen educators in settings that exemplify trustworthy practice. And as a preparation ground for professionals, the education school must unequivocally embrace the kind of academic preparation that readies one to work comfortably with the ideas and technologies appropriate to an advanced society on the brink of a new century. Medicine delves into the molecular level, architecture renders on computers in three dimensions, law searches for precedents on LEXIS. Many professions and occupations have been altered to such an extent that neither practitioners nor future practitioners can afford to cling to old ways. Meanwhile, far too many of those who prepare teachers and other educators continue to dwell in a bygone era, guided by outmoded conceptions of teaching and learning, and not conversant with the nature of professional work in schools.

Too many education schools maintain low standards for the public schools in which their students carry out apprenticeships. They often place students in schools where the conditions of work are almost identical to those encountered generations ago. In these outdated schools, the dominant work confines teachers to isolated classrooms, and the primary technology remains chalk and eraser though the slate has turned from black to green. These future teachers and principals learn in schools where understanding is sacrificed at the altar of coverage and knowledge is measured through the expediency of true/false, short-answer, and multiple-choice responses. Some universities still allow their education students to learn exclusively in monocultural schools when today's educators must prepare themselves to educate the most highly diverse culture on earth. Relevant university theory on individual differences has little effect, even if taught well, when apprentices get their first taste of teaching in schools that remain disconnected from the real lives and needs of children, particularly minority, poor, and non-English speaking children. The university's standards for field placements must acknowledge the diversity of America's next generation, recognizing that many schools today house a Babel of languages among their pupils.

Research and development studied by future educators in university classes fades quickly when mentors in the schools show disdain for such knowledge, or when school policies and practices run counter to the ways the university faculty claim they should be. The university faculty and the schools with which they form partnerships must ensure that theory and practice converge. For educational knowledge to be useful to future and practicing educators, it must first be credible and effective in helping them think and act more successfully in the interest of youngsters' learning. The school of education must link its educational research and development to the service of school improvement and to the preparation of university students who will learn and be evaluated for their knowledge of the changing roles and responsibilities in the schools.

Kansas State University's Colleges of Education and Arts and Sciences have entered a partnership with the Manhattan-Ogden School District to transform teacher preparation and the district's elementary schools. The venture is based on the premise that education should be viewed as a continuum from kindergarten through

> university, and that improvement in one part of the sys-
> tem is not possible without improvement throughout.

The enormity of the challenge that society poses today requires indomitable effort on the part of educators. Schools and education schools must address these challenges. Many children arrive in elementary school lacking the bare essentials of good health. The media seduce children with messages of immediate gratification. Illicit drugs poison their will and violence cuts them down before puberty. Youngsters hardly finished playing with dolls bear children. The old order will not suffice.

In a world that has changed, education schools, too, must change. School professionals must now learn to educate effectively a new breed of student. Many of those who would have become dropouts in former years now remain enrolled. Academic demands have risen and instructional strategies must be adjusted to fresh realities. Research in education and the cognitive sciences sheds new light on ways to improve student learning and understanding. Those who go into the public schools to make their careers must know how to provide the best possible education to a cross-section of children who personify a new America.

Simply put, the need for greatly increased, higher quality teaching and learning expands at a rate much faster than the education system's ability to offer better teaching and learning. While some achievement statistics have improved, the performance of too many students resembles a swimmer who treads water just enough to keep from going under. Some youngsters confidently carry themselves far out into the academic sea with bold, sure strokes while others risk being swept away by the next wave. The country cannot afford such uneven performance among its students. The education system has to discover and implement ways for many, many more to catch up and maintain the pace. This is why The Holmes Group and many others advocate the formation of Professional Development Schools to increase the amount and influence of educational research, development, and demonstration addressing the needs of America's children, especially those at greatest risk.

The kind of far-reaching change needed to deal with new situations requires concentrated and coordinated reform that cuts across many parts of the system at once. Piecemeal reform has proven inadequate because of the web of connections among the system's various parts—curriculum, pedagogy, assessment, texts and materials, and professional development, for example. All of these parts must be tied together. Attempts to change only one part at a time are obstructed by the stasis of the larger system. Imagine, if you will, a new math curriculum that calls for a different kind of teaching so as to stress problem-solving, a curriculum in which performance assumes the dual character of both learning the material and being assessed on one's learning. New books and materials and more demanding instructional assignments are other pieces that make up this puzzle. Ideally, the pieces will fit together so the picture makes sense. Successful improvement requires coordinated changes in all of these various parts.

Changes of the kind we describe depend on the knowledge, skills, and dedication of the professionals charged with carrying them out. If education schools do not equip school professionals to perform in new ways, then as surely as fifth grade follows fourth grade, most educators will continue to regard teaching as show and tell, learning as passive listening, knowledge as a litany of facts, tests as memory samples, and accountability as something about which only students must concern themselves. If the education school continues to equip people for organizing and managing schools as the factories of old, plans for improvement will be dead on arrival.

How can university-based schools of education stand by and not lend their support to those in the public schools who struggle to overcome practices and policies they know are hopelessly dated? Some education schools, joined by their counterparts in the arts and sciences, have begun developing innovation sites in Professional Development Schools. But support for broad-scale outreach to the schools is inadequate, even as policymakers mouth the expectation that students, regardless of race, gender, ethnicity, or social class can and must learn and that educational institutions will make fair and reasonable opportunity for such learning. Little changes, even though new understandings from educational research provide insights about learning and about ways in which it can be brought about more effectively to meet ambitious learning goals.

Elementary and secondary schools must transform themselves into places where teaching and learning take more complex and more flexible forms, where teachers guide students in the development of curiosity, and where teachers engage students with important ideas that enrich their daily lives. Such learning is not the stuff of drills and worksheets, but of learning rooted in rich experiences for students. Technology in all of its glorious manifestations can perform as a partner in promoting learning of this sort. But the public remains largely unaware of these possibilities because too few examples are available for them to observe as a new norm.

If members of The Holmes Group and other leading colleges and universities in each of the fifty states joined in partnership with the state's most innovative elementary and secondary schools to foment bold but responsible change in education, then surely the public would know and understand that a learning revolution was under way. The public has already seen abundant evidence of the capacity of the great universities for research and innovation in a host of areas. Collectively, the universities and the schools that educate educators—working together to ensure that research and development guides and accompanies change—could push aside the boulders that block the path of change in the public schools. A field that accounts for a tenth of our nation's undergraduates and almost a quarter of our nation's graduate students will have significant impact if it rises to the challenge. It is time for the universities to weigh in on the side of elementary and secondary education as they have done for medicine, engineering, agriculture, management, and other fields. It is time for universities to modify whatever policies they must concerning research, teaching load, and tenure to make these changes in quality possible.

For the universities, altering the way they go about educating educators means a reordering of priorities. Universities are accustomed to conducting research and development activities on behalf of other fields, but they give short shrift to the study of teaching and learning as it is carried out in the public schools. Furthermore, the research of education schools disproportionately concerns itself with describing the troubles of the education system as it now operates, rather than exploring new avenues for more fruitful teaching and learning. Universities will have to redirect their investment in education R&D to take account of long-term applied work on what needs to be done to improve the public schools. Also, they must confront the schism between educational research and educational practice.

As matters now stand, especially in many of the most research-intensive institutions, the faculty who get time and opportunity for educational research often have little responsibility for preparing practicing educators and may, in fact, hold teacher preparation in disdain. Meanwhile, the faculty members involved predominantly in teacher preparation get little if any time to conduct research on the problems of teaching and learning and hardly any encouragement to study and develop solutions to these problems. As a consequence, too many faculty members educating teachers have limited entree to the study of the most serious problems of the schools and do not investigate the innovations that might remedy such problems. And while all professional schools struggle with the distancing effects of academic specialization and the subsequent loss of concern about and understanding of broad societal problems, educaction can ill afford this lack of connection. Education is an expansive public undertaking in America and requires broad study and clear application of its inquiry to the problems of practice.

Universities and their education schools let down America when they fall short in these ways. Public education, to a great extent, becomes what higher education leads it to be through the educators it prepares and the knowledge and tools it contributes to school improvement. Just as medical schools created teaching hospitals and agriculture schools created experimental stations and extension services to lead their fields in significant ways, so, too, can education schools fashion new mechanisms for aiding elementary and secondary education.

All of this is not to say that serious participation in education renewal by some colleges and universities and by individual faculty members has not been noteworthy or appreciated. Or that government, corporations, and philanthropic foundations have not participated in trying to simultaneously improve schools and education schools. These contributions, however, emerge in stark relief against a larger background of business as usual in far too many university-based schools of education. Elementary and secondary schools and their education schools require something more extensive and more enduring than casual connections. The public schools need the aid and collaboration of colleagues from higher education who regard the schools as professional education's paramount concern—and the professional schools need the aid and collaboration of colleagues from elementary and secondary education who value quality educational research and professional education.

> Work by teacher educators from the University of North Dakota's Center for Teaching and Learning with Lake Agassiz Elementary School in Grand Forks has constructed curriculum increasingly responsive to student interests as documented through portfolios and parent consultations.

Thus, the member institutions of The Holmes Group rededicate themselves to the renewal of professional education for those who work in America's elementary and secondary schools. We will join other universities and schools that share our commitment to ensuring that youngsters throughout our states and regions have opportunity to learn from highly qualified educators. This means that students in education programs must experience learning environments where learners search for meaning, appreciate uncertainty, and inquire responsibly so they can recreate such circumstances for their own students. It also means that our graduates must possess the ability to provide the knowledge and skills needed to give even the most downtrodden children the opportunity to advance through education. The public schools remain the last best hope of this country and, in setting the following goals for Tomorrow's School of Education, we launch a crusade in quest of exemplary professional practice.

Goal I: To make education schools accountable to the profession and to the public for the trustworthy performance of their graduates at beginning and advanced levels of practice
Competence in subject matter requires that education students experience first-rate learning in the liberal arts. Some colleges and universities still offer prospective educators watered-down studies in the arts and sciences, especially at upper levels. Sometimes they segregate education students from others studying the same discipline or provide them with less challenging content or don't give them the chance to study with leading professors in the disciplines. Prospective educators taking a content course in English or chemistry or mathematics should sit alongside liberal arts majors even at advanced stages. Education credentials should not be printed with shoddy ink. The TSE will therefore refuse to admit or recommend for a teaching license

any student whose studies in the arts and sciences have been diluted in any way whatsoever.

Likewise, the education courses for those who will teach must be of high quality. Learning must be based on the best available research about how to teach subject matter, how to tailor it appropriately to the understanding of the youngsters, and how to evaluate and improve their instructional outcomes. To ensure that graduates can sustain high standards of practice, the TSE will provide internships in PDSs where students enjoy exceptional opportunities to learn and to demonstrate quality practice. Recommendations for degrees, licensure, or certification will rest on performance assessments made by school and university faculty who are themselves accomplished practitioners. Concern for the trustworthy performance of our graduates will not be limited to the initial preparation of educators, but will pertain to TSE students at advanced levels as well. Our doctoral students will apprentice in research and teaching with faculty who are proven masters in both.

Goal 2: To make research, development, and demonstration of quality learning in real schools and communities a primary mission of education schools

We will bridge the pernicious gap between researchers and practitioners by conducting much of our work in real schools and communities. School and university faculty will collaborate regularly in sustained educational inquiry over time, much of it in schools educating at-risk youth. Our PDSs will connect much of our TSE inquiry to the teaching and learning of young students as well as to the professional development of novice and veteran educators. Many of our recommendations in this report cannot be achieved in the absence of the PDS, for it functions as a place where the best from our current research is applied to the everyday events of teaching and learning, and where promising new possibilities are developed and tested over time.

Goal 3: To connect professional schools of education with professionals directly responsible for elementary and secondary education at local, state, regional, and national levels to coalesce around higher standards

Educators need professional development of high quality from the time they enter their initial programs and throughout their careers. The only way each future generation can be better educated than the last is to have educators continuously engaged in quality learning. Advanced studies at the university and continuing professional development in the schools must be first rate—informed by the best we know from research and study, as well as from documentation of wise and effective practice. At the local level, starting with at least one PDS, the education school will build a network of these pre-collegiate institutions as places where TSE students learn and are evaluated for professional practice in the context of ongoing school renewal. The PDS, not just any elementary or secondary school, functions as a place where prospective and practicing educators from the school and the university immerse themselves in a sea of inquiry in pursuit of ever more effective learning. These local partners join with other professional schools and groups of educators at state, regional, and national levels to accumulate trustworthy educational knowledge, and to encourage its inclusion in professional development programs, performance assessments, and in standards for licensure, hiring, and promotion.

Goal 4: To recognize interdependence and commonality of purpose in preparing educators for various roles in schools, roles that call for teamwork and common understanding of learner-centered education in the twenty-first century

Because success in the future will depend on an ability to collaborate on behalf of every youngster's learning, we will no longer prepare educators for isolated roles. Instead, we will get them ready to work together on behalf of children in learner-centered schools and communities. Administrators, counselors, teachers, and other faculty influencing the learning and development of youngsters from early childhood through adolescence need opportunity to study and develop common language and understandings. They also need the chance to prepare for interaction with others whose work affects the lives and learning of the young, others whose professional work is often most needed for the learning success of students at educational risk. Thus, we will develop a core curriculum for educators at initial and advanced levels, and encourage experience and study across the various professional educational fields.

Goal 5: To provide leadership in making education schools better places for professional study and learning

We will ensure that our faculty are competent teachers and researchers, comfortable in both college and school settings, and committed to an education of quality for all children in an interdependent world. Our faculty and student body will come to reflect the rich diversity of American society and our education schools will offer a curriculum that all can respect. We will strive to see that outmoded and faulty assumptions about teaching and learning no longer determine educational policies and practices in our respective states and across the nation. With our practicing professional colleagues, we will set new standards for our professional schools, see that our own institutions meet them, and work to develop policies that require all schools of education to achieve high standards.

Goal 6: To center our work on professional knowledge and skill for educators who serve children and youth

We will sharpen our focus and concentrate our programs so that we offer studies more closely aligned with the learning needs of children and youth in a democratic society. Many schools of education have been trying to do too much with too little, dividing their curriculum into a succession of sub-specialties and stretching themselves too thin: Education schools trying to be all things to all people fail everyone. Our priority will be on program quality for those working to improve learning for children and youth. To sustain or increase the program quality needed to address rising standards in the nation's schools, TSEs must judge their offerings in terms of the collective contributions they make to the educators who serve each new generation of young citizens, including contributions to educators who address the learning needs of the poor.

Goal 7: To contribute to the development of state and local policies that give all youngsters the opportunity to learn from highly qualified educators

The value of the education school rests, in part, on its ability to contribute knowledge, information, and policy analysis that leads to informed decisions about educational quality. This requires checkpoints along the path—at admission and throughout preparation, licensure, hiring, certification, and professional development. Schools of education must promote standards of quality in their home states and oppose forces that allow youngsters to be "educated" by less than fully competent, caring professionals.

■|■|■

The Heart of the Matter

Three Kinds of Development

Tomorrow's Schools of Education (TSEs) must place children first and, in so doing, underscore a commitment to emphasize the connection of the TSE to the education professionals closest to the students, those in elementary and secondary schools. It may seem odd for this report to speak of stressing the TSE's mission to serve children and youth. Isn't that what schools of education have always done? Not necessarily.

Ambiguity surrounds the purpose of schools of education. Many of these institutions have been less than clear about their mission. The confusion arises, largely, from the tendency of many education schools to support too many different programs and to invest too little in work with the schools. As a consequence, a disproportionate number of faculty members separate their work from that of the elementary and secondary sector. Many professors go about their teaching and research with hardly a nod toward the public schools, seldom if ever deigning to cross the thresholds of those "lowly" places. Such attitudes transmit an unmistakable message. The people most intimately responsible for children's learning in elementary and secondary schools are not sufficiently valued by the education school. Schoolteachers and young learners, who should be the focus of the education school's concern, are kept at arm's length. They are a sideshow to the performance in the center ring, where professors carry out their work insulated from the messiness and hurly-burly of elementary and secondary education.

Schooling in America cannot renew itself so long as the links between universities and public schools languish. Dysfunction, instead of healthy symbiosis, characterizes the relationship between many university-based education schools and the schools. Sustained involvement in the public schools, predicated on mutual interest in the learning needs of children, must become an enduring feature of the TSE. For this to happen, a good number of professors in schools of education must identify not only with their disciplines but more actively with the public schools themselves. Research in the education schools should be directed toward groundbreaking work on matters involving both the creation and the application of knowledge. This will require a shift in many places, and necessitate reorienting the faculty reward system in the education school and in the university. Scholars who respond favorably to this call for more involvement with elementary and secondary schools and for more research into applying knowledge must suffer no penalties for their pioneering efforts so long as high standards are upheld for their work.

> The education of teachers has become a major focus of research and teaching agendas of faculty throughout the Graduate School of Education at Rutgers University.

In their rush to emulate colleagues in the arts and sciences, many faculty members of education schools lose sight of their responsibilities and opportunities as part of a professional school. Traditional forms of academic scholarship have an important and proven place in professional schools, but such institutions are obliged, as well, to learn from practice, and to concern themselves with the scholarship of applying knowledge. Teacher education and investigations connected to teaching and learning in the public schools must hold central positions in the TSE. Like schools of medicine, dentistry, law, business, architecture, and veterinary medicine, for example, a school of education should properly explore issues involving the practice of the profession. Tomorrow's Schools of Education must not try to garb themselves in guises that hide their true identity as professional schools. They will wither into deserved irrelevancy if they are unwilling to stand up and display their concern, above all, for children and their learning.

The voices heard most frequently amid the ferment surrounding elementary and secondary education are not those of faculty members of the education schools, but those of business people, politicians, and policy analysts. Some university educators speak out about the public schools, but they are few. The TSE needs to muscle its way aggressively into the fray. By hitching its wagons to public schools that are striving to transform themselves into Professional Development Schools, the TSE can ensure that the experiences of practitioners who are closest to the day-to-day learning of children figure more prominently in the great debate. To these ends, every TSE should embrace and conduct quality work on three complementary agendas—knowledge development, professional development, and policy development.

The seeds for developing knowledge take the form of investments in basic and applied research. Then, like all good scholars, educational investigators screen and document that research, cautiously estimating its value and the extent to which generalizations may be drawn. Professional development results from creating new meanings and layering on coat after coat of knowledge, gradually building up expertise that is both deep and strong. The process begins with selecting and preparing future educators and then by adding to their advanced and continuing education. Finally, policy development emerges from a synthesis of this knowledge and professionalism to produce thoughtful and sober analysis, constrained by guidelines that promote educational quality and provide protection from untrustworthy practices.

Knowledge Development

An essential and defining feature of the TSE is its production and application of new knowledge. In paying more attention to the public schools, the schools of education will inevitably reposition themselves to extend more of their knowledge development beyond the Academy and closer to the lives of youngsters. Previous investments in knowledge development by schools of education have, to too great an extent, remained tangential to core questions regarding teaching and learning in elementary and secondary schools. Research that is relevant and accessible to practitioners holds the greatest promise of transforming the field.

Professional education, in general, does not always discharge this responsibility as diligently as it ought to. Research by architecture faculty, for instance, may not take sufficient consideration of users; research by medical faculty may not take sufficient consideration of patients; and research by law faculty may not take sufficient consideration of clients. Faculty members in a professional school must remember always that their profession exists because it produces a service for someone. Without its clients or patients, the profession loses its raison d'etre, and study of the disciplines in arts and sciences suffices. The "inconvenience" of having to apply and study the apparent value of new knowledge and technologies over time in real contexts, and with real clients, is avoided. But scholars who follow this route ignore the recipients of the profession's service at a certain amount of peril. A profession disconnects itself from its lifeblood to the degree that the research severs its links to those who are supposed to receive a service. This reality, then, should shape the essence of professional schools for educators as we see them.

Fortunately, the Professional Development School (PDS) movement that we and others advanced in the late 1980s has taken root and promises to grow into something substantial that can cast its nurturing shadow over more and more of the education enterprise, allowing knowledge development to take greater cognizance of teaching and learning in elementary and secondary schools. Inquiry in the PDSs challenges the traditional relationship between research and application and gives promise of creating a new conception of that relationship.

For one thing, research in the PDS is conducted in the real context and complexity of educational practice. This tends to make research and application inseparable. Researchers create instructional environments in accord with particular theoretical principles. The creations are not only real instruction, but they are also experiments. Researchers collect data in these circumstances, using it both to correct their theoretical ideas and to improve instruction itself. Many researchers who use this method create such instructional environments in direct collaboration with teachers, and some of these "experiments" last for a semester or a year or longer. Such extended studies require the collaborators to monitor progress and problems all along the way rather than merely administer some kind of test at the end. No one has to figure out how to apply the research because it emanates from practice.

Another conception of educational research makes collaborators of teachers and other practicing educators, building on their intimate knowledge of learners in the context of particular schools and communities. Documentation of their observations and interventions into the learning lives of the young promises new insights and a synergy that some researchers argue may transform the field of educational knowledge. The PDS therefore represents a source of hope for those who want to see the knowledge mission focused closer to the thoughts and learning experiences made available to genuine young learners over time. The tie of research to the PDS opens a broad new avenue for the TSE to follow in collecting, evaluating, and demonstrating in practice the best of what is learned from new lines of study, or what is gleaned from traditional research and applied in a variety of circumstances. Already, in a good number of incipient Professional Development Schools, schools of education share the benefits of knowledge development and application with prospective and practicing teachers.

The University of Arkansas College of Education funds university/public school collaboration to study various educational practices. They have examined the effects of cooperative learning on attitudes of middle-level students, classroom management strategies for elemen-

tary students, a parent-child take-home drug education program, and field-based and campus-based methods courses on the reading orientations of prospective
teachers.

Experienced and beginning teachers do not learn about research by reading
articles or listening to lectures alone. They learn by seeing research findings applied
by others, talking about questions and findings with like-minded colleagues, and by
developing knowledge themselves. The PDS offers a venue for such opportunities
to novice and veteran practitioners alike. In such a setting, knowledge of change and
how to bring it about bursts beyond the confines of library shelves. Practitioners and
those who collaborate with them evaluate and disseminate research-based ideas,
practices, and tools by using them in the PDSs. By highlighting these emerging
lines of educational research, we do not seek to denigrate the other forms of educational inquiry in and outside PDSs that are also valuable. We are not trying to be
exclusionary, but only to note emerging work that holds promise for a field that has
historically slighted improvement-oriented work, teacher perspectives, and long-
term study of youngsters' learning in the schools.

Professional Development

University-based education schools inadvertently contribute to the de-intellectual-
izing of teaching when they favor professional development programs that accord
greater prominence to non-teaching roles or when they minimize the importance of
deeper knowledge for those who remain in positions in the classroom. This happens,
for example, in programs that claim that prospective teachers can learn to bring
about quality learning for groups of diverse young clients in a variety of subjects by
simply having these future teachers take some university courses in methods and foundations and then apprentice for ten weeks with a supervising teacher unknown to
the university. This approach contrasts sharply with the education school's requirements for counseling psychologists that call for extensive advanced study and selected
placements to gain experience with highly qualified mentors. Such differences in expectations imply that classroom teaching represents only a "starter position" and that
serious educators study substantial knowledge only in connection with higher level,
non-classroom assignments. The folly of this reasoning sustains a dangerous hierarchy in public education and suggests that those at the bottom—the classroom teachers—should not trouble themselves with the deeper theories of teaching and learning,
matters best left to curriculum coordinators, other specialists, and administrators.

The TSE posits a different philosophy—that teaching must be regarded as intellectually challenging work and that prospective and practicing teachers should be people capable of making informed professional judgments. This philosophy suggests that TSE faculty will collaborate with their PDS partners to adapt and recreate the role of teacher so that those in the position have greater opportunity for reflection, thought, and colleagueship. This idea applies to teaching at all levels of experience. Teaching should infuse itself with intellectual challenge from the outset of preparation through the length of one's entire career in schools and classrooms. The TSE will treat the prospective teacher as one expected to delve deeply into the intellectual side of teaching and learning. Thinking, judging, deciding, adapting—all are part of the ethos of teaching, minute by minute, day by day, year by year. The status of those working in the public schools suffers when they are excluded from policy decisions and treated like instructional robots.

The blame for denigrating the teacher's role rests not only with the school of education. If the education school has been preparing people for routine work in the classroom, that is largely because teachers were not permitted to do more. Schools that now take the professionalism of teachers more seriously afford them opportunities to make judgments and to participate actively in the development and implementation of education policies. In the more enlightened school districts, teachers are now prepared and encouraged to participate as primary players in curriculum selection, standards development, evaluation design, and other areas that call for professional judgment. But many principals, school boards, superintendents, state education agencies, and federal policymakers still downplay teachers' professionalism even while paying lip service to the concept. Schools of education must no longer lend themselves to this disturbing denigration of teachers.

Fresh evidence attests to the importance of teacher judgment and to the necessity for teachers to tailor curriculum to suit individual students, a practice that certainly demands professionalism. This new foundation for enriching the intellectual life of teachers—to which the research of some teacher educators has importantly contributed—provides a basis for a fresh start in how society regards its teachers. Increasingly, schools of education recognize that the professional knowledge of teachers must be built on more than how-to admonitions for keeping order in the classroom. Substantial issues of teaching and learning have to figure more prominently in the knowledge base of teachers. Schools of education must strengthen their alliances with school districts and states so as to ensure that those whose preparation equips them for decision-making receive the chance to exercise discretion in regard to appropriate professional practice.

It makes abundant sense for the professionals in closest contact with youngsters, those well educated by an education school, to make judgments about the education of those children. When this happens, students in elementary and secondary schools gain in two ways. First, the professionals who know them best will decide more of the details about their education, immediately matching practice to learning needs. Second, only by respecting the teacher's mind will the public schools be able to compete for more of the best and the brightest candidates and then be able to hold them. Smart people don't want to be treated as mindless ninnies. They are most apt to consider teaching if they perceive it to be a job for thinkers. The ablest college students, those for whom the public schools would like to vie, want jobs in which they can grow intellectually. Thus, the need for teachers' continuous learning and development throughout their careers calls for universities to rethink their roles and relationships to schools in regard to continuing professional development. If educators no longer need to leave teaching to advance as professionals, then the entire continuum of advanced professional education must be reconsidered.

Policy Development

The new TSE merits a place at the table where policymakers gather even if it has been omitted from the invitation list in past years. These are new times and policy-driven efforts to improve education are too important to cede to representatives of government and business, who seem to have taken up many of the chairs in recent years. If the TSE elevates the needs of children to unprecedented levels of concern, as we advocate, then surely the added attention to elementary and secondary schools and the resulting interest in professional development and in knowledge development for school-based educators ought to help insert the TSE more actively into the debate about public education. These contributions to policy can arise from two sources within the TSE. On the one hand, research that ties itself more closely to the most pressing issues in pre-collegiate education will lead the way to policy insights. On the other hand, simply by immersing themselves deeper into the everyday issues of elementary and secondary schools, faculty members at the TSE will be more in touch with the most pressing issues.

Policy Analysis for California Education (PACE) is an independent, nonpartisan education policy research center in the School of Education at Berkeley. Collaborating with education faculty from Stanford and USC as well, PACE informs policymakers, educational professionals, and the general public by researching and analyzing issues facing California's K-12 education system. The Research and Development Center established at the University of Delaware, with help from the state's Business

Public Education Council, models itself after PACE. The
director of the center is a member of the education faculty and the state superintendent's cabinet.

In making this argument, we don't mean to exaggerate the TSE's importance in
policy development. By itself, the TSE cannot remedy the social and economic circumstances that conspire to undermine the good intentions of the schools. The
roots of some of the problems run so deep that even the best insights of professors
at the TSE or of experts from any other sector might only begin to lay a foundation
for solutions. Furthermore, the idea should not be for the TSE to try to hold itself
out as a font of all knowledge, but for it to combine its wisdom with that of foundations, think tanks, and, yes, business and government, to help elementary and secondary education set a course that will avoid some of the shoals of the past. We
believe that the newly-constituted TSE will have much to offer in this regard.

Surely, though, policymaking in education can only benefit from the input of
informed faculty members of the TSE. Individual professors have long been involved
in policy work, but we envision institutionalizing this function and making it a formal part of the mission of the TSE. Quite possibly, consortia of education schools
will collaborate on some of these activities to avoid needless duplication of programs. At some point, for instance, schools of education in the same state must
almost certainly develop policies together to coordinate their recruitment of new students and to tie their credentialing programs to the needs and realities of the public school marketplace. The policy collaboratives we discuss later in this volume
address this need.

However they decide to pursue the development of policy, this activity should
be a major item on the agenda of TSEs. Like their colleagues throughout the departments of the university who influence public policy on transportation, labor, hous-
ing, and health care, those who educate educators should similarly strive to bring their
expertise to bear for the public good. Precisely because we expect faculty members
of the TSE to be experts in teaching and learning, we believe they can add valuable
points of view. They certainly would do no worse than some of those whose influence has been greatest until now. Look at the impact of current policy initiatives: The
nation's schools have gotten mandated tests for student promotion, ability tracking,
minimum basic skill tests for teachers, moments of prayer, and use of the SAT for
purposes for which it was never intended.

Daily decisions in Congress, in state legislatures, and in school districts could
gain from enriching the mix of ideas considered. Universities and their education schools
can play a fundamental role in this process, supplying reliable and impartial knowledge as a basis for policy formation. The public desire for greater quantities of quality learning will remain unfulfilled without acting on the basis of what we know. Analyses

provided by the TSE could help influence future directions in school finance, performance assessment, teacher testing and hiring, and a host of other areas. Legislation to increase the granting of emergency teaching licenses, for instance, has bubbled to the surface in some states. Lawmakers need and deserve to know about the synthesis of policy relevant to this subject. The TSE can help. It also can oversee, pilot, and test versions of programs that might be studied as a prelude to legislation.

Thus, knowledge development, professional development, and policy development lie at the heart of the education school's mission. Virtually everything the institution does will be shaped by these three fundamental concerns. In this regard, the TSE stamps its imprimatur on the educator as a professional. This approach distinguishes schools of education from trade schools. The TSE equips its graduates for careers in which their work can be respected for the depth and range of intellect it requires. The TSE equips them for decisions about knowledge that stem from a willingness to set priorities for teaching and learning, and it equips them for practice that provides insight for pertinent policy formation. Perhaps most important, however, the TSE grounds its critical examination of knowledge development, professional development, and policy development by connecting it to the public schools and to the long-range effects of schooling on young learners.

Special Knowledge for Educators

University-based education schools should devote themselves to producing knowledge and putting it into the heads, hands, and hearts of educators. The creation and sharing of knowledge, after all, lies at the very core of the university's existence. These institutions already make substantial investments in the advancement of knowledge for the betterment of society in many other fields. Why not in education as well? Imagine the impact on elementary and secondary schools if the nation's universities that already award a quarter of all of their advanced degrees to educators turned their attention to harnessing knowledge in behalf of the public schools, too, not unlike what they have done for medical science, physics, agriculture, engineering, business management, the humanities, and the social sciences.

Right now, some universities go through the motions of educating school professionals without taking the crucial steps that would connect that education to trustworthy knowledge about the renewal of elementary and secondary schools. A vigorous move to further research-based knowledge, its connections to practice, and its inclusion in the full range of professional programs for school-based educators would lead to better education for all children. Such a commitment would demand closer attention to lodging research and development in real classrooms, in the places where teaching and learning actually occur for youngsters from preschool through high school. It would also call for greater collaboration among the research universities and other institutions that educate educators.

Outsiders frequently misunderstand schools of education in terms of their potential contribution to the knowledge and expertise of professional educators, their value-added function, so to speak. The public and much of the university itself harbor suspicions about education schools and wonder whether they serve a useful purpose. Teaching, according to the average citizen, involves merely knowing something and explaining it to others. Can't any reasonably intelligent person with a decent general education carry out this job without special training? Perhaps a few courses in classroom management might help, but all those other education courses? In truth, education schools have failed to make their case. The public actually wonders, if they stop to think about it, why the country needs schools of education. People understand the utility of studying an academic discipline in college and doing some practice teaching in the school, but the rest of what happens under the auspices of the education school baffles them.

The confusion of the public has its counterpart in the minds of many faculty members in the rest of the university. Their colleagues in the education school perplex those in the institution's other colleges and they tend to view the education faculty from the perspective of one perched high on a ladder eyeing the laggards on the lower rungs. Faculty members throughout the rest of the university, after all, know their subjects well and teach them without special pedagogical preparation of any sort. What's the big deal? You get up and talk about what you know and those who listen either get it or they don't. Right?

What, then, is distinctive about the contributions of a school of education? Good schools of education provide substantive expertise for education practitioners, policymakers, and researchers. A focus on complex issues in context produces expertise otherwise unavailable. Multiple disciplines are brought to bear. No matter the issue—school finance, the lives and potential careers of students, intellectual and moral development of youngsters, professional development for teachers, assessment, educational equity, worthy goals for instruction, the uses of technology— that issue is linked to others. Insights from many perspectives are needed to address any one of these issues properly. Thus, the work of bringing diverse disciplines to bear on the key issues and problems of educational practice is a central challenge confronting the education school, which must help students weave together the strands of knowledge they glean from various sources. Four areas of educational knowledge frame the distinctive contributions of the professional school. Some are more developed than others, as education schools move forward unevenly in developing these areas of expertise. But these areas of growing knowledge and expertise, more than any others, provide the raison d'etre for the education school:

- Special Knowledge About Children and Their Learning
- Special Knowledge About Knowledge Needed by the Next Generation
- Special Knowledge About Education Systems
- Special Knowledge About Culture and Young People's Learning

Special Knowledge About Children and Their Learning

America takes its children for granted. Sometimes it seems that little progress has been made since the time when children were regarded as nothing more than small versions of adults.

This country did not even adopt compulsory schooling laws until it was clear that such statutes were needed as a device for ending the exploitation of children in mills and factories. It was not that reformers desired to promote schooling, but that they wanted a place to send children to keep them away from the oppression of the workplace. Today, the United States appears almost in a state of reversal after decades of improved regard for children. Many youngsters are without adequate health care in one of the wealthiest countries on earth. So horrendous has lawlessness become in parts of the country's inner cities that five-year-olds think that diving under the furniture at the sound of gunshots is a normal rite of childhood.

But America knows better even if it does not act on its knowledge. The healthy development of children is at stake every step of the way in their growing years. Children are complex organisms whose distinctive stage of life must be studied and understood in order to provide properly for their changing needs, especially in connection with formal learning. People can appreciate the work of naturalists who earn a living studying and reporting about the development of insects or birds. Great fascination surrounds advances of knowledge about chimpanzees who learn human language or about the intricate social system of ants. Well, the special study of children is no less valuable, particularly when its observations and findings lead to the design, implementation, and evaluation of interventions that enhance learning and development for each next generation.

Studies demonstrate, for example, the need for pedagogy to link a child's previous experience to the subject matter at hand. Furthermore, researchers have found that even very young children engage in complex thinking and problem-solving, a realization that underscores the need to customize learning tasks to suit the learner's experiences. Learner-centered education of this type requires an understanding of and respect for children and their ways of knowing, however informal, that they bring with them to school. For this reason, educators talk less today about whether the child is ready for school and more about whether the school is ready for the child. The school can't be ready if educators lack these valuable insights.

Schools jeopardize the education of children when educators disregard the powerful effects of out-of-school influences. The impact on each child of, say, interaction with adults, television, and peers affects learning and, in turn, should be considered in determining teaching approaches. More graphically, the out-of-school experiences of too many children, particularly those in depressed inner-city and other poverty-ridden areas, often teach them of the meaninglessness and futility of schooling. Clearly, teaching approaches, content selection, and content organization ought to consider these stark influences.

A rich body of literature provides insights for educators who are conversant with the findings. The needs, interests, and capabilities of the young have long interested those faculty members in schools of education who have led efforts to move the field from simplistic views to deeper understanding of the thought processes of children. The psychological, historical, sociological, and comparative perspectives brought to the study of children's cognition form a basis for entirely new teaching applications. Ongoing studies in these areas hold important implications for teaching and learning, although substantial numbers of practicing educators remain unaware of the findings. Similarly, studies of motivation and of the propensity of individual children to learn in different ways hold promise of revitalizing the life of our classrooms and schools.

In the first of Oregon State University's Professional Development School sites, considerable student improvements in mathematics have already been demonstrated. In addition, classroom teachers, intern teachers, and students have initiated action research projects.

Researchers in education schools have shed light, for instance, on how youngsters can appear to be learning when, in fact, they're not. This distinction between "faking it" and "knowing it," the issue of what constitutes understanding on the part of learners, has emerged as a crucial issue in teaching and learning. Prior to gaining this insight, educators thought students in elementary schools were learning better than they actually were. When students reached junior and senior high school and the sheer volume of "memorized stuff" overwhelmed their ability to pretend, it became all too apparent that they didn't know or understand the material in the first place. As a result, educators familiar with this research are revising their views about what it means for students to know subject matter. Parroting the right answers was never enough, but many teachers didn't recognize it. Now the importance of students' *understanding* and making *meaning* in their own terms is clear.

Findings gained from research inform the work of many educators on a number of such issues. For example:

■ Research shows that young people's competence is better served by learning a few things deeply and well, than by learning a wide variety of things superficially.

■ Students can greatly improve their effectiveness by learning to manage their own learning, thinking, and problem-solving, and research has shown how teachers can help them to do so.

■ Further work reveals not only how schooling can erode the learning potential of some groups of children, but how it can be reshaped to enhance their learning as well.

■ Young people cannot use the knowledge they memorize in manageable packets of information. Knowledge takes hold better when it evolves over long periods of time into coherent structures. Teaching, then, must be refocused on fostering deep understanding rather than just the memorization of facts and mechanical procedures.

■ We often assume that most students have similar conceptions of a given subject matter domain. In contrast, research shows that students have startlingly different conceptions of the same domain.

■ Young people don't become good problem-solvers because of innate ability or by learning general techniques they apply to all types of problems. Instead, they learn distinct problem-solving strategies for different knowledge domains (e.g., engineering vs. economics), and these strategies can be effectively taught to students.

This kind of contribution—providing educators with knowledge about how children learn, how their individual development is influenced by the different experiences of culture, race, and class, and how they understand and retain important ideas—must be central to the mission of Tomorrow's Schools of Education. Educators' knowledge of important content has to be wed to both understanding and to skill in applying the pedagogy most appropriate for helping youngsters acquire knowledge. If a teacher knows something, but lacks an understanding of how best to teach it, then neither effective teaching nor effective learning is apt to occur.

Special Knowledge About The Knowledge Needs of Each Next Generation

Questions about what should be taught in school provoke contentious debates, within and outside the Academy. Just look at the furor over outcomes-based education, culturally-responsive pedagogy, and the new national history standards. Education schools must clarify these complex issues, often illuminating the deep conflicts in values that undergird them, offering guidance on how the dilemmas might be managed, or suggesting ways of setting priorities under conditions of uncertainty. The criteria for deciding what is most important for young students to learn are not straightforward. While education scholars have addressed these questions for many decades, it is fair to say that this area of expertise has received less sustained study and investment than issues associated with how children learn. Nonetheless, curriculum theorists have long contributed sound criticism and analyses of what young students have opportunity to learn in school, and how it may or may not serve individuals and the society.

Other education faculty have drawn on future projections to analyze likely learning needs for the next generation. The need for greater multicultural learning, for example, has long been recognized in light of an increasingly global society. The growing interface between man and machines, combined with the seemingly unending information explosion, provokes questions about how youngsters can best be helped to make sense out of all the "stuff" that is traveling across the information highways. And as knowledge grows, while time to study and learn remains constant, the issues and questions about what constitutes needed and important learning for children become ever more critical. This area now calls for further investment and new approaches to the work of curriculum theorists.

Members of the education school faculty must prepare future and practicing educators to participate in the many debates over content and to inform the various points of view, all the while balancing respect for what the individual child needs to know with what children in general need to know. Above all, this means providing students in elementary and secondary schools with an education that prepares them for participation in a democracy, gives them the ability to reason and solve problems, and, eventually, leads to a productive and rewarding life. No inherent genes predispose children to grow into good citizens or able workers. Democracy's health depends on people accumulating participatory skills and appreciating the need sometimes to subordinate one's will for the good of the social contract. Success on the job demands taking possession of a body of knowledge, mastering skills, and acquiring good work habits and a cooperative attitude. Formal schooling helps shape students for these outcomes.

We do not pretend that school alone implants the knowledge and values that determine the kinds of adults that students will become. The neighborhood, the peer group, the media, the religious institution, and, particularly, the home stamp their marks on the child. But the role of the school looms ever more important in an era when the influence of other sectors is either diminished or out of proportion. The home and the church, for example, exert waning influence on some children, while peers and the media have grown ever more powerful. The school has the awesome responsibility of offsetting negative out-of-school factors while bolstering potentially positive ones that have lost their potency.

Knowledge about the knowledge needed by the next generation helps professional educators decide, each step of the way, what children should know. While steeped in only one or maybe two disciplinary areas, teachers must have sufficient grasp of other fields to draw on them and to interact with other teachers about them, ensuring that education in elementary and secondary schools is coherent and integrated. In addition, those who work in the schools must be ready at times to infuse the curriculum with viewpoints that take cognizance of a variety of intellectual, social, and artistic traditions and accomplishments. Few other workers in any field face so daunting a task as teachers do.

The responsibility rests with educators to resist pleas to insert inert esoterica into the curriculum. Educators must also reconcile divergent viewpoints of advocates, such as those who would either keep all knowledge separated into pristine disciplinary boundaries or those who would dispense with study of the disciplines as totally artificial conceptions. At the same time, public school educators must deal with those advocates who want only more and more time to cover their particular subjects and passions. A school professional, in other words, must be equipped for the difficult task of sorting out competing claims on the curriculum. Students need more depth, not more coverage that skims across material that students forget almost as soon as they have encountered it. Furthermore, students need more experiences in school that integrate the disciplines so that they learn about knowledge instead of merely about subjects.

Special Knowledge About Education Systems

If, as we said earlier, change in schools should be approached systemically, then surely school professionals must come to understand the workings of the system. Historically, the importance of such studies may have been held in low regard because those enrolled in the education school assumed that merely spending time in a public school provided all the knowledge they needed to understand the whole. But whence was this understanding to come? Most people in school systems have assumed ownership over only a small part of the system and worked in relative isolation from other parts. The modest goals of the schools of yesteryear permitted relative "success" under these arrangements. Not all students were expected to learn, and it was all right for many to do poorly and drop out. The elders decided what should be learned.

Teaching was showing and telling groups of students what needed to be learned, learning was listening and memorizing by oneself, testing was sampling what students remembered on standardized instruments, evaluating was comparing and distributing students along a normal curve. Teachers needed only to manage their individual classrooms; principals would manage the schools and superintendents would manage the district. And central office staff would each manage a function of the district—the evaluation office or the staff development office or the business office, for instance. Individual educators were prepared each to carry out his or her part in keeping the "schooling machine" operating smoothly.

In contrast, today's education professionals have new goals and rapidly changing work requirements. Parents and community members are directly involved in helping to shape the nature of the school. All students are expected to learn, and at increasingly higher levels of accomplishment. If anything, schools suffer a deluge of information and educators have to decide how they will invest their time and talents. No longer will educators simply be judged by how smoothly the enterprise operates, but by the extent to which they effect ambitious learning for the entire student body. Today's educators succeed only when the students for whom they share responsibility learn effectively throughout the length of their schooling. The students and their learning are now the centerpiece.

Professional educators must now understand the system as a whole, knowing the contributions of the interdependent parts, so as to draw on those parts in the service of students' learning. They must now involve themselves in seeing that all parts serve the interests of all students, assuring their regular progress toward high learning standards. This means, for example, that second-grade teachers now care about and accept certain responsibility for what happens to their students in the first and third grades as well. For what if second graders could learn more if they had a richer experience in prior years, or what if second graders who do well and learn to like mathematics suddenly develop a lasting distaste for it in subsequent years?

> Teachers College, Columbia University, promotes the concept that the teaching/learning process is usually more effective, at all levels, as a collaborative rather than an isolated activity. TC accepts its responsibility to build trust and communication among school and university faculty—and from that foundation it generates innovation, creativity, and constructive change.

Working in schools today ought to mean knowing and sharing responsibility for what happens to youngsters in their prior or subsequent years and knowing and sharing responsibility for what happens in other subjects. The workings of the system itself must be understood. This means knowing how educational policies and practices throughout the system impinge on youngsters' learning—everything from evaluation policies and practices to financial decisions, professional development opportunities, responses to federal and state mandates, and so on.

America's education system comprises many actors and many complex parts distributed across local, state, regional, and national jurisdictions. Inquiry into educational systems may extend over a horizon so vast that the points along it cannot be discerned without turning one's head far in one direction and then far in the other. The particulars of the system are almost inexhaustible: governance, policies on instructional grouping, selection of textbooks and multimedia, writing across the curriculum, multicultural education, uses of technology, policies for desegregating schools, counseling, finance, professional development, and many others.

Learning of this kind requires study and experience beyond any single school or classroom. A practical examination of the education system would resemble nothing so much as a perusal of the proverbial elephant by the three blind men. One, holding the trunk, reaches certain conclusions about the animal. Another, stroking one of the great flapping ears, comes to a different verdict. And the third, leaning against the elephant's side in a futile effort to push him, forms yet another opinion about the nature of the beast. Each person in a school or school system tends to view the entire enterprise through the lens closest to him or her. Advanced students in schools of education may work as teachers, principals, and district administrators. They may coordinate transportation services, buy materials for the library, supervise paraprofessionals, specialize in the teaching of mathematics, or balance accounts in the business office. Each such position contributes to the larger education system of which it is a part. But few individuals ordinarily gain a comprehensive view of the system itself. Some observers say that this is why educational reform has not enjoyed greater success.

How may an individual school professional gain a full perspective of so vast an enterprise? As difficult as it may be to bring into focus, the larger picture, once fully and clearly viewed, provides a multitude of entry points for observing interconnections between and among the parts of the system. Altering what one does as an actor in the system has consequences for colleagues and for the roles they play. Thus, as professional roles and responsibilities change to increase youngsters' learning in one part of the system, it is important that others change in compatible ways. Successful reform depends on those who understand the interdependence of these parts and how they must change in mutually beneficial ways for greater student learning.

A crucial new element, technology, also makes it both easier and more difficult to gain a grasp of the entire system. In just the last decade or so, education has grown more intricate with the introduction of the computer, not to mention the CD-ROM and other items of technology. Students in the same classroom can engage in a multitude of lessons as they sit shoulder to shoulder, each gazing at the monitor of his or her own computer. Teachers fashion new kinds of assessments using technology to allow for simulations and for computer-aided design. How can all of this be coordinated and exploited to the benefit of students by educators whose career-long orientation and support system has been built around paper-and-pencil? Those are some of the complications that technology has added to the system. But, fortunately, technology has the potential to facilitate and simplify work, as well. Classroom management and the operations of the entire school and even the school system can be more readily coordinated if connected appropriately to advanced learning about technology's role. Banks, hospitals, and courts all have altered and streamlined themselves by incorporating computers into the core of their existence. Education lags, but eventually similar changes will occur and when that happens the system itself may be more comprehensible.

Once, in what observers now acknowledge were simpler times, change was ordered by fiat, from the top down. This approach was thought to be dictated by common sense. Now, more is known about the change process because research has lifted the curtain that obscured the hidden obstacles to change. One of the most important disclosures has to do with the need for systemic change from the bottom up. Simultaneously, greater comprehension of the complexities of the education system and of the need to interact with families, social service agencies, communities, and other entities now places reformers on the cusp of what could be a glorious and productive era in American education. Much will depend on the education school's ability to seize the moment so that it can marshal this knowledge of the system on behalf of desperately needed reforms.

Special Knowledge About Culture and Young People's Learning

Teaching and learning, like all human activities, are usually culturally specific. Perhaps the most obvious and overdrawn example of cultural specificity is language, the most fundamental of all teaching and learning tools. Language conveys most content and important ideas made available in schools, and teachers are responsible for seeing that the language is in forms that have equally powerful meaning to the diverse array of students they must help to learn. If the metaphors, examples, and illustrations used for instruction are unknown, unfamiliar, or basically irrelevant to students, they lose meaning.

America's students come from multiple cultures and from homes where the first language of the parents and often of the children, too, is a language other than English. But cultural uniqueness is not limited to language, though it develops, like language, from the time youngsters are born. Children learn continuously at home, in their neighborhoods, at school, and wherever they happen to be. They acquire funds of knowledge, often culturally specific, from these varied experiences and it is this knowledge that they bring to school and use in response to demands made upon them. We know that culture, like language, makes a deep imprint on the mind and helps to shape thoughts, values, and behaviors. It becomes a filter through which the world is seen and interpreted, and it is powerful and enduring.

Children and youth are shaped by their culture and cannot be expected to disconnect from it when they come to school. Their culture is neither right nor wrong; it simply is what it is—and the school must help youngsters learn and develop with and through the cultural meanings that are uniquely theirs. Teachers and other educators should have the knowledge and skill to foster this enabling process. This makes the relationship between teachers and students a critical aspect of the teaching-learning process.

> The University of New Hampshire, Old Dominion, Norfolk State, Hampton, and Howard Universities collaborate through a Holmes mini-grant on a multicultural education project involving teacher education students and faculty. The group engages in seminars, panel discussions, and shared experience to consider needed program revisions for today's educators.

Research has revealed that students learn best by building on and revising what they already know. What they already know and what they are willing to learn, they acquire from the contexts in which they live. To foster their students' learning, then, and to provide instruction and instructional environments in which their students can thrive, those preparing to teach must gain a deep and extensive knowledge of the contexts of their students' lives.

Education scholars now recognize, though, that future educators cannot become experts in the cultures and languages of all the diverse students they may eventually serve. Nonetheless, prospective educators must learn to value each student's background and perspective—for in it reside the keys that can unlock the mysteries of successful teaching. Teaching is successful to the extent that students find meaning, and if teachers fail to connect youngsters' current meanings with the new ones they seek to engender, the students will simply not learn effectively.

One of the great challenges in good teaching is that of helping learners whose cultural backgrounds differ substantially from the teacher's own. Educators in this country, the most pluralistic on earth, must develop a repertoire of skills that enable them to understand how diverse youngsters think about various subjects, and how they, as teachers, can present knowledge in a variety of ways for their students. The good education school not only provides prospective and practicing educators with opportunities to work with diverse youngsters, but also gives them practice and assistance in representing disciplinary knowledge in a variety of ways that can reach the variety of youngsters that comprise America. Educators can no longer see or relate the world to the next generation through a singular set of lenses. They must respect and reach all sorts of youngsters—boys and girls, rich and poor, those of different races, ethnic backgrounds, and disabling conditions.

■|■|■

Participating in Policy Development

The schism between practice and policymaking in education must be bridged, and we think that the TSE is uniquely situated to develop capacity for spanning the divide. TSE faculty members and their partners in the Professional Development Schools are increasingly able to address the compatibilities and incompatibilities of educational practice and policy. Recently, for example, discrepancies were noted between testing programs for students and those for teachers. Higher level learning was asked of high school sophomores on their state assessments than was asked of the future teachers on their state tests. As school and university faculty observe factors like these, factors that obviously influence educators' and youngsters' learning, they must bring them to the attention of policymakers. But they ought not wait only until the problems present themselves. TSE faculty and their PDS colleagues are increasingly able to anticipate policy interventions needed to improve teaching and learning. These insights could be valuable in any consideration of policies affecting elementary and secondary education.

We said at the outset of this report that the TSE should embrace three complementary agendas—knowledge development, professional development, and policy development. Now, we will pursue that idea in greater depth in regard to policy development, pointing out how in its mediating role the TSE could help address policy issues, all the while advocating for young learners and indicating what might be best for them.

In examining how the TSE might involve itself in informing policy, we will concentrate on three areas by way of example, though the possibilities are endless. The three that we have in mind involve policies for standards for teaching, learning, and schooling; policies for equity and access in education; and policies for school-based coordination of services to children and youth. Policy development, for whichever of these purposes, must link itself to educational improvement. This guiding principle should properly underlay virtually all considerations of policy relating to elementary and secondary schools as well as to education schools. Better schools give students a foundation for fuller, more productive lives.

In essence, therefore, policy analysis and policy influence by the TSE go hand in hand with democracy-building, which depends on people attaining a certain level of education. The schools, in their purest and ideal form, prepare young people to take their rightful place in the American democracy, as old-fashioned as this may sound. To the extent that the schools fall short, democracy is imperiled. If the TSE sees its role in policy development as helping elementary and secondary education to fulfill this mission, then surely the policies emanating from the TSE will be good ones.

Policies on Standards and the TSE

The recently-enacted goals legislation calls for incentive funding for developing voluntary adoption of national standards at the state and local levels. As the TSEs create networks of PDSs, they become a major resource for studying issues that must be resolved to develop workable standards. What would prod and encourage the schools to respond favorably to the standards? Do public schools harbor the capacity to implement the standards? Must teaching and learning change in any appreciable way to realize the spirit of the standards? Teachers and other school educators will likely require additional learning to achieve and adapt new standards for their own work and to see that students achieve the new standards. Many talented educators will be needed to help reach these new levels of learning, and the universities will be among the institutions needing to respond. The growing numbers of teachers certified by the National Board for Professional Teaching Standards can help.

The potential role for the TSE assumes even greater importance now that most states have embraced the national goal that "by the year 2000, the nation's teaching force will have access to programs for the continued improvement of their professional skills and the opportunity to acquire the knowledge and skills needed to instruct and prepare all American students for the next century." We suspect that the TSE will carve a special niche for itself on issues involving professional development, which must be revised to ensure the success of new policies affecting the teaching and learning of students. The learning of educators has emerged as a critical policy issue because the intent of the reform movement cannot be realized without substantial investment in professional learning. Higher levels of student learning and increased performance among young learners will not automatically result because people call for it. New knowledge and new approaches to educators' work are needed, and, in turn, professional development as we know it must change substantially.

Currently, professional development ties itself too thoroughly to credentialism and pay scales. The course-taking and the ensuing credential-granting that is now the norm often have little impact on actual practice. States and districts, in cooperation with organized educators, are exploring alternatives to the system, and TSEs are lending expertise to framing new and better policies on professional development. Newer approaches use investments in professional development to educator learning, that is tied to school improvement or to demonstrated achievement of high performance standards (e.g., such as with the National Board for Professional Teaching Standards). Most states and school districts have yet to alter their policies, which, ultimately, must support learning at the job site that promotes collegiality and leadership. The extent to which educators' professional development continues to rely heavily on the universities' current master's degrees remains to be seen, but districts will probably soon want more for their investment than a record of seat time in university courses.

> Many Holmes institutions have assisted the National Board for Professional Teaching Standards. Faculty members from Stanford University and Michigan State University contributed to the basic conceptual underpinnings for the Board's work.

The TSE should align its interests in standards for educators with the activities of the National Board, which has begun administering assessments to identify worthy veteran teachers. At the same time, the TSE must formulate policy standards for beginning teachers in line with the work being done by the Council of Chief State School Officers. So far, few states or districts have embarked on the road leading to comprehensive reform of professional development. This is a garden waiting to be sowed. Whether the weeds of old reappear or new flowers blossom will depend on the quality of the policies that cultivate professional development in the future.

Policies on Equity and Access and the TSE

As an agency promoting opportunity, the public schools must serve the least as well as the most privileged. Struggles around equity and access, however, have produced a mixed record. The nation has witnessed desegregation and resegregation. Courts have overturned finance systems, and new finance systems have arisen to bring hardly any relief to hard-pressed school districts. All-black faculties have been dismantled along with the all-black school systems that they served, only to see the black representation in the country's teaching force dwindle to alarmingly low levels. Title I and then Chapter I have contributed to an apparent increase in basic skills among the most economically disadvantaged students, but the programs infringed on the quality of their classmates' and their own education by pulling children out of classes. Similar paradoxes confound programs for bilingual education and special education.

The promise remains, frayed but enduring, of public education as society's great equalizer, a potential source of opportunity and unity for a diverse and divided nation. More than ever, though, the public schools require sagacious guidance to stay the course. At this crucial juncture, the quality of policymaking as regards equity and access will determine whether the United States moves into the twenty-first century offering a sense of hope or a sense of despair to many of its people. Among the issues on which the TSE should focus its expertise are those having to do with race relations, cultural diversity, inclusive education for students with disabilities, improved ways of providing bilingual education, sensitivity to gender inequities, and implementation of new guidelines for Chapter 1.

What makes the TSE so qualified to contribute to forming these policies is the fact that the TSE itself and the PDSs that it helps create are fundamentally committed to supporting education that promotes rights, equity, and access. Throughout this report, we repeatedly pronounce our belief that such commitments must underpin all aspects of the TSE and its activities. If the PDS operates as we propose, it will be one of the leading proving grounds for the testing of policy. In essence, the PDS spans the gulf between theory and practice, permitting the TSE to formulate policy with full awareness of practical realities. Results, both empirical and scientific, can inform all aspects of TSE policy analysis in regard to equity and access.

As the debate over tracking grows, for instance, policymakers will need hard evidence to speak authoritatively on the topic. The PDS, founded on the premise of equity and access, will be a de-tracked institution that can provide living examples of what happens when a school adopts and adapts well-established research findings and extends respect to all children for their ability to learn. No guesswork here. Look at the record. Examine what outcomes in the PDS say about schools that change approaches to tracking. We foresee the TSE, in alliance with its PDS, poised to offer many such policy insights.

Policies on Coordination of Services and the TSE

In much the same way, the activities of the PDS in coordinating social and health services for its students will build a record that can be scrutinized for policy implications. We don't pretend that the PDS will be the only such site, but we do know that, unlike most other schools that coordinate services, the PDS will keep extensive data and that the findings of able researchers will be available to shed light on the impact of coordinated services.

Policy issues abound here. The configurations of the various school models for coordinating services lead to questions about educators' preparation for such activities. If a teacher or principal, for instance, is expected to blow the whistle on child abuse in the home, then careful and thoughtful training for that specific purpose must be provided. And just how much of that kind of work can be imposed on the teacher or principal without compromising the main goals of the curriculum?

We project that the TSE and its affiliated PDSs will develop service delivery models in conjunction with new policy approaches that create new structures, programs, and funding opportunities. We expect the schools of the future to feature coordinated services that operate year-round and that require professional educators to take on tasks that they do not now perform. Perhaps in an ideal world the public schools would be able to restrict themselves to academic concerns, but in the real world all sorts of messy matters such as poor nutrition, uncorrected vision problems, family mobility, and parental unemployment impinge upon a child's education. Educational interventions on a child's behalf may be all but impossible without extending the long arm of concern into the home through the conduit of the school. Even after acknowledging this necessity, however, the schools must take the next step and figure out how to deliver the needed services effectively so that the services enhance teaching and learning. The TSE can be a beacon to those searching for ways to strengthen such efforts.

■|■|■

A Commitment to Diversity

What must be done above all else to improve the learning of the children most ill-served by America's schools? How may professional study within the TSE better prepare educators to respond to the needs of such students? How might changes in research and policy alter our capability for response to their learning needs? These questions pose matters of pressing urgency for schools of education.

Knowledge about effective practice for a diverse range of children is starting to emerge and can be accumulated to an even greater degree by TSEs, for they will not shun these most salient issues. Studies of teachers who are successful with all students point to familiar themes. They hold high expectations for these students and provide them with academically-demanding work. Furthermore, students benefit from role models and from teachers who show a sense of caring. Teachers must help connect school and home, and the TSE must educate school professionals to forge the needed links.

Two critical principles present themselves: First, the languages and cultures of learners should be incorporated into the school milieu. Second, the codes and customs of the school should be explicitly taught so that all children can participate in the mainstream. But without the knowledge and skill that the TSE can impart to both novice and experienced educators on how to implement these principles, chances are that the principles will be honored in the breach. Educators, even gifted ones, aren't born with the ability to teach what they don't know. Furthermore, those who work in schools often need assistance in their efforts to link the classroom and the home. A growing body of literature pertains to the home-school connection and educators need the opportunity to engage in guided reflection on this topic.

Educators increasingly recognize that effective practice in public schools involves schoolwide arrangements with a host of service providers, as well as direct engagement with families, especially those that historically have felt excluded by the public schools. Research attests to the fact that parents from all social classes are more interested in their children's schooling than many educators and policymakers believe. Schools have to do more to engage parents as allies in the education of their children. This prospect threatens some school professionals, who perhaps grow anxious about their lack of knowledge about how to foster relationships with the home.

Serving a diverse group of students more effectively requires knowing more about the out-of-school lives of these children. For the TSE, the mission is clear: Those who work in the schools cannot do the best job possible for students whose lives outside the classroom are a mystery to them. The TSE has to become a repository of wisdom and a center of research about the diverse cultures of the United States and, in particular, about the interventions in teaching and learning that will enrich the school experiences of all children.

Self-knowledge is a foundation stone of this quest, ironically, for both student and educator. A TSE should strive to ensure that adults who work in schools begin their professional quest by taking a personal inventory as a prelude to trying to help their students get to know themselves. Self-knowledge extends to searching one's own beliefs and attitudes, not unlike the training of a good psychoanalyst who cannot minister properly to others without becoming better acquainted with oneself. Coming to terms with one's feelings and confronting one's prejudices prepares a teacher to help students gain comfort and assurance in their own cultural identity inside and outside the school. Many students otherwise end up with feelings of alienation and irrelevance.

Professional studies should contribute research-based findings on learning differences that stem from cultural backgrounds. Education professionals can be taught procedures for gathering information about children, families, and communities and for assessing their teaching in light of children's preferred learning and the interaction of the school with styles in the home and in the community. The implications for developing a multitude of teaching strategies are implicit, though an educator must always remember that, cultural backgrounds aside, students are individuals whose separate needs cannot be dictated solely on the basis of cultural origins. In other words, a skilled teacher uses this knowledge not to shove students into cultural pigeonholes but, like a good tailor, to sew for each youngster a garment that fits his or her unique contours.

The classroom of the TSE offers one important setting for equipping members of the education profession for these tasks. As part of their education, professional educators should spend time in schools with diverse populations, observing and learning from successful teachers. But the classroom cannot be the sole venue for this kind of learning. Students from the TSE should shadow principals and work with various service providers in such schools as well. Finally, the TSE should also help the student fashion field experiences in neighborhoods and even in homes where they can get to know more intimately people who are unfamiliar to them. Ultimately, to know a child or anyone else, is to become familiar with the texture of the soil from which that person sprung.

For a variety of reasons, few TSEs are as well prepared to take on this responsibility as they might be. Their faculties, for instance, are overwhelmingly white and monolingual, people who for the most part have had little experience teaching those different from themselves. Fewer than five percent of education school faculty nationally have taught for even a year in inner-city classrooms. Likewise, many schools of education lack field settings that would enable their students to come in contact with diverse populations. Nor have the institutions aggressively recruited classroom teachers from those settings to act as clinical or adjunct professors. As for the students entering studies in the field of education, they generally share the demographic characteristics of the faculty and often express a preference to work in schools that are middle-class and suburban. Those who venture into inner-city classrooms, unequipped as they are to cope with an unfamiliar setting, frequently conclude that they lack the ability to teach, administer, and counsel in such settings.

Schools of education must launch vigorous recruitment campaigns to enlist more minority teachers. Efforts like Recruiting New Teachers, an organization that runs an advertising and information campaign to induce more members of minority groups to enter teacher preparation programs, must be intensified. The TSE should align itself with such programs and strive toward the ideal of an inclusive community in its own programs and in the composition of its faculty and its enrollment. The children in America's elementary and secondary schools deserve no less.

An equity council has been established at the University of Mississippi for recruiting minority students and faculty as well as for connecting with historically black institutions for faculty exchanges.

Teachers of all backgrounds must understand and be better prepared to act on the growing knowledge of human cognition which enables them to accommodate the needs of diverse learners and be more effective in their teaching. Youngsters understand a lesson in their own way, but may not be able to articulate what they know in a manner comprehensible to their teacher. So teachers must be able to project themselves inside each learner to see how the student conceptualizes the material. This is not simply the empathy of caring, as important as that might be. What we have in mind is a teacher's working knowledge of cultural-based learning. Such expertise enables teachers to reach youngsters and communicate with them through metaphors and experiences that have meaning in their terms as well as in teachers' terms alone.

More than this, though, equity demands that faculties of elementary and secondary schools and of education schools, too, wear the face of America. To settle for less is to deny the potential of a significant portion of the population. This is a country, statistics tell us, in which children from minority groups will constitute the majority of the enrollment in twenty-three of the twenty-five largest cities by the year 2000. By 2020, they will make up fully forty-six percent of the nation's entire school-aged population. And the number of students from homes where a language other than English is spoken constantly grows. Poverty complicates the changes by engulfing one in five schoolchildren in circumstances utterly unlike those with which most schools are equipped to deal.

These children need to see people with whom they can readily identify in positions that indicate that they can make something of themselves, that they, too, can aspire to teach. They need people who readily understand them and their plight. They need role models. We would not be so foolish as to say that white, monolingual teachers cannot play this role or that all teachers of color are automatically expert at such matters. Of course, white teachers can relate to minority students, and many have with great success. Some teachers, though, clearly harbor destructive biases and an even larger number have not the foggiest idea of how to cope with a classroom full of students whose backgrounds vary greatly from theirs. The possibilities of greater progress will in all likelihood be enhanced by building a more diverse group of professional educators. It will especially give poor minority students who need the most help something extra on which to grab hold as they try to scale what for them is a very slippery slope indeed. In the final analysis, then, it flies in the face of reality for schools and colleges to continue to have faculties and student bodies that are so disproportionately balanced.

What we urge will not be easy. Among the country's full-time faculty members at institutions of higher education in 1991, only 2.1 percent were Hispanic and 4.7 percent were African-Americans and nearly half of them were at historically black colleges. The numbers for Native Americans and Asian Americans were lower still. Nonetheless, TSEs must try to carry out the education of educators in circumstances that respect equity and diversity. Schools of education should model the kinds of communities that they hope to see established in elementary and secondary schools and in the United States itself. Issues of racism, sexism, and other forms of prejudice must be faced squarely.

The Holmes Group set up two programs to help advance this priority. Its Equity Critique and Review Panel reviews the publications and other work of Holmes in order to provide feedback on the handling of issues of equity and access. The Holmes Scholar Program sponsors one to four fellows on each campus, minority students who study at the advanced undergraduate or graduate level and who eventually will be candidates for faculty appointments. These four goals characterize the Holmes agenda:

- To create a more racially diverse community of faculty, staff, and students and to prepare additional persons of color who are excellently trained to become professors on the tenure track at schools of education and on the clinical faculties of Professional Development Schools;
- To create a more racially diverse membership in The Holmes Group so as to benefit from the participation and contributions of a more diverse group of faculty and students;
- To increase the number and quality of graduate professional education programs that have substantial numbers of faculty and students from minority groups; and
- To structure ongoing evaluation mechanisms by which the reform efforts of The Holmes Group and its member institutions may be assessed for their impact on progress toward equity and cultural/racial diversity.

As part of the response to the Holmes agenda, Oklahoma State University's teacher education program has sponsored six Holmes Scholars since the inception of the program. These doctoral-level students have included four Native Americans, and one African-American, and one white woman pursuing a field in which few females are employed.

Future actions affecting the education of educators should flow from these goals. The TSE must establish, for example, specific initiatives to recruit and support the graduation of more minority students from the education school. The attendant strategies might include creating an advisory panel on the recruitment of minority students, forming tighter links with public school systems as sources of applicants, organizing trips to campus by students from high schools and community colleges, targeting professionals in other fields who might consider career changes, and involving alumni in these various efforts. An evaluation by the Equity Critique and Review Panel of progress to date in the Holmes Scholar Programs stated:

Although the Holmes Scholars believed that peer networking was the most significant experience in Holmes, their networking with each other cannot replace the needed association with and guidance of faculty and administrators. Graduate students of color need advocates, sponsors, and counselors who support and guide them through their programs. Admitting and providing financial aid to Holmes Scholars are mere beginnings; teaching, promoting, and socializing them into the professoriate are subsequent and more significant next steps in the process.

The Holmes Group has an uneven record when it comes to assessing progress towards these equity goals. Some institutions have documented their progress and some others have no data whatsoever. The Equity Panel has developed and tested an instrument for monitoring progress that Holmes members are now using. While the TSEs cannot alter the past, the future remains to be shaped. The inclusion of more diverse voices will necessarily produce conflict and challenge in the TSE and PDSs from time to time. But the contributions from our research and development activities, our professional development, and our policy work can only improve American education by giving greater attention to its rich diversity. The TSEs have it within their grasp to fashion a future that speaks to the American ideal of equality of opportunity for all.

Footnote: To increase the diversity of the candidate pool available for faculty positions in their own and other universities, The Holmes Group created a Holmes Scholars Network in 1991. Currently over 180 graduate students of color are pursuing advanced studies in member universities. As of this writing, seventeen have graduated and hold positions in education; thirteen are in tenure-track positions in U.S. universities.

■|■|■

Human Resources

Making People Matter

What is true for students in elementary and secondary schools is equally true for students in the education school, namely, that the most effective learning results from having teachers who are competent and caring. Of all the resources that can be marshaled in the students' behalf, the overall talent and composition of the faculty matters most. Whether attending schools or colleges, students deserve the opportunity to learn from diverse and highly qualified teachers.

No educational institution at any level would readily admit that its faculty consists of teachers who are less than "highly qualified." Yet, the common parlance in higher education refers to "teaching institutions" and "research institutions," and we all know on which side of this divide the members of The Holmes Group tend to fall. The country's great research universities wear their appellation proudly, but, by extension, this research distinction implies that teaching occupies second rank. Of course, some institutions excel in both research and teaching and, to be fair, some members of The Holmes Group attain this status. Many of the large research universities, however, often turn over much of the responsibility for educating educators to volunteers, part-timers, and graduate students, and to the least experienced members of the regular faculty.

Furthermore, students enrolled in the education school often must contend with a faculty so dispersed and so divided as to rob their education of all coherence. This faculty comprises arts and science professors offering studies in the general liberal arts and in the students' major and minor areas of concentration; other arts and science faculty teaching methods courses to education students; the regular faculty of the school of education; the scattered corps of cooperating teachers in the public schools; adjunct faculty who are mostly doctoral graduates working full-time in the education field and teaching part-time at the university; and finally, graduate students and staff who teach, advise, and supervise field placements.

New arrangements would better allow the school of education to provide the best possible instruction for professional education students. The TSE must become a different kind of institution, where the teaching responsibility gets the attention it merits. To move in this direction, the TSE will have to find new ways to carry out its mission and it must do so in concert with arts and science colleagues who help to heighten the importance of teaching campus-wide.

The Students

As one of the most important changes, we recommend that the TSE organize its students into what we call "cohorts," the members of each cohort journeying together along a common path of professional learning and socialization that leads to lifelong personal and professional growth and development. No longer should any student in a school of education lack the support of a group of students who form their own small learning community. Each student would be part of a group in which fellow students take an interest in each other's attainments. We expect that the members of a cohort will form a mutually supporting network that endures for many of them throughout their professional careers.

A cohort, for the most part, would include students pursuing the same program. The TSE would have to find the right size for a cohort over time, seeing if perhaps a dozen or twenty students might be the most practical number. Their class assignments might often call for students in the same cohort to function much as a group does in, say, cooperative learning, carrying out a project for credit together. Other times, the cohort could act as a study group, with students preparing together for examinations. Some education faculty still struggle with the concept of cohorts for part-time students, while others report improved retention and learning with cohorts of part-timers. Networking around how these new arrangements are variously developed and managed will be key to their eventual success as innovations for personalizing learning and building community. The TSE will serve the students through the cohort and individually by improvements in these five areas:

- *Recruitment*
- *Learning Experiences*
- *Assessment*
- *Placement*
- *Continuing Education*

Recruitment

Students will be admitted to the TSE, both at the initial and advanced levels, with the idea of fitting them into cohorts that will remain intact so that they encounter a set of learning experiences together. Individuals can, of course, go off to take electives in which other members of the cohorts may or may not enroll, but much of the study in education will be pursued as a group. Just as the TSE will seek diversity in its enrollment, the membership of the cohort, too, will be diverse, taking into consideration such factors as age, race, ethnicity, gender, and life experience.

> The Department of Education Administration at the University of Utah's Graduate School of Education has a field-based Ed.D. program for practicing administrators. It emphasizes the use of theory and research to frame problems of administrative practice and to seek, critically examine, and apply information to solve problems of practice in educational organizations. In an attempt to put into operation ideas on curricular integration, faculty members in Purdue University's Teacher Education Program offer their respective methods courses to a cohort of pre-service students in a block schedule.

Diversity within cohorts at the graduate level is especially important because of the specialist's need to achieve a broad understanding of youngsters. Members of the cohort can provide insights to each other so as to gain the ability to step back from a particular situation and see the larger picture. Otherwise, specialists view problems only from within the confines of their own limited perspectives. If this happens, a special educator may chalk up a child's failure only to the school's curriculum or pedagogy, or the counselor may see the cause of failure only in the child's family situation, or the school psychologist may see the problem only in test results, or the administrator may see the problem only in terms of school organization, or the teacher may see the student as not personally investing enough effort. Each professional, drawing on his or her specialization, forms a working hypothesis about the pupil's learning difficulties and conducts his or her analysis in isolation of the others, implying simple and single causes for the behavior of students. Educators should not be educated in ways that suggest that the solutions to students' problems are so elementary.

Recruitment and admissions procedures in the TSE will go beyond grade-point averages and standardized test scores to apply strong, but liberal, entrance standards. The TSE wants students who possess a service ethic and who place a high priority on diversity. It wants students who value learning for themselves and enjoy helping others learn. Members of the cohort should be people who assist each other, just as one hopes that they will help their students and colleagues as professional educators. That quaint trait, altruism, persists through these selfish times and we hope to see it manifested in as many educators as possible. Financial assistance to students admitted to the TSE will be as available when possible so that need does not prevent a qualified applicant from attending, thereby helping to create the kind of enrollment from which diverse cohorts can be assembled.

Learning Experiences

Specific faculty members will be assigned to various cohorts so that both groups, education students and faculty members, get to know each other through sustained contact over a period of several years. The TSE will underscore the importance of knowing and caring about students by building these close associations between faculty and students. The faculty members working with a particular cohort should be aware, of course, of the various activities in which students engage under the auspices of the TSE, and nothing should isolate the student from the faculty, as practice teaching so often has done. Collectively, the faculty members will assume responsibility for seeing to it that quality learning experiences are afforded to all of their students. And they will strive to ensure that learning that takes place away from campus—in the PDS and at other field placements, for instance—also adheres to high standards.

What we describe here pertains to students at advanced levels, those pursuing graduate programs, as well as to undergraduates. The responsibility of the TSE to its students assumes an added dimension at the post-baccalaureate level. The TSE will demonstrate its concern for advanced students by more closely monitoring their teaching assistantships in the education school so as to banish exploitation. It makes sense for qualified graduate students to play a role in the instruction of undergraduates, but we object to the education school using them primarily as a source of cheap labor. Teaching assistantships should be educationally valuable for the graduate students, who, after all, attend the institution as students themselves.

Assessment

Reports to students in the TSE ought to keep them apprised of their academic progress, periodically assessing their competence. Portfolios and performance evaluations based on high professional standards will be part of the record on which assessments are based. Substantial information will be garnered by PDS faculty judgments of students' performance throughout their internships. Some students will turn out to need assistance to meet high standards, and the TSE should provide it; other students may be aided by counseling them out of the program. Proper monitoring should prevent the possibility of a student not finding out until the end of the program that he or she has not measured up.

Hiring Networks

If the TSE believes in its programs and considers the students who complete them well qualified to work in elementary and secondary schools, as indeed they should be if they get credentials, then the TSE will take every step possible to get them into positions from which they can help America's children. It is that simple. The TSE must commit itself to its students, and the obligation does not end with the awarding of a degree or a credential. Holding educational professionals to high standards does little good if they can't use their well-honed talents in the workforce. The TSE will maintain contacts with groups of school administrators and school boards to promote the interests of the students that it educates.

Continuing Education

The responsibility of the TSE for its graduates continues in another way. The TSE will provide opportunities for them to keep growing. Lifelong professional development will be every bit as much of a primary function of the TSE as initial credentialing. In coming years, school districts and individual schools will probably increase their involvement in the ongoing development of their professional staff, but the TSE must act whether or not school districts accept this responsibility.

By tradition, most universities have provided their continuing education for teachers and other educators through added course work, offerings they typically make available both on- and off-campus. These courses accumulate credits that count toward step-ups on the salary schedules of most school districts. Summer school programs for educators who wish to pursue continued studies in education have also been popular, as most districts don't yet have year-round schooling, and teachers can use their vacation time accordingly.

Another popular form of continuing education, supported in part by universities, has been that of individual professors going out to consult in the schools. Universities typically allow their professors one day a week for consulting, and the school districts select and usually pay individual faculty as speakers, workshop leaders, and advisors. Typically these "consultations" are limited to one- or two-day contributions and don't involve course credits, although they do frequently count toward the accumulation of CEUs (continuing education units) that have been mandated by state governments for educators' continuing certification.

The weaknesses of these continuing education offerings have been their overemphasis on seat-time in university courses, their lack of continuity or sustained assistance over time, and their lack of close connection to educational practice as it affects youngsters' learning. Prior to the systemic suggestions made here for comprehensive professional development, universities wanting to contribute regularly to the continuing education of educators didn't know how to handle the problems of scale. The magnitude of the education workforce in each state's elementary and secondary schools dwarfs that of higher education, and since all educators need to be continuously educated to ensure that each new generation is better educated than the last, the challenge takes on an overwhelming dimension. The proportional differences in faculty size appear insurmountable.

But now we suggest the possibility of changing these circumstances in ways that address the long-standing problems of quantity and quality in the continuing education of educators. We recommend that universities develop a collaborating faculty of very high quality in Professional Development Schools, a faculty that would have a magnifier effect in terms of the qualified human resources available for continuing education. Instead of spreading the university's human resources thinly and sporadically across the schools in the state, the institutions would focus their resources on collaborating PDS faculty. A one-time, up-front major investment in these school-based educators would create a top-flight set of practitioners as full partners in their educational research, demonstration of best practice, preparation of novices, and in the continuing education of other educators in the state. The idea is to produce a synergy by combining heretofore separate, highly distributed, and scattered functions.

Here is how it might work: By focusing its resources, the university develops a set of PDS sites that serve, eventually, as the internship sites for prospective educators. Because of their extended and stronger preparation, interns approximate today's beginning teachers, yet they do not yet practice with full autonomy. They are still learning and being screened for their professional expertise, although, importantly, they provide an added human resource for the Professional Development School sites. The interns' presence, with some of the university faculty's presence, provides real-located time for the school faculty. During this time, the school faculty—as both expert practitioners and collaborating faculty for the university—conduct and demonstrate quality lessons and make themselves available for teaching prospective and practicing educators via sophisticated human and technological networks.

Thus, the university extends its expertise and outreach through this set of continuously educated partners. These partners collaborate in education research and professional education at all levels. When technological updating is completed in PDSs, these outstanding practitioners can also reach their colleagues throughout the state via a great range of interactive media. We foresee the time when the PDS networks might actually blanket the state through cooperative arrangements among universities and schools. This network could frame the professional development infrastructure in each state, giving virtually every educator access to research-based knowledge and skill in more flexible and responsive ways. But the human and technological networks needed to connect schools and universities must first be in place, and such changes require significant adaptations in many long-held traditions.

A new kind of professional development would emerge, one that would inevitably lead to reconfiguring faculty roles and graduate programs to increase relevance, quality, and accessibility. Relevance would increase because the focus of continuing education would now be placed on improved learning in the schools. Quality would rise because continuing education would be grounded in research and competent practice in actual schools. And accessibility would increase through greater numbers of university faculty—including the collaborating faculty that the university helps develop and bring into true partnership—and the technological infrastructure built through university and school investment in the PDSs.

The human resources and capacity gained by establishing this promising new institution and set of networks on the American landscape—the Professional Development Schools—affords a more flexible university contribution to continuing education. For example, the TSE with its PDS collaborating faculty would have real demonstration sites available, in which educators could actually see and experience the changing nature of education. And by grounding the substance of professional development in trustworthy study of educational practices that have real consequences for young people's learning, we stand a chance of diminishing the "every-new-fad" nature of contemporary continuing education in the schools. The TSE also can help graduates who want to prepare to sit for the examinations of the National Board for Professional Teaching Standards, and as the National Policy Board for Educational Administration brings forth standards and assessments, the TSE can also assist the administrators and aspiring administrators among its graduates. In speaking of what the TSE owes to its graduates, we do not mean to indicate that non-graduates shall be excluded from the TSE programs. But if the continuing education programs of each education school concern themselves primarily with their graduates, this will at least assure each professional of a place to turn for this kind of advancement.

As the TSE increases its capacity for outreach with PDS faculty over time, it is likely to play a more important role in professional development for neighboring schools and even for more distant schools that can participate by way of computer hook-ups. We expect increased capacity for outreach as PDS faculty from the school and university together develop more familiar routines, as university interns become more regular parts of the PDS resource, and as all participants develop greater confidence and expertise in their new arrangements. The human and technological networking capacity that the PDS develops should eventually become an important resource for dissemination of research, tested theory, and wise practice throughout our professional development networks nationwide. Together, the various school districts and the TSE should be able to design more meaningful and more lasting professional development activities than either could offer if left on its own. Certainly this "can do" cadre of professional development specialists working in the PDSs will be more valuable than the traditional consultants who come from various government or private consulting firms, typically from out of state.

The Faculty

The TSE should take an expansive view in defining the faculty community involved in the education of school professionals. Some are further from the center of the circle than others, but somewhere within the circumference reside many people whose professional activities touch upon students studying for work in the schools. Students in the TSE will gain to the extent that the institution nurtures the connections among members of the faculty. All of those whose work has any link whatsoever to the TSE should be encouraged to regard themselves as unselfish resources for the students of the education school. This means changing the mindset of some people.

Through its participation in Fordham University's National Center for Social Work and Education Collaboration and its Stay-in-School Projects, Fordham's Graduate School of Education is developing elements of collaborative professional education for social workers and educators. The efforts focus on an examination of in-service

and pre-service preparation of professionals for work
in full-service schools.

Faculty members in the arts and sciences, for instance, play key roles in providing liberal education, depth in the disciplines, and sometimes in subject-specific teaching methods, but they pledge primary fealty to the liberal arts and especially to their disciplines. And within the TSE itself, some faculty members play similar roles in such disciplines as educational sociology, history, or psychology. Other people who teach education students are mentors in the school and not even integrated into the campus community. The allegiance to the goals of the TSE of these men and women should be strengthened so that the majority of the faculty supports the general mission of the TSE. We acknowledge the difficulty the TSE will have in attaining this goal. Surveys show that faculty members in higher education regard their loyalties to their disciplines as superseding those to their institutions. But the TSE must cultivate the faculty so as to make them comfortable with their place within the orbit of the professional education of educators and to encourage their support of the TSE and its programs.

A troubling aspect of the faculty continuum just described has to do with the uneven balance in status, rewards, and integration into the professional community. At one end, university-based scholars enjoy the greatest advantages. At the other end, the more one's work ties that faculty member to the public schools, the more marginal the rewards and the status in the education school. Thus, few of those with university appointments want to accept assignments that bind them closer to the public schools. The situation resembles that which formerly existed in public education, when teachers who taught the youngest children occupied the positions lowest in pay and prestige and their colleagues in high school got the most recognition and the highest salaries. In the years ahead, the TSE must correct this imbalance and underscore the belief that professional proximity to elementary and secondary school students means being nearest to the fundamental mission of the school of education.

Some institutions have recruited and appointed young faculty members in order to further these objectives, but by working as extensively in the PDS as they do, these newcomers place themselves at a disadvantage. The university's reward system continues to favor a steady stream of publications over all other criteria for promotion, tenure, and merit pay. Likewise, the elevation of the clinical professorship remains problematic so long as such field-based positions get marginal backing from the university. Criteria for judging excellence in faculty contribution to the schools should be developed as soon as possible so that the university has tangible standards for evaluating the kind of faculty work that verges away from more traditional activities.

The University-Based Faculty

The TSE cannot fulfill its goals unless it welcomes a full range of scholarly approaches among its faculty members. Many kinds of faculty roles will prove vital to the university-based school of education of the future—the statistician developing new quantitative tools for research syntheses; the historian exploring gender relations in schooling; the policy analyst consulting on reform of federal education policy; and the developmental psychologist studying the emergence of social competence in children. The TSE requires a broad, eclectic mix of scholars who bring cutting-edge knowledge to the programs of professional development. For that reason, nothing in this report should be read as hostile to this free play of scholarly inquiry or to the marshaling of many disciplinary perspectives on a wide range of issues, questions, and problems. These scholarly pursuits have brought distinction to the Holmes institutions in the past and will continue to do so in the future.

A fresh emphasis in the revamped school of education, though, will be put on forming a tighter bond between scholarship and practice. The creation of the PDS promotes that objective. Thus, the TSE agenda has implications for the composition of the university faculty and for faculty work commitments. Tomorrow's School of Education unabashedly seeks to employ more faculty members who want to use their research abilities to pursue interests in the settings provided by elementary and secondary schools, grounding their scholarship in practice.

> Nine of the twelve professional development schools with which the University of Louisville is working are in urban areas. The first and most well-developed efforts are two urban high schools where the university teaches secondary education courses. Practitioners help with the planning and the teaching. University faculty, in turn, are involved with teaching, restructuring, and research projects in the schools.

If one were to observe such scholars' workdays or work weeks, they might look something like this: The professors divide their professional time mainly between two locales, the TSE and PDS, shuttling regularly between campus and public school. Sometimes they teach classes on campus, as professors have always done, and other times they provide professional development for practicing educators at the PDS itself through study groups and other means. Sometimes they co-teach children in the public school; other times they confer with school teams as part of their shared responsibility for TSE interns. They spend some of their time at the PDS testing hypotheses through action- and intervention-oriented research projects, carrying out this work alone at times and sometimes collaborating with school faculty members. When the findings are published, the authorship may reflect a sole investigator or the names of practitioners in the PDS, and maybe even education students who are listed as co-authors in recognition of their scholarly contributions to the publication.

This new breed of professor must learn to walk the new walk, keeping one foot in the traditional scholarly community of the campus, where one must satisfy rigorous canons and norms, and keeping the other foot in the public school, where one respects the realities of practice and honors the need of educators to serve children, schools, and communities. Only a few brave and dexterous souls have mastered this unusual walk so far. Those who try to combine work in the public schools with assignments on campus often stumble because the university hobbles them by withholding the support they need to work with the public schools. As we said, even the university's standards for judging such practice-based research remain inchoate.

Given the right backing, however, an exciting array of bold scholarly ventures emerge as possibilities once connections between the TSE and the PDS are made on the levels we envision. These are just a few such examples:

- A psychometrician might work with PDS faculty to develop new methods of student assessment in the schools.
- An expert in special education might try out new approaches to inclusion of disabled students in the mainstream of the schools.
- An expert in literacy might develop, pilot, and study the effects on learning of integrated approaches to reading and writing.
- A professor of educational administration might develop and study the exercise of team-based leadership and shared decision-making in the PDS.

These scenarios predicate themselves on the assumption that the PDS will be a resource for all faculty members at the university, not just for a few in the school of education. To realize the fullness of the vision, members of the arts and science faculty must be drawn into the work of the PDS. We realize we propound an ambitious agenda, one that demands changes in the faculty culture for all of this to happen. Long-standing discontinuities and contradictions that have plagued the professional education of educators can be remedied only if liberal arts and education professors work together, if the education school creates close relationships with a set of PDSs, and if professionals across fields collaborate around models of integrated service delivery to children and youth.

The Field-Based Faculty

We propose to integrate the field-based portion of the faculty fully into the TSE faculty so that they no longer have the standing of second-class citizens. Prior to the rise of the university in America, apprenticeship sufficed as the principal form of professional education. The professional school, vested with pretensions of the larger university of which it became part, obviated the simple arrangements of the apprenticeship in the name of uplifting the profession. This shift can be counted as progress insofar as the professions developed a theoretical and scientific basis for practice that could be conveyed through a rigorous course of study. But, in education, some of the benefits of the older mode of learning on the job from a master disappeared and the vestiges of the master's role lost its prestige—largely because standards were not maintained for selecting the masters.

Thus, particular attention must now be given to the clinical professors whose work primarily is in the public schools. The clinical professors—we wish another, less medical, title were used—must come from the ranks of distinguished practitioners with substantial experience in the schools. These faculty members form a living bridge between campus and practice and will share with colleagues on campus responsibilities associated with the Professional Development School agenda and with the development and operation of professional studies programs. Differentiated roles will be developed, where faculty having their tenure with the schools collaborate with faculty tenured with the university in making significant contributions to programs of teaching and inquiry. Clinical professors must be made to feel a part of the university even if their work commitments are away from the campus and focused substantially on the PDS and its youthful learners. Upon these educators fall a main part of the responsibility for ensuring that education students experience quality in practice, and are prepared to meet high standards.

The Holmes program at Louisiana State University has been well served by the creation of clinical faculty roles for eleven new members of the faculty. Clinical faculty are primarily responsible for helping Holmes students integrate theory and practice through guiding and supervising their practicum experiences. A critical outgrowth of The Ohio State University's PDS initiative is the creation of a "clinical educator" role wherein expert veteran teachers are released for fifty percent of their time to interact directly in the initial teacher preparation program and to provide leadership for continuing profes-

sional development and school improvement at PDS
sites.

The Holmes Group case studies conducted in conjunction with this report
indicate that most universities are revisiting the issue of field faculty and making appointments with an eye toward diversifying and upgrading this role. Many of these
appointees are seen as integral to the PDS. We must build on these efforts, insisting that reciprocity agreements be in place with the schools, and work out collaborative staffing arrangements. Members of the TSE faculty should treat those in the
PDS as peers—not as glorified graduate assistants. To bestow upon the clinical professor some of the luster of the masters of old, the TSE must invest in planning and
professional development for both school and university faculty as shared assignments
are explored. As no single model exists for this renewal, we suggest that each university further its own exploration, and share with others the various approaches that
best work with the public schools.

At the most modest level, a TSE might arrive at an arrangement under which
PDS faculty guide novices engaged in field experiences by providing observation, individual and small group instruction, projects of short duration, and extended internships. A more far-reaching approach might involve creating formal positions with
pay and dedicated time for designated PDS faculty who will teach at the university,
as well as at their own public school.

Whether the TSE chooses either of these approaches or some other arrangement,
the participating PDS faculty members should be selected with care and given good
preparation for their additional duties so that they will be full colleagues of the
university-based faculty, partners in a renewal of professional education based on integrating practice with theory. Field-based faculty members should be viewed as potential colleagues of university-based faculty in research and development activities, as
professionals comfortable with serious intellectual work. Field-based faculty members should be expert and exemplary practitioners, very much in keeping with the
apprentice tradition, to whom the TSE should commit stable, long-term resources.

A New Professional Identity
for All Members of the Faculty

Taken together, these various recommendations affecting both the university-based
faculty and the field-based faculty, aim to create a new institutional culture and a new
professional identity, aligned more directly with the country's elementary and secondary schools. Schools of education have been under pressure to adapt to the cul-

ture of the Academy and to distance themselves from the public schools. The TSE, by comparison, dedicates itself to joining research, development, and preparation to the service of improving education as practiced in elementary and secondary schools. To reach this goal, the school of education must support the emergence of a new faculty culture and the university itself must modify some of its policies. These five steps, then, must be taken by the TSE if needed changes are to occur:

1   Graduate students given teaching and other service-related assignments will be carefully selected and supervised, and provided the support required for success.

2   The TSE will implement the recommendations of the Holmes Equity Panel, thereby increasing targeted efforts to recruit and retain students, staff, and faculty of color. This will mean developing and using indicators of progress toward an inclusive community and integrating diverse perspectives into the life of the TSE and into the curriculum.

3   The TSE will make a top priority of increasing the numbers of regular faculty committed to working in the PDS as a primary site for their teaching, scholarship, and service.

4   The TSE will encourage and assist a significant number of regular faculty members to connect their talents, interests, and experience to the TSE agenda, particularly to activities in the PDSs and to the professional studies curriculum.

5   The TSE will review and revise its policies and procedures for promotion, tenure, and merit pay in light of high standards for this work, and then negotiate to make appropriate changes in university-wide policies.

The range of policy reformulations required in the TSE and in the university at large will differ according to the conditions that already exist. In general, though, institutions will need new indicators and standards to evaluate an expanded range of faculty tasks at the PDS, including the work of teaching, advising, and supervising, as well as participation in curriculum development, collaborative research, governance, and professional development. Some questions about how to apply these standards can be answered only over time. How, for instance, will this new configuration of assignments affect considerations for promotion and tenure?

In addition, institutions must reconsider policies in regard to workloads and scheduling to accommodate these broadened activities. Finally, institutions will have to weigh whether to adopt such new kinds of faculty incentives as small grant programs to fund faculty projects associated with pursuits in the PDS. This report does not provide the proper forum for thrashing out the details of the many policies that will affect field-based faculty; we attempt only to suggest a few of the issues that will have to be tackled. These include hiring criteria, titles, compensation, training, and relationships to the university and school districts.

■|■|■

The Core of Learning

What All Educators Must Know

Images of a core evoke many thoughts. A core is something central. A core is a uniting element. A core is the pith that defines and establishes the character of something. The core of learning for an education professional consists of the essential knowledge that everyone—the eleventh-grade chemistry teacher, the middle-school assistant principal, the second-grade teacher, and all others who pursue a career connected to the teaching and learning that occur in the public school—ought to possess.

The core is essential, but not all essential knowledge resides in the core. By this we mean to say that while all educators will have had the same core experiences, individuals will have gone on to acquire specialized knowledge. Thus, the chemistry teacher and the assistant principal each have advanced knowledge that goes beyond the core and enables them, separate from one another, to perform functions vital to the school. Education in both the core and in the specialties accumulates from a wide variety of learning experiences, in the larger university, in the TSE, in its PDSs, and at other sites in the field, as well as through independent study. Much of the learning will probably be done toward the attainment of degrees and certificates, but we also foresee some of the core and special learning being provided in informal, noncredit situations.

The professional core that we envision connects itself strongly to the teaching and learning of the classrooms of elementary and secondary schools. By implication, almost everyone who goes to work in public education should be prepared to teach and—with few exceptions—should launch their careers as teachers working directly with children. Among the possible exceptions are those, for instance, who work as school nurses, accountants in the district business office, and some university-based professors in the foundation areas. As we see it, all major advanced positions in education would build on a base of demonstrated knowledge and competence related to the teaching and learning of school-age children, who, after all, provide the reason why the schooling enterprise exists.

The TSE will create a professional force of educators bound to each other and to public education by a set of common experiences. All will have shared a core education that ensures that they speak the same professional language, that a certain body of skills has been mastered by all, and that they cherish professional values that unite them, not divide them. In addition, as teachers and former teachers, they will all resonate to the heartbeat of the classroom, the life force that sustains every fiber of elementary and secondary education.

We do not advocate a single approach to providing core knowledge. Each TSE must experiment with a range of structures and programs that it develops to offer initial and advanced common learning. Institutions will pursue various structural and programmatic alternatives, differing in points of entry and exit, duration, terminal degree, as well as in content and focus. The institutions will be bound together by an uncompromising commitment to high-quality learning for educators.

Each TSE need not reinvent the elements of the core. Major efforts to identify the base of learning for teaching have yielded considerable consensus. These include the syntheses of research and practice commissioned by the American Association of Colleges for Teaching Education, the Association of Teacher Educators, and the American Educational Research Association, as well as the standards put forth by the National Board for Professional Teaching Standards, the National Council for the Accreditation of Teacher Education, and the INTASC project of the Chief State School Officers. John Goodlad's reports on teacher education and the background review of the literature conducted for this Holmes study indicate a growing consensus, but not one free of controversy. An important set of moral and epistemological issues has been engaged—issues that must continue to be addressed around questions of equity and diversity, the nature of knowledge, power and privilege, and evidence.

The same areas that comprise the knowledge, skills, and dispositions required of beginning teachers also serve to organize the advanced core that brings together educators preparing for multiple roles including administration, counseling, social and health services, and further work in teaching. The specialized and role-specific knowledge and skills that reflect both requirements for licensure and consensus within particular professional associations provide a base for learning at the advanced level.

Faculty members at education schools apparently support the idea of a core professional curriculum for entry-level students more readily than they do for advanced students. But since we assume that good professional development for educators must foster teamwork and learning throughout one's career, we believe that concern about a core of knowledge should not be limited to initial preparation. The knowledge of working educators will grow outdated and increasingly useless if they do not deepen and extend it. The TSE, with its PDSs and collaborating school districts, can be a partner in supporting such professional development. The idea of the "spiral curriculum" described by Jerome Bruner captures the essence of this approach. Educators in elementary and secondary schools will revisit and rework core concepts and topics at increasing levels of sophistication and complexity.

The extension of the core into the graduate level in education puts our goal at odds with the dominant approach to graduate studies taken by many working professional educators, for whom advanced learning is, at best, a part-time activity to be squeezed into one's busy schedule. Regretfully, we found in our case studies that education school faculty resist the prospect of altering the traditional pattern, a stance that surely poses an obstacle to the reforms we wish to introduce. In our view, the current system operates as if credentials and pay increases, not professional knowledge, were the point of advanced programs. Many programs have recently undergone redesign in light of changing expectations, while others follow a slower, more phlegmatic pace. We expect the new curricula, program structures, and faculty relationships called for in this report to emerge over time, but the bulk of the change remains unrealized at almost all schools of education.

> Students at the University of Colorado seeking elementary and secondary teaching certificates get their degrees in Arts and Sciences, reflecting the commitment of the education school to prepare a cadre of teachers who have strong liberal arts backgrounds and subject matter knowledge, as well as training in pedagogy, child development, assessment, the social and cultural aspects of schooling, and professional ethics.

What we describe in these pages may sound somewhat familiar. This discussion grows directly from previous declarations and publications of The Holmes Group.

In *Tomorrow's Teachers,* for instance, we recommended abolishing the undergraduate education major so as to strengthen prospective teachers' general education and their depth of content knowledge in the subjects they would teach. We assumed that many (though not all) future teachers would begin at least a portion of their education studies as undergraduates, but that they would not major in education until the extensive professional sequence started in the fifth year.

We urged that teachers ground themselves in the arts and sciences, reasoning that if it took students majoring in arts and science disciplines four years to complete their liberal studies, then teachers, too, would need at least the same length of time. The Holmes Group remains fundamentally committed to securing more time for the education of teachers. Future teachers must have a firm foundation in the arts and sciences in order to make teaching intellectual work. A period of internship adds further substance to this foundation. We hold fast to what we stated in 1989:

> Across Holmes Group campuses a variety of structures are taking shape. These include revisions of undergraduate programs, integrated five-year programs, fifth-year programs coordinated with undergraduate education, master's degree programs for liberal arts graduates who wish to enter teaching, and alternate route programs that rely heavily on apprenticeship . . . The Holmes Group claim for more time to prepare teachers is being staked out in the form of "integrated extended" programs— usually five (or more) years in duration, including an internship that is both intensively supervised and formally reflected upon. (p.1)

The Elements of the Core

Our initial report proposed that the profession recognize three categories of teacher: the "career professional teacher" prepared not only to teach but to assume a range of schoolwide responsibilities; the "professional teacher" prepared to assume full classroom duties; and the "instructor," a novice with a temporary certificate who practices under the supervision of a career professional. We still believe in these categories and urge that they be institutionalized through state policy. The elements of the core draw on the education school's unique areas of knowledge, though they are organized conceptually in ways more compatible with existing frameworks. They concern themselves with the following:

- Human Development and Young People's Learning
- Subject Matter, Technology, and Pedagogy for Young People's Learning
- Instructional Management for Young People's Learning
- Inquiry, Reflection, and R&D in the Interest of Young People's Learning
- Collaboration in Support of Young People's Learning

Human Development and Young People's Learning

Teachers must acquire substantial, rich, and varied knowledge about learners as an indispensable foundation for their practice. Of course, the eleventh-grade chemistry teacher, the third-grade teacher, and the reading teacher will each need to know something different to handle their specialties. But all require, as a starting point, a broad, general understanding of human development and its implications for learning, and a deep knowledge of the core of their teaching subjects. This knowledge should enable teachers to delve into the psychological, social, and cultural aspects of students' learning and to focus on the most important and enduring ideas of their disciplines. Teachers well versed in these areas use the knowledge to motivate students, to judge their responses, and to help students gain confidence as learners. Armed with this knowledge, the teacher recognizes how relationships between language and cultural background affect students' learning.

The stakes here revolve around whether or not the teacher knows enough to understand what the student brings to the learning situation and to appreciate what steps she must take to match the material and the pedagogy to the child's formal and informal experiences. Equipped with this knowledge, the teacher can step out of her own skin and empathize with the student and his distinctive needs as a learner. Knowledge of human development allows a teacher to avoid traps and heightens the likelihood of the teacher accepting the student's thoughts and actions as perfectly reasonable given the student's experiences. The issue is not whether the child has had the "right" experiences, but whether the teacher can seize on those experiences, whatever they may be, and help the student use them to greater advantage for learning. A skilled teacher structures the learning so that it builds on what the student knows to move him or her to higher levels of competence and understanding.

Subject Matter, Technology, and Pedagogy for Young People's Learning

Teachers acquire most of their subject matter knowledge in studies in the arts and sciences, though education courses that tie pedagogy to developmentally appropriate content for youngsters of different ages augment this background. Moreover, in the TSE, this learning will not be monochromatic, but will take on interdisciplinary shadings to give it richer, fuller colorings. Additional input on the integration of subject matter gives educators the acuity to recognize the many artificial barriers that divide subjects, both when they learn about them and when they teach about them.

Interdisciplinary seminars, for instance, should make up a portion of the core learning curriculum. At their best, these seminars are the products of collaborations, developed and taught by members of the education and liberal arts faculties or by professors and schoolteachers. Where else are students of education going to delve into the relationships between and among the disciplines or the ways in which the same concept might be taught from various disciplinary perspectives? Such learning has characteristically been absent from more traditional programs, although we emphasize that interdisciplinary studies grow from sound learning in the disciplines. The matter of co-mingling the disciplines for purposes of additional important learning is a complicated and complex matter that educators need to understand.

We fear that without an approach of this kind, education professionals will be unprepared as teachers to help their students jump disciplinary barriers. It's an old story: Teach something to someone the way you would like that person to teach it. If students think their universities do not value interdisciplinary knowledge, then surely those students, as teachers, will also deem it unimportant. The TSE can demonstrate its commitment to pedagogy that embraces both knowledge in the disciplines and cross-disciplinary approaches by making it a prime concern of the professional core.

Today's educators must also learn and have opportunity to develop facility with the rich array of technologies they can now exploit to help youngsters learn important ideas and powerful skills. No longer limited to texts, paper, and chalk boards, educators need the chance to explore the range of alternative technologies available for students' learning. They must experience and have opportunity to develop facility in the use of various technologies during their internships, giving attention to the study and examination of technology's power in helping youngsters learn their subject matters more effectively.

And just as educators must learn to select developmentally appropriate subjects and technologies for learners, so must they experience and develop expertise in constructing pedagogically appropriate tasks for students' learning. Often, this will mean providing youngsters with enriching experiences in and out of school, opportunities for self-evaluation, and skills in record keeping. Today's technologies open a new world for both learning and better documentation of that learning.

Instructional Management for Young People's Learning

Good intentions will come to naught if a teacher cannot organize for instruction. We are talking, for example, about the ability to link curriculum planning, classroom management, instructional strategies, assessment, and conferences with parents. Teaching and learning are undermined without smooth links among a number of predictable activities. And without some of these connections, the parts would spin loose and chaos would reign.

We oppose the idea of teachers performing as clerks who manage preordained learning packages, but we know that a classroom functions best as a community and, as such, must be well organized. To send new teachers into classrooms without the technical knowledge related to fundamental duties is to drop someone into the ocean without swimming lessons. The person may survive, but it won't be a pretty sight. As in the other areas of the professional core, the knowledge imparted grows gradually more sophisticated so that from an initial emphasis on the classroom and on school instruction, the emphasis for advanced students, who already work in the schools and in district offices, revolves around such topics as cross-school analyses of students' learning, staff development policies, and out-of-school learning opportunities for students. At this level, the school professionals who are advanced students may scrutinize and evaluate methods of school improvement and examine how state and local requirements might be better aligned with national goals.

At the risk of repetition, we repeat the idea that schools are complex systems and that districts and state systems, too, are networks of complex systems with an overlay of additional complications. Those in education who fail to appreciate these intricacies labor at a decided disadvantage. Education left to chance is education that may not happen, and so every professional carries some responsibility for making the system effective for the students it is supposed to serve.

Inquiry, Reflection, and R&D in the Interest of Young People's Learning

Educators should learn not only how to cope with recurring problems, but also how to reflect productively on their students, their actions, and their learning. This area of professional education usually gets scant attention and most of the practitioners for whom reflection and inquiry are important parts of the job gained their insights outside of formal preparation. It does not have to be this way. Work in schools should be thoughtful employment that engages one's intellect and stimulates one's inquisitiveness. Reflective educators learn how to harness and discipline their insights for the benefit of students. The TSE should ensure that its students are predisposed to act in this way. Educators need not look beyond the learner-centered schools and communities they are developing to find the building blocks on which to construct this kind of education.

> Inquiry and reflective practice are infused as a way of life throughout professional preparation in teacher education at the University of Connecticut.

Everyday concerns, not abstractions, provide points for educators to ponder and to explore. Worthy questions pour forth like water from a faucet: Why are some students and not others confused by a new concept in mathematics? What experience could help them come to better understanding? Why is it so difficult for students to come up with a topic when they are told that they can write a paper about anything? Why do high schools teach biology before they teach chemistry? Professional education should equip school professionals to set sail for voyages of discovery. Every educator, in effect, has through his or her access to a classroom a fascinating source of material on which to reflect and about which to inquire. The advent of technology, like the steam-powered ships that replaced the clippers, makes this voyage of discovery faster, easier, and more productive.

Reflection and inquiry in the service of better teaching and learning must be lifted to a prominent place in the core of the TSE. As the reflection of PDS faculty becomes more sophisticated and disciplined, and as they get increased time for it (largely through contributions of PDS interns), they will profit from opportunities to learn again from inquiry—just as the university faculty will profit from opportunity to learn again about educational practice. Students will have around them to serve as models, professors and veteran practitioners who themselves strengthen their work through careful reflection and inquiry. The TSE should socialize its students to a norm that accords priority to the intellectual side of teaching. We expect the TSE to become a community of learners in the fullest sense.

Collaboration in Support of Young People's Learning

Collegiality appears to be only for those outside elementary and secondary schools. Practitioners in the schools remain isolated, working alone and spurning offers of collaboration because the education school and the public schools that hire them expect it to be that way. Like solo pilots in small planes, education professionals always run the risk of going into free fall with nothing to cushion their landing. However, school professionals owe it to their students, if not themselves, to dispel the curse of isolation and join with partners who can help with their students' success. The partners might be colleagues in neighboring classrooms or on college campuses, youth service providers, parents of students, local activists, or any of a multitude of others whose experience will enrich the classroom. In other words, the entire community should be enlisted in behalf of the students.

Schools treat teamwork as some exotic commodity, still unknown and untested. But those employed in business and industry—as well as a small but growing number in education—know that much more can be accomplished in unison, by delegating portions of the work that probably would not be done if left to individuals.

Not only should the TSE encourage education professionals to accept this idea, but it must teach them how teams operate and how to work with colleagues. Education students can start absorbing the fundamentals of teamwork by performing as members of teams while in the TSE and in PDS cohorts. Similarly, while some public schools have turned to health and social service agencies as partners, most schools have no such experience. At one time or another, many of those who work in these schools pass through the TSE as they pursue advanced studies. The TSE should infuse the studies of its students with the lessons they need to form partnerships.

We acknowledge, incidentally, that many faculty members in the universities and in schools of education, too, spurn the idea of collaboration and that much proselytization will be needed. Our case studies reveal that activities that increase interdependence in working relationships receive least support from the faculty members. Some professors in departments of teacher education, for instance, do not want to work with those in departments of school administration, and neither may want to work with the department of counseling. A note of encouragement, however, can be heard in the response of education faculty to the surveys we conducted, indicating that they support collaboration with public school educators. This interest extends to research partnerships, as well, where a majority of the faculty said that shared inquiry in public schools was highly desirable.

Professional Foundations

Foundations courses in education schools bring together perspectives from history, philosophy, sociology, and political science to examine American education. Some educators disparage foundations courses, but we believe these offerings, when taught well, have much to say about why educators do what they do and why public schools are the way that they are. The TSE can revitalize foundations courses by teaching them better and by showing students how the content relates to conditions that confront educators in the schools in which they work today. As taught in the core of professional education, foundations courses ought to be a wonderful vehicle for interdisciplinary knowledge that draws extensively on the humanities and social sciences. This approach should underpin the preparation of all practitioners.

Through interdepartmental collaboration, a set of foundations courses has been developed for all teacher licensure students at the University of Minnesota. This core provides students with crucial ingredients for classroom success: (1) a comprehensive understand-

ing of the aims of education and the role of schools in society, including the current dilemmas facing teachers; (2)
the importance of literacy and critical thinking skills; (3)
inquiry into the nature of teaching and schooling; and
(4) assumptions underlying school reform, including
school organization, pupil grouping, curriculum, and
parental involvement.

Foundational knowledge can also be integrated into other courses rather than
being left only to be taught in separate courses. Novices and advanced students
might be helped to make connections between what they encounter in public schools
and the content of the foundations course. Free-standing studies in the foundations
of education should be included in the initial core, but with an eye toward deepening treatment of the various topics as part of ongoing professional development.
We recommend that in revising foundations courses the TSE include studies in educational ethics, which otherwise might not be supplied at all. Also, teaching about
foundations should link itself to contemporary events, such as disputes over busing,
choice, or outcomes-based education, to demonstrate the enduring and relevant
nature of knowledge about the foundations of education.

What It Would Look Like:
A Scenario for Tomorrow's School of Education

The twenty-first century began just a few years ago and the school of education, though
still housed in its former site, feels very different once one enters the old red brick
structure. Let us walk through the building, a place where the entire milieu supports
the education of school professionals who will be grounded in a common core, people linked by their devotion to teaching as an intellectual pursuit. A visitor cannot
help but notice the amount of cooperation among those who teach education students and among the students themselves. Faculty members work together to plan
and co-teach courses: the professors from the TSE, the professors from arts and sciences, and the clinical faculty from the PDS. The curriculum is the product of their
collaboration. They meet regularly to discuss the programs of the cohorts of students
they share and to identify the learning needs of individual students. The students
follow the lead of the teachers, often pooling their talents and energies to learn
together.

The visitor is impressed by the portability of the education. These students take
it as natural to change their places of learning continually, rotating from campus to

the PDS, and to other field sites that are locales for their learning. Off-campus experiential education flourishes to a degree far beyond that described by today's reformists, who talk about this sort of learning principally in regard to high school students. Some education students even use social service agencies and other community facilities as locales for their learning.

Active, student-centered forms of pedagogy predominate, though lectures are used when appropriate. Every classroom seems to bristle with VCRs, CD-ROMS, and computers. Often, students gather in learning groups to solve problems or review cases. Frequently, they pursue independent projects. Camcorders sit on shelves for students to take into public schools to document their work. Faculty members accept as part of their basic work some responsibility for developing learning materials for professional education students, sometimes writing cases or problem scenarios. Other times they sit at word processors, writing comments onto "papers" that students submitted electronically, or else they record videotapes in public schools that they incorporate into the lessons they teach on campus.

Sometimes students scrutinize work in the PDS without actually going to the school. The media lab permits them to observe PDS classes as they happen or to review videotapes of past classes. Cameras mounted inconspicuously in the corners of certain PDS classrooms create this running documentary. Interactive communications allow an instructor at the PDS to engage the students who are watching the class in the media lab on the college campus in a full-blown exchange of ideas. Furthermore, the work of the children in the PDS class can be called up on a disk in the media lab so that the TSE student can follow up on the results of the whole-class instruction that he or she has viewed.

Flexibility is a hallmark of this new TSE. Instead of every student being expected to do the same thing, education students, even those enrolled in the same course, may get different assignments in their studies, particularly in the PDS and at the various field sites. The approach resembles what happens when architecture students take internships in offices and some work on computer-aided design, while others build models, and still others help in the marketing department. The amount of time education students spend at field placements also varies; one student may go to the third-grade classroom solely to observe only once a week for two hours; another may act as a teacher's aide for a full day every other week.

Undergraduate and graduate courses for pre-service and in-service teachers at Texas Tech University are taught regularly in the six professional development schools.

To a remarkable degree, almost without being conscious of it, faculty members in higher education have by this time in the first decade of the twenty-first century adopted many of the reforms that they once urged upon elementary and secondary schools. The changes have thrust education students into a new situation in which the TSE models for them the very kinds of behaviors that teachers were for years being asked to incorporate into the public schools. The proliferation of teamwork into the TSE is yet another of the reforms that once were urged only on pre-collegiate education. Just as they were telling classroom teachers in elementary and secondary schools for so many years, those associated with the education school have cracked through barriers of isolation. Small groups gather to collaborate on projects in rooms of the TSE that once were used only for classes.

A sense of community pervades the TSE. The pall of cynicism so familiar to those who knew this school of education just a few years earlier seems to have lifted. Maybe this happened because the studies root themselves so thoroughly in the issues of teaching and learning that dominate day-to-day life in the public schools. No one, professor or student, any longer scoffs and says of the content of the education courses that "this is out of touch with reality."

■|■|■

The Professional Development School

Integral To Tomorrow's School of Education

When we created The Holmes Group in 1986, we invented the idea of the Professional Development School and we joined with practicing educators over the next several years to construct guidelines for developing this new genre. Early in 1990, we published *Tomorrow's Schools: Principles for the Design of the Professional Development School,* and most of our member institutions have been refining the PDS ever since.

The concept of the PDS took hold, but like all other good ideas it attracted cheap copies. The label "PDS" has been slapped on to all kinds of schools that do not begin to approach what we had in mind at the beginning. The most dangerous result of this wave of imitation is that the copies threaten to devalue and drive out the real currency. When nothing more than a school to which students are sent for their practice teaching automatically carries the designation PDS, the deepest and most radical intentions of this innovation fade away. As a matter of fact, such deceptions, intentional or inadvertent, are inimical to the very essence of the PDS, which means to stress the professional integrity of the teaching profession.

We are concerned not because it is our idea that is being co-opted, but because the PDS remains integral to what we envision as Tomorrow's School of Education. Without the authentic PDS, the TSE will not be all that we know it can be. Nothing like the PDS has ever before existed in American education. Analogues can be found

in medicine with the teaching hospital and in agriculture with the experimental station and the extension service, but the PDS contains characteristics that are sui
generis. This institution and the network of continuous innovation that it is designed
to sustain are meant to bring about substantial improvement in public schooling.
The PDS is no McDonald's franchise to be set in place ready to operate simply by
acquiring the proper equipment and following the rules in a manual. Sweat and
tears make the PDS. It is as much a process as a place, and its dynamism means that
the PDS evolves constantly. Human interactions shape each PDS and so no two PDSs
look exactly the same, though all possess certain characteristics in common.

Completed research from Colorado State University's
most fully-developed high school professional development school confirms that teacher candidates who
participate in the PDS route to licensure are better
prepared for their student teaching internship than
those who attend the traditional program. The University
of South Carolina has established seventeen professional development schools, all of which reflect the six
design principles for PDSs outlined in *Tomorrow's
Schools*. Now, the South Carolina Commission on Higher
Education and the State Department of Education have
outlined a plan to create and fund PDSs for all teacher
education programs in the state by the year 2000.

The PDS injects school-based and traditional research into teaching and learning in the context of school and education school renewal. It allows for educational
theory to be examined under the strains and tensions of practice and readily discards
those practices that don't bring improved results. Functionally, the PDS demands a
close interplay of education faculties in higher education and in public schools.
When it works, the PDS produces more engaged learning and greater understanding among students. Furthermore, it releases educators from the grip of ennui and
immerses them in collaborative personal and professional growth so that they may
join a learning community of education professionals. The PDS stands potentially
central to three basic commitments of the TSE—professional learning in the context of sound practice, improvement-oriented inquiry, and educational standard-setting. We shall discuss each of these commitments.

Professional Learning in the Context of Sound Practice

A student of professional education benefits from a setting in which he or she may observe, be guided by, and participate in discussions with a cross-section of excellent practitioners. This the PDS provides, taking advantage of the expertise of educators throughout the building, as well as those from the participating TSE. Contrast a stimulating environment of this sort with what the student of professional education typically encounters in practice teaching—a supervising teacher who has little or no connection to the rest of the student's program and who works in isolation from the rest of the faculty. This absence of strong practical connections between the knowledge and skills taught in the classroom of the education school and their application in practice represents a central, glaring weakness in most university-based professional learning for educators. Opportunities for practice in this kind of pre-service education usually limit themselves to a single classroom and seldom offer the entire school as a crucible in which to forge knowledge into practice. Where a seamless connection between preparation in the university and preparation in the school should be expected, only gaps appear. Teachers in the public school are not brought into the work of the university and the professors are not involved in the public school.

The worst manifestations of this incongruity appear in places where the public schools fail most egregiously to serve their students. These overwhelmingly are the elementary and secondary schools populated by indigent children, where teaching and learning plumb the depths of despair and, for the students, the passage through the system amounts to little more than a march to oblivion. The PDS has a special mission in these settings. Good education for all depends on good practice in elementary and secondary schools everywhere, including the neighborhoods that historically have been the worst served. The PDS offers a format for realizing that goal, exemplary not only of best practice but also faithful to what we spell out in these pages as the objectives of the TSE in regard to equity. The TSE enjoys company in this quest. We have in mind James Comer's School Development Program, Henry Levin's Accelerated Schools Project, Theodore Sizer's Coalition of Essential Schools, and Robert Slavin's Success for All Schools. If the TSE fails to take the best of what it can offer to the settings where public education fails worst, then the TSE will aid and abet the preservation of a system that eschews that toughest challenge and settles for high scores where they are easiest to attain.

Ultimately, the stakes involve the level of practice carried out in elementary and secondary education, and especially in the most troubled schools. These schools most urgently need the attention of the nation's schools of education, which must accept the challenge of reforming and strengthening the connection between professional education on the campus and in the field. Most current models fail the test. Our response is the Professional Development School.

Improvement-Oriented Inquiry

Educational inquiry provides a second rationale for the PDS. One kind of inquiry calls for acquiring and exercising the habits of reflecting, questioning, and trying out and evaluating ways of teaching by one's self and with colleagues. Such habits redound to the advantage of both new and veteran educators. A second kind of inquiry at the PDS involves systematic research and development aimed at generating and applying new knowledge by members of both the school and university faculty associated with the PDS. Practice becomes the locus of inquiry.

The PDS, in effect, redefines the relationship between researcher and practitioner, bringing the latter closer to the scholarly investigation while easing the way for researchers to tie their investigations more readily to actual situations. We assume that the practitioner's perspectives are vitally important to furthering research that aspires to be useful to practice. These perspectives tend to get overlooked in the usual research projects or else the practitioner's perspective gets simplified by researchers who do not appreciate the sophistication of the insights of some teachers. The PDS approach sets the stage for research to be a collaborative activity, combining the experience of the university-based investigator and the savvy of the classroom practitioner. PDS inquiry devotes itself to understanding a particular case, while traditional university-based research seeks more universal explanations and contributions to general theory. This emphasis on the close study of cases in context has precedent. Precursors include, for example, Piaget's pioneering investigations of the young pupil's thinking about basic school subjects, studies in which Piaget rejected the traditional methods of basic science in favor of extensive interviews with children.

All is not roses and sunshine, though, in attempting to bring about the collaborations that the PDS seeks. The cultures of the public school and the university easily clash and various tensions must be reconciled before teachers and researchers can work together comfortably and productively. Nonetheless, our optimism sustains us. TSE faculty members who responded to our survey expressed strong support for collaborative research with schoolteachers. More than half of the respondents indicated that schools of education "to a great extent" should:

1   Integrate faculty from schools, school districts, and other educational settings into the research and development activities of the school of education;

2   Create opportunities for faculty research in a variety of field settings affiliated with the school of education; and

3   Create opportunities for faculty research in collaboration with field-based practitioners.

Educational Standard-Setting

Attention to standards of all kinds, including those related to assessment itself, figures prominently in today's educational reform movement. Standard-setting, subject by subject, dominates the concerns of the disciplinary organizations. New instruments to measure the abilities of both teachers and students are being fashioned for use nationally. At the same time, the nature of testing faces challenges as performance-based exercises, portfolios, and other forms of assessment come to prominence in an attempt to de-emphasize the influence of multiple-choice and short-answer questions.

We believe that the PDS should become a central resource to the standard-setting movement and that its contributions can be made in several ways. First, the public schools in the TSE's orbit can be locales in which to gather together the various strands of the movement so as to form frameworks for piloting these innovations. Second, because assessment will increasingly be embedded in practice, the PDS can gain and disseminate expertise on how best to incorporate assessment into the curriculum. Assessment reform must have a formative dimension. It should contribute to learning, not simply enhance the ability to measure the learning that has occurred. Third, as assessment methods become more judgment-based, educators must become adept at administering them. While outside authorities at the district, state, and national levels will create frameworks for standards, the teacher in the public school classroom will be asked to carry out the assessments. Pilot projects will be required to perfect the procedures, as schools in England discovered when they instituted a new curriculum and new assessments in the late 1980s. Again, the TSE and the PDS can work together to cultivate this expertise.

All of this said, we do not want to exaggerate the promise of assessment reform nor discount the technical difficulties that must be overcome for the new methods to be any better than the old ways of measurement. Studies reveal a range of problems and complications associated with both performance assessments and with portfolio assessments. We can best characterize our stance on educational standards as cautious optimism. In any event, the PDS can contribute greatly to educational standard-setting. This involvement by the PDS can help prevent the adoption of assessment practices that are not in the best interests of teaching and learning for all children.

What we have outlined here establishes an ambitious agenda for the PDS and causes us to acknowledge the many challenges and problems that lie ahead. Our case studies provide a further basis for closer examination of the future of the PDS. What have we learned about the PDS? What are the main difficulties to overcome?

Most of the case study sites have at least one PDS, but these early efforts to create PDSs typically involve only a vanguard of faculty members from the school and from the university. Most other faculty members of the two institutions remain on the sidelines, watching and perhaps criticizing. The air crackles with tension, even amid the early triumphs. The participants struggle to accommodate the demands of two very different cultures that differ on mission, reward system, recruitment patterns, clientele, working conditions, and governance.

While practitioners at PDSs perceive and report that they are making significant changes in their practices, researchers often attest to less dramatic results. So far, teacher education has received more attention than research in the collaborations between professors and schoolteachers. The reward structure of the university inhibits the involvement of many university faculty. Younger members of the faculty tend to participate in the PDS more than senior colleagues, but with problematic consequences. Not having tenure, the younger academicians worry about how they will be judged and rewarded by older colleagues who control the promotion and tenure process. Certainly, those in higher education who willingly involve themselves in the life of the PDS ought not to receive penalties. This work deserves rewards and, if the people from the campus earn no academic recognition for their efforts, then future participation by their colleagues will be jeopardized. Considerations of time weigh heavily. Regular participation in the life of a school means establishing oneself as a member of the community. The human relationships make increased demands on time, as does the travel time. As it is, faculty members say that the kind of research and development that they carry out at the PDS takes longer than traditional research to reach the publication stage. The TSE can ease the burdens by making allowances for these demands on time.

The School of Education at the University of Missouri-St. Louis and its school partners collaborate on their evaluation efforts. They collect basic data on the numbers and types of activities involving PDS participants, as well as conduct case studies and focus-group sessions that reflect on and review the quality of their program.

On the school side, teachers report additional burdens on their time, too, and the emergence of tasks that they feel unprepared to handle. If such situations are not managed carefully, the extra work can overwhelm participants, leading to fatigue and decreased effectiveness. Teachers are torn between their obligations to the children in their classes and to the interns from the schools of education whose induction they oversee. How does one reconcile the demands of such a schedule? Even temporary exhilaration may not be enough to compensate for the extensive demands. In addition, the start-up costs for PDSs can be great in terms of time and resources, and, in all honesty, many of these sites remain largely an idealized blueprint with much still on paper. The framework rises slowly across the country, as tests of its durability and quality remain.

Nonetheless, the early successes demonstrate that the PDS holds great promise for improving education in both pre-collegiate schools and in education schools, and that augers well for our recommendations. So, the battle has been joined and, however rigorous, it must continue, because the quality of education at all levels will be lifted by the struggles and by the accomplishments that we anticipate. To that end, we propose a four-part agenda:

- The creation of at least one full-fledged PDS affiliated with each TSE;
- A set of standards for evaluating the progress of the PDS;
- Long-range plans for expanding each PDS into a local, state, regional, national, and international network; and
- Support from government and private sources at local, state, and national levels to help institutionalize the PDS.

At least one PDS

Given the work required, many of those developing the PDS will choose to concentrate initially on a single site and make a success of it. While we expect eventually that every TSE will sponsor a network of PDSs, trying to spread the effort too widely at first might mean diluting it since the involvement of only a portion of the faculty from each of the participating institutions can be expected. Experience suggests a range of starting points for creating a PDS network. The first site might be a school with a tradition of collaboration with the university, providing a history of trust and shared work as a foundation on which to erect this initially shaky structure. In this case, the PDS could be launched by nurturing the already existing informal relationships and allowing them to expand.

Standards

Without the imposition of standards, we worry about attempts to pass off imitations of the PDS as the real thing. As we noted earlier, we don't want to see the PDS discredited as just another flawed innovation when, in fact, what receives scrutiny is not even a PDS.-Standards can be developed in stages as the PDS matures, so that the incipient effort does not totter under the burden of a tome of regulations much too heavy for an infant to bear. The standards should be a collaborative product of the school and the university and should draw on the findings of such organizations as the National Center for Restructuring Education, Schools, and Teaching and the National Council for the Accreditation of Teacher Education, both of which have started framing standards for the work of education professionals in the PDS. The standards might cover such conditions as the number of school and university faculty to work regularly with the PDS, the budget, the number of student placements, and the review process. The entire relationship should be regarded as voluntary and unofficial until it proves itself. This way, outside organizations such as state agencies and accrediting groups are less apt to impose judgments and requirements while the PDS gestates.

Long-range plans

The PDS is not, we repeat, IS NOT, just another project for the education school. It must be woven into the very fabric of the TSE, its many strands combining with those of the institution's other programs. Beginning small, the TSE must plan to increase eventually the number of such sites so that learning experiences for most TSE students can occur at a PDS. This suggests the need for careful planning for a lengthy future for what will be an integral and integrating part of the TSE. The education school may, in fact, have to trim the breadth of other outside involvements, and researchers may have to submit to some restraints so that they focus more of their investigations through the PDS prism.

Support

We recognize that for the PDS to occupy so pivotal a position in the future education of educators, The Holmes Group will have to secure allies in the larger policy community. Holmes must make the case for the PDS over and over again. The national goals and accompanying state systemic reforms will require capacity-building at the local level. The proponents of the PDS must insert the interests of the PDS into the debate early and with vigor. Furthermore, advocates of the PDS should seize on the emerging interest in revitalized professional development to ensure that these discussions dovetail with the spread of the PDS.

■|■|■

New Commitments and New Kinds of Accountability for the TSE

Many of the institutions that belong to The Holmes Group have embarked on the long and difficult road that should lead to a new era of professional education for teachers and other educators. But advocates of simultaneous renewal of schools and schools of education face an uphill battle. Many of the obstacles encountered during the initial stages of their journey demonstrate that the movement will be neither quick nor easy. In fact, some of the ground gained with considerable struggle has already been lost, as several institutions have actually had to retrace early steps. Like a column of tanks halted in their advance, the nation's research universities have had to reassess the strategies for change that they have been using.

So far, reforms in most schools of education have been neither wide enough nor deep enough to impact significantly on practices in elementary and secondary schools, which, as we noted at the outset of this report, should be the focal point for measuring the effect of changes on the TSE. The changes to date have had too much of the quality of projects that can readily be dismantled when the impetus for change disappears.

The universities and their schools of education need an approach to change that is more comprehensive, more long-term, and powerful enough to knock aside obsolete traditions and cultural norms that block their path. The increasingly ambitious goals of the schools necessitate a more ambitious response by the universities. But we must be candid. While progress has definitely been made, most universities find it impossible to implement fully the worthy goals that they have endorsed for the education of school professionals. Yet, the aims of this battle remain eminently reasonable. Why then are the objectives of reform—which we have set forth on previous pages—so hard to attain? We think that the unwieldiness of the change process at university-based schools of education is due largely to three factors:

- Not developing a strong enough collective will to take on what amounts to a major challenge;
- Not adequately supporting a critical mass of faculty needed to do the serious work of change; and
- Not creating alliances of the external forces needed to overcome obstacles over which they cannot prevail alone.

Collective Will

The Holmes Group assumed that the country's great universities wanted to improve education in America, which, of course, calls for doing a better job of educating educators. And while we see progress in a number of universities, we see considerable inertia in others. Excuses abound—not enough time, not enough money, not enough people to take on the tasks, not enough cooperation from the outside. The rhetoric amounts to a lack of will.

This lack of will speaks to the generally negative attitude in higher education toward matters relating to elementary and secondary schools. Forming serious connections with pre-collegiate education—as the TSE is being asked to do—yields some public relations kudos, but few rewards within the realm of the Academy. A university can win prestige by strengthening the medical school or the law school so as to improve the professionals they serve. But strengthening programs between higher education and the public schools produces few accolades in most parts of the university. Despite these firmly entrenched attitudes, we continue to believe in the inevitability of progress. Higher education has a history replete with examples of overcoming obstacles. Properly nurtured, the will to change can create a TSE that accords pre-collegiate education the serious attention it deserves.

The importance of changing the culture of Teacher's College at the Univeristy of Nebraska-Lincoln to reach certain goals is well recognized. The college is devel-

oping modifications to its promotion and tenure criteria, its merit pay plans, and its criteria for graduate faculty membership to make those criteria fully consistent
with work as scholar-practitioners and collaboration
with professionals in the elementary and secondary
schools.

When research and development were needed in support of the war effort in the 1940s, higher education provided it. When sacrifices had to be made to accommo-date a flood of veterans who arrived after World War II under the G.I. Bill, higher education reconfigured itself. When a new kind of post-secondary institution was required in the 1950s and 1960s, higher education created dozens of community col-leges each year. When equity demanded that privilege be extended to groups that had been excluded, higher education in the 1970s admitted women and members of minority groups in unprecedented numbers. Clearly, higher education can turn itself inside out when it has the will. But this current challenge involving elemen-tary and secondary schools is even more difficult because it is not just an added function for the professoriate, with massive amounts of funding or strong govern-ment pressures for the changeover.

Can it be that when it comes to the public schools, the magnitude of the prob-lem paralyzes the university and prevents it from summoning up a will equal to the task? Is higher education intimidated? After, all, the changes will be judged not sim-ply by what the TSE does to alter itself, nor by corresponding changes in the arts and sciences, but by how these changes in the university play out in the elementary and secondary schools with which the TSE affiliates. Some in higher education may fret over their ability to meet a challenge so far removed from the university and so linked to the troubles of society itself. Ergo, a challenge avoided is a challenge that cannot be lost.

In their most confessional moments, faculty members and administrators at education schools admit to worries over miring themselves in the morass of the problems of the public schools. Many academicians have had scant professional contact with pre-collegiate education and were appointed to perform work largely unrelated to day-to-day teaching and learning in public schools. But their reticence, while understandable, cannot be allowed to hold back change in Tomorrow's Schools of Education.

The reasons for linking the reform of the education school to the fortunes of elementary and secondary education are multiple. Even self-interest dictates a need for this kind of commitment. Like record stores that refuse to stock compact disks, schools of education risk being abandoned to irrelevancy, if they won't change. Education professionals who accept employment in the public schools have to prepare themselves for duties very different from those assigned to their predecessors. University education programs that do not make themselves relevant to the altered circumstances in the schools and to new discoveries on ways to improve practice will fall into disfavor with students whose careers cannot be built on outdated concepts and outmoded practices. Students will attend education schools that offer them what they need and bypass the others.

In places where university-based education schools have not given sustained attention to some of the most pressing educational issues of the day, students of education tend to learn only part of what they need to know. "All children can learn," for instance, is taken to mean "no tracking," but education students do not learn the appropriate range of instructional strategies. "Authentic assessment" is taken to mean "no multiple-choice tests," but education students do not learn to handle performance assessments. "The importance of working with parents" takes on a romantic notion of school-home cooperation as many of the complexities of today's families are glossed over. Education schools that fail to ground their work in well-studied practice inhabit a make-believe land, a Potemkin village of reassuring facades.

If building a connection to elementary and secondary education were just another project for the education school, it might hold greater attraction. A one-shot effort to improve mathematical reasoning by fifth graders in one particular school district would be manageable. An isolated attempt to introduce more writing in the biology classes in a network of high schools in the corner of one state seems achievable.

But fundamentally altering the way that almost three million educators develop their professional expertise so that they, in turn, can reorient the totality of their work for the more than forty million children in pre-collegiate education throughout the country? The very thought of it boggles the imagination. As individuals, we can each understand the failure of will. One of the greatest examples of insufficient will on a personal level revolves around the spate of diet books, published one after another in the United States. Why? Because it requires less effort to read and talk about losing weight than to marshal the will to do it. Unfortunately, the will often arises only under great personal threat to life or limb, when life itself depends on summoning the will. But our future does depend on better educated educators and young citizens. A visit to any of the most troubled high schools emphasizes that point.

The time has arrived for universities to discipline themselves to a new regimen, one that involves thinking in new ways about reforming the professional education of educators. Perhaps the will for change might be more readily aroused if the task were viewed in a different light. The Holmes Group may have given universities the impression that each institution was on its own in creating a TSE. Now, to rectify that error, we want to stress the collaborative nature of our education renewal. Universities exercising leadership must speak up, but if their voices are to be heard and have effect, they must be amplified by joining together. Acting in unison enables us to consider alternatives, develop strategies, and amass support that none of us could do alone. Together, our sense of possibility and will should enable us to do what needs so badly to be done.

The Holmes Group intends to underscore this call for collective action by sending a copy of this report, *Tomorrow's Schools of Education*, to the trustees, presidents, chief academic officers, deans, and others at institutions of higher education. We will assess their willingness to exercise leadership in behalf of our agenda. We will invite them to participate in a national movement in behalf of implementing the recommendations of this report. We want those most responsible for making decisions at universities to understand that they have support and that no one wants them unilaterally to put themselves at risk by being the only ones advocating a bold new agenda. The common agenda that we hope appeals to a good number of leaders in higher education calls for determination to take the following actions:

- To commit to the development of a TSE that makes complementary contributions to educational knowledge, professional development, and education policy that sets and maintains standards of excellence for the country's educators and their students;

- To establish enduring, formal partnerships in which both universities and schools adhere to and follow PDS principles, and together develop the range of human and financial resources needed to sustain a set of Professional Development Schools for quality professional education and applied study;

- To work to change policies of universities and states that impede the development and retention of a highly qualified education workforce for the nation's public schools;

- To raise scholarship money to ensure that education schools can have diverse enrollments at initial and advanced levels; and

- To hold our own institutions accountable for progress on this agenda by monitoring the efforts and encouraging public and professional scrutiny.

The will to change can be demonstrated through clear and public statements, leaving no doubt about the institution's intent. An action agenda should be offered to underscore the seriousness of the commitment. It may perplex some observers to see us go through these machinations so that institutions of higher education can change. But we understand why the reform of professional education has lagged, and we need allies to counter the many impediments. We hope to generate greater collective will than has ever been behind such change before, for while we have a good base of support, it is insufficient to the challenge. Furthermore, education deans, provosts, and faculty members who step out in front in this struggle for improved education must not isolate themselves by their acts of courage. They deserve backing from their trustees, from university administrators, and from faculty leaders, as well as from allies in other universities.

A Critical Mass of Faculty

Too many spectators and not enough players. That sums up the situation facing those who would like to create Tomorrow's Schools of Education. As a practical matter, transformation demands a sufficient number of participants to put change in motion and to sustain it during the difficult periods when countervailing forces will try to bring it to a halt. The university faculty sorts itself into several factions when we examine reactions to the agenda we propose. Some people, usually fewer than a majority, are willing and prepared to pursue a new agenda. Another group has the capability, but insufficient backing—at least not until a different sort of reward structure lends them the support they need. Still another group contains people sympathetic to the goals of the TSE, but ill-equipped to help without pursuing professional development. And yet others, the diehards who hold the potential to undermine the entire effort, refuse to promote change in schools of education. Strategies must be fashioned to deal with each of these various groups. The change process is riddled with complexities, but the scholars who have studied change give us ideas that have practical application.

What we propose for the TSE calls for more work and requires more pairs of hands. It also demands new kinds of faculty expertise and new approaches to collaboration. Professional development of our university faculty and of our faculty colleagues in the schools will be needed to increase chances of success. Constructing the requisite critical mass for this enterprise depends, of course, on enlisting adequate numbers of people in the efforts. The numbers can be bolstered by incentives and staffing changes. The steps outlined in the paragraphs that follow embody simple and logical measures for giving the education school the human capacity to accept a changing mission.

Incentives

Faculty members, no less than other people, want to feel appreciated. They will more readily shift assignments or take on extra work if they know unequivocally that the university and the school of education value their contributions. Incentives and rewards help deliver this message from a university that wants to demonstrate its support for those who work with elementary and secondary education. The backing may take the form of extra attention, extra time, or extra money.

Cincinnati Public Schools and the University of Cincinnati have developed new staffing patterns for teacher education that include half-load, half-pay, fifth-year internships

that are supported by allocation of staffing dollars and
some added district and university stipends for intern
support teams composed of a lead teacher-mentor,
career teachers, and university faculty.

Added attention might approximate no more than words of appreciation so
that those who take on expanded roles know explicitly that the education school and
the university consider these efforts important to higher education. More concrete
incentives might include assistance with the extra clerical load, say, to keep records
on site-based research resulting from work in the public schools, or such amenities
as car phones and fax machines that can demonstrate concrete support for this work.
Even providing a van to make it easier for university faculty to travel to the school
can encourage their participation.

Time for work in the public schools can be squeezed out of the schedule by adjust-
ing faculty workloads so that the hours spent in the public school do not have to come
on top of everything else. Also, interns and graduate assistants who fill in occasionally for regular faculty members can free them to perform other jobs. And, finally,
raises in salary and bonuses can spur participation. If the faculty member decided
over a several-year period to go on to other duties, the bonus would lapse. The concept of added pay for people doing high-priority work during a period of transition
seems worth considering.

Staffing

A TSE can increase the number of faculty members prepared and willing to work
in the schools simply by hiring new people who are so inclined. Despite tight budgets, hiring looms as a possibility because the demographics of an aging faculty suggest that openings will be created by an increasing number of retirements during the
next decade and a half. In addition, hiring might be authorized to promote the
commitment to diversity that should be part of the restructuring of the school of
education.

The school of education should also regard the PDS as a potential source of talent for carrying out new roles. The very concept of the PDS demands a partnership
between school and university, including the assumption of certain clinical faculty
roles by school professionals. Each person who affiliates himself or herself with the
university through the PDS represents a potential addition to the formation of a critical mass. As the number of teachers certified by the National Board of Professional
Teaching Standards grows, they, too, can be regarded as potential contributors to the
critical mass of universities in their areas. Professional development can be a vehi-

cle for converting some of those already on the faculty—but unprepared for the new mission—to become productive contributors to the TSE. No less than in elementary and secondary education, professional development in higher education can be used to retrain those whose knowledge and skills are insufficient to meet new expectations. Sabbatical leaves and post-doctoral grants can augment professional development and provide others with time for learning what they need to participate in the TSE.

Whether through hiring or professional development, the TSE must attend to the need for having more faculty members who can assume responsibility for knowledge development in the areas designated for expanded work—developing knowledge about knowledge, knowledge about professional development, and knowledge about policy development. Existing faculties almost certainly must be enlarged or retooled to fulfill this mission. With this added capacity comes the critical mass that can be a foundation for creating a successful TSE.

External Forces

If The Holmes Group stands alone, solitary and exclusive, it places its future and what it seeks to accomplish at peril. The organization must add members, form regional networks, and ally itself with a broad range of partners. These strategies will bolster individual TSEs by weaving them into a web of external forces. The time has arrived for this outreach. Holmes launched itself by inviting the affiliation of at least one university in each of the fifty states, and at least one for every 25,000 teachers, assuring itself of an elite membership. Ten years later, we realize the limitations of this conception. To create and realize the potential of the TSE, the universities must widen their connections and form coalitions with education organizations and agencies and with the vendors of education products and services.

The commitment to raising levels of quality and to broadening access to the educating professions means that The Holmes Group must face outward, not inward. To achieve inclusiveness, a larger number of institutions of higher education can join our efforts, for instance, through consortia that unite universities with extensive research capacity but limited capacity for professional development with universities with extensive capacity for professional development but limited capacity for research. These universities will complement each other and the resulting synergy will produce an impetus for change more powerful than any institution could provide on its own.

Alliances with partners outside the universities offer the opportunity to spread understanding for what we seek to achieve and to enlist support for our goals. To these ends, The Holmes Group proposes to enter into partnerships with such organizations as the American Association of Colleges of Teacher Education (AACTE), the American Association of School Administrators (AASA), the American Federation of Teachers (AFT), the National Board for Professional Teaching Standards (NBPTS), the National Education Association (NEA), the National Policy Board for Educational Administration (NPBEA), the National Staff Development Council (NSDC), and other groups sympathetic to advancing the goals of our three reports—*Tomorrows Teachers, Tomorrow's Schools,* and *Tomorrow's Schools of Education.*

The Auburn University College of Education, with support from the Alabama Power Foundation, has for the last two years provided leadership to a network of professional development schools involving six universities and nine school sites.

In addition, the cause of educational reform can only gain if The Holmes Group cultivates friends among the leading companies, both for-profit and non-profit, whose products and services are integral to public education. Educators often overlook the makers of computers, textbooks and materials, tests, and other school resources when they reflect on potential partners for school improvement. But vendors, too, have an interest in the well-being of America's elementary and secondary schools and probably would welcome the chance to be allies in bolstering the education of educators by joining in research and development activities in PDSs.

External forces of all kinds figure prominently in our plans for lifting the quality of the education of educators. Right now, schools of education meet minimum state regulations for initial teacher preparation, but are free to do what they choose in most other programs. Many universities reject national professional accreditation of their education programs, a fact reflected by the fact that fewer than two-thirds of the Holmes members have accredited programs. Some university-based education schools perform in exemplary fashion, while others ride the distinguished coattails of the great institutions of higher education on whose campuses they reside.

The 250 schools of education in the United States that now offer degrees for doctoral and master's study as well as initial education preparation should be accountable to the public and to the profession for the quality of their contributions to educational knowledge, to professional practice, and to education policy-setting. We will ask our professional partners and allies to join us in framing new standards for the TSE. Those schools of education that cannot meet these new standards after a reasonable length of time should be closed.

No education school that offers a questionable program for initial preparation should be permitted to offer advanced programs for educators. No education school should conduct research on educators or produce research for educators if it cannot provide quality professional development for educators. If an education school contributes good research but poor professional development, it should become a laboratory or a center or a department in arts and sciences and cease to pose as a professional school—for education schools bear the unique expectation that their faculty will themselves be good educators, and their students will indeed learn important things. And if an education school claims to offer professional development of quality at advanced levels without strength in research and education policy analysis, its programs should not be recognized, for the faculty are ill-prepared to educate professionals at advanced levels.

Like any business that has customers, the TSE must concern itself with the market, which in this case comprises the school districts that employ TSE graduates. We reject the philosophy of caveat emptor. The abilities of students who come through the TSE should be guaranteed by assiduous documentation and evaluation of their performance in actual work situations. Those with assignments in the PDS will be assessed by highly qualified practitioners over a sufficient period of time under conditions that permit employers to have confidence in the graduates' ability to practice. Nothing about the professional education of educators should be left to chance. The Holmes Group will take several steps designed to promote standards, collaborating with the Educational Testing Service and the Council of Chief State School Officers to develop assessments for use during our students' internships. We will work also with our national and state school board associations to encourage local school boards to support policies that require performance assessments as a precondition for hiring. Finally, we will invite universities to give hiring preference both in the TSE and in their PDSs to candidates with National Board certification and with successful TSE internships.

The external pressure of public opinion can be another force for improvement. Tomorrow's Schools of Education should raise public awareness about the professional education of educators by maintaining a dialogue with the public. Universities and public schools owe their very existence to the public whose taxes, donations, and tuitions sustain educational institutions. The new era that we envision should include public information campaigns that help people understand exactly how meritorious professional education for educators can promote the goal of making excellent learners of this nation's children.

National professional accreditation is yet another important lever in strengthening the education profession overall and assuring quality learning for those pursuing careers in schools and ed schools. We intend to help to develop new advanced standards for schools of education that are compatible with TSE goals. These developmental standards should promote improved contributions to educational knowledge and its application, to quality education of professionals at both initial and advanced levels, and to education policy. Toward that end we will ally ourselves with the National Council for Accreditation of Teacher Education to incorporate these new standards into the expectations for all institutions offering advanced programs—developing new accreditation processes and procedures for TSEs. We eventually expect national professional accreditation of all TSEs, and we will work with our new partners and allies and the public to impose sanctions on those that demure.

In the Final Analysis

We realize that the dose of reality we have administered here may be too strong for some tastes. But universities and their schools of education that fail to assess the current public mood or choose to ignore significant changes in the educational environment around them, do so at some risk. The collapse of public education will be at hand in the absence of action to address the failings of educators—both those in schools of education and those in pre-collegiate education.

In this document, we have assumed the peculiar posture of talking to ourselves. On the one hand, The Holmes Group uses the occasion of this report to affirm its intention to improve schooling in America for all children, and especially for those worst served. On the other hand, we speak to ourselves to admonish some of our colleagues and to reaffirm our own commitment to the difficult course we have set for our future. We do not seek simply to lecture others. We want to be clear about our commitment to the improvement of public education in America—to our intent to build authentic professional schools for educators who work in them—and to an action agenda to put our own houses in order to serve them better.

Henceforth, the schools of education that commit themselves to implementing these recommendations to establish Tomorrow's Schools of Education (TSEs) will take all necessary steps to transform words into deeds. The greatest challenge to democracy as the country nears the twenty-first century revolves around access to knowledge and to equitable opportunities to learn. The TSE accepts its role in trying to avert the tragedy of making permanent the two-tiered educational system that now characterizes American public education. Three generations ago, W.E.B. DuBois observed: "Of all the civil rights for which the world has struggled for 5,000 years, the right to learn is undoubtedly the most fundamental." His enduring statement continues to guide us.